Complete
David Norris

The publisher has used its best endeavours to ensure that the URLs
for external websites referred to in this book are correct and active
at the time of going to press. However, the publisher and the
author have no responsibility for the websites and can make no
guarantee that a site will remain live or that the content will remain
relevant, decent or appropriate.

For UK order enquiries: please contact Bookpoint Ltd,
130 Milton Park, Abingdon, Oxon OX14 4SB.
Telephone: +44 (0) 1235 827720. *Fax:* +44 (0) 1235 400454.
Lines are open 09.00–17.00, Monday to Saturday, with a 24-hour
message answering service. Details about our titles and how to
order are available at www.teachyourself.com

For USA order enquiries: please contact McGraw-Hill
Customer Services, PO Box 545, Blacklick, OH 43004-0545, USA.
Telephone: 1-800-722-4726. *Fax:* 1-614-755-5645.

For Canada order enquiries: please contact McGraw-Hill
Ryerson Ltd, 300 Water St, Whitby, Ontario L1N 9B6, Canada.
Telephone: 905 430 5000. *Fax:* 905 430 5020.

Long renowned as the authoritative source for self-guided
learning – with more than 50 million copies sold worldwide –
the *Teach Yourself* series includes over 500 titles in the fields of
languages, crafts, hobbies, business, computing and education.

British Library Cataloguing in Publication Data: a catalogue
record for this title is available from the British Library.

Library of Congress Catalog Card Number: on file.

First published as *Teach Yourself Croatian* in UK 2003 by
Hodder Education, 338 Euston Road, London NW1 3BH.

First published in US 2003 by The McGraw-Hill Companies, Inc.

The *Teach Yourself* name is a registered trade mark of
Hodder Headline.

Copyright © 2003, 2010 David Norris

Typeset by MPS Limited, a Macmillan Company.

Printed in Great Britain for Hodder Education, a division of
Hodder Headline, 338 Euston Road, London, NW1 3BH,
by CPI Group (UK) Ltd, Croydon, CR0 4YY

Hodder Headline's policy is to use papers that are natural,
renewable and recyclable products and made from wood grown
in sustainable forests. The logging and manufacturing processes
are expected to conform to the environmental regulations of the
country of origin.

Impression number   10 9 8 7 6 5 4
Year   2014

Contents

Credits

Front cover: © pavelr – Fotolia.com

Back cover and pack: © Jakub Semeniuk/iStockphoto.com,
© Royalty – Free/Corbis, © agencyby/iStockphoto.com, © Andy
Cook/iStockphoto.com, © Christopher Ewing/iStockphoto.com,
© zebicho – Fotolia.com, © Geoffrey Holman/iStockphoto.com,
© Photodisc/Getty Images, © James C. Pruitt/iStockphoto.com,
© Mohamed Saber – Fotolia.com

Meet the author

I graduated from the University of London with a first-class degree in Serbo-Croatian language and literature. My first visit as a student to the country then known as Yugoslavia was to Croatia, staying in Zagreb and Dubrovnik. Since finishing my degree I have taught at the University of Nottingham in the Department of Slavonic Studies where I also gained my PhD. I specialize in the language and culture of the region in which Croatian and Serbian are spoken. I have lectured abroad as an invited speaker and have published books and articles on these topics. Previous editions of this textbook have been translated into German and Polish. I have been a constant visitor to the region both for professional reasons and for leisure.

My students from Nottingham have found employment in a variety of ways doing business in the region or using their linguistic knowledge for the United Nations and other governmental and international organizations.

David Norris

Only got a minute?

Croatian is a Slavonic language written in the Latin alphabet, its spelling based on a simple phonetic principle: each letter represents one sound and each word is spelt as it is pronounced. It is not a difficult language to master and modern Croatian incorporates many words that will be familiar to English speakers, including **taksi** (*taxi*), **kava** (*coffee*) or **auto** (*car, automobile*; pronounced in Croatian with three syllables as written a-oo-to). It is also similar to the language spoken in Bosnia or Serbia, with many people regarding them as dialects of the same language.

The first Croatian kingdom disappeared in 1102, after which the country was ruled by Austrian, Hungarian and Venetian overlords. Much of the north of the country was incorporated into the Ottoman Empire for some 200 years, the result being a rich mix of all these cultural influences over the whole country. The capital, Zagreb, looks like a smaller version of a Central European city such as Prague, while, on the Dalmatian coast, the atmosphere is more Mediterranean with Italian influences in cuisine and in local dialects. For most of the 20th century the country was part of Yugoslavia and there are numerous reminders of this in monuments and sites recording the many achievements of the united state of the South Slavs, many of them celebrating Partisan victories in the Second World War.

The independent Republic of Croatia in the 21st century is a favourite tourist destination for many people travelling from Austria, Britain, Germany and other European countries. Such a small country is easy to get around whether using public transport or driving yourself. Independent travel is made all the more pleasurable with even slight knowledge of the language since locals respond warmly to visitors who have made the effort to speak their language with them.

Only got five minutes?

Croatian is a member of the family of Slavonic languages. This family is divided into three groups: the eastern Slavonic languages including Byelorussian, Russian and Ukrainian; the western group with Czech, Polish, Slovak and Sorbian; the southern group, which numbers Bulgarian, Croatian, Macedonian, Serbian and Slovenian. Croatian and Serbian are particularly close and were formerly regarded as one language called Serbo-Croat, although most native speakers now recognize differences that are of not only a linguistic but also a cultural nature. Serbian and Croatian remain mutually comprehensible as the standard forms of language spoken across most of today's Bosnia, Croatia, Montenegro and Serbia. Croatian has three main dialects with their names based on their respective words meaning 'what': **kaj**, **ča** and **što**. The **kaj** dialect is spoken in the region to the north of Zagreb and is most similar to standard Slovene. The **ča** dialect used to be widespread throughout Dalmatia but is now confined to the islands and the Istrian Peninsula. It displays traces of Italian influence in some of its words and its continuing existence in Istria reinforces the strong sense of local identity evident there. The **što** dialect is the most widely spoken and was singled out as the basis for the linguistic reforms of the 19th century. These reforms were intended to bring a sense of unity at a time when Croatian spelling and pronunciation varied greatly from region to region. Renewed interest in political freedom sparked a concern for national cultural identity. The Illyrian Movement, led by Ljudevit Gaj, was active in the 1830s and 1840s. Its members proposed a series of changes to codify Croatian grammar and to produce an alphabet system compliant to the demands of the spoken language. They introduced accents above certain letters to represent a greater range of sounds. A description of these letters as used today follows later in the book. The reforms of the Illyrian Movement in the 19th century have evolved into the modern Croatian language presented in this book.

Today's Republic of Croatia is a crescent-shaped country with its northern arm stretching from the border with Serbia in the east to the border with Italy in the west before turning south down the coast of the Adriatic Sea. For the practical needs of most visitors, it can be divided into three convenient areas. The flat northern plains of Slavonia contain the most fertile agricultural land with some commercial and industrial centres such as Varaždin and Osijek. Croatia's capital, Zagreb, standing on the very western edge of this region is a typical Central European city, with an old town raised on a hill overlooking an elegant central part built largely in the 19th century. Travelling west from Zagreb visitors come to the Istrian Peninsula and the northern coastal region, with the industrial port of Rijeka and tourist resorts of Opatija, Poreč, Pula and Rovinj. To the south lie the long coast and mountainous hinterland of Dalmatia stretching down the Adriatic Sea. This region attracts the largest number of tourists from abroad to the Mediterranean atmosphere of its old towns like Dubrovnik, Šibenik, Split and Zadar along with the islands of Brač, Hvar and Korčula.

For much of their history, Croats have been ruled by foreign overlords. The independent medieval kingdom of Croatia reached the height of its power and prestige in the 10th century but later disappeared. Hungarians, Turks, Venetians and Austrians have taken their turn at conquering and administering different parts of Croatia. The architecture of many Slavonian cities stands as a monument to Habsburg influence in the region. The remains of a Venetian presence can still be felt in the Istrian Peninsula and Dalmatia where Italian influence was a key element in promoting the arts, literature and architecture of the Renaissance that flourished here from the beginning of the 15th to the end of the 17th century. After 1700 southeastern Europe was divided between the Catholic Habsburg Empire and the Islamic Ottoman Empire. Croatia represented the frontier of Christian Europe, with the Croats as a nation living on the periphery. They were a colonized people, used by the Austrians and Hungarians as their last outpost before the Turks. The local aristocracy took to speaking German or Hungarian, which became the languages of government, education and trade.

Croatian was reduced to the tongue of an illiterate, feudal, peasant class of people who lived in villages and worked the land.

Croatian society in the 19th century was polarized between those who wanted liberation from Habsburg rule and those who were satisfied with seeking accommodations within the status quo. The Croats could not hope to win their freedom alone and their plans included some degree of cooperation with other Slavs in the Balkans, principally with the Serbs. Their chance came at the close of the First World War when the Croats were united in one state with their neighbours called the Kingdom of Serbs, Croats and Slovenes. The new state was the first Yugoslavia, meaning 'land of the South Slavs'. The promise of national freedom was greeted enthusiastically but initial euphoria turned to disillusionment during the 1920s and 1930s when it was felt that the new country was dominated by Serbia. The Croats demanded a greater degree of local autonomy to run their own affairs. In 1941 Yugoslavia was attacked by Germany and the country capitulated in less than two weeks. Yugoslavia was dismembered and an independent Croatian state was created under the Ustaše, the Croatian Fascist Party supported by the Axis Powers. The Ustaše followed a rigid policy of racial purity against Serbs, Romanies and Jews. Following Germany's defeat in 1945, Yugoslavia was resurrected under the Communist Party of Yugoslavia and its leader Josip Broz Tito.

Croatia was one of six Republics (the others being Bosnia-Hercegovina, Macedonia, Montenegro, Serbia and Slovenia) in the socialist federation of Yugoslavia. The Republics had little or no local autonomy and real political power was firmly held by the Communist Party's Central Committee. However, in 1948 Yugoslavia was expelled from the Cominform organization of states in Eastern Europe, which was dominated by the Soviet Union. The country embarked on a series of economic reforms and undertook measures towards political liberalization bringing Yugoslavia closer to the West. Croatia began to attract tourists from Britain and Germany to its beautiful coastline and eventually became a favourite tourist spot. President Tito insisted on the unity of Yugoslavia until his death in 1980 after which members of the federation began to pursue individual rather than joint interests. Consequently, the state lurched from one crisis to another in the 1980s until tensions reached breaking point and the socialist federation faced collapse. The first free elections in Croatia were held in April 1990 and were won by the nationalist Croatian Democratic Union. Croatia and Slovenia wanted independence and they were granted international recognition as sovereign states in January 1992. However, civil war had already broken out and spread to Bosnia later that year. Peace returned to the region with the Dayton Agreement at the end of 1995. Today's Croatia, entering the second decade of the 21st century, is looking forward to membership of the European Union and full integration with all its institutions.

Introduction

About the book

The book is intended for absolute beginners. By following each section in each unit, you will gradually build up a stock of words and phrases to be used in everyday, practical situations. The central purpose of the book is to teach you how to make your way around on your own, order meals and drinks, buy travel tickets, read notices and write messages; in short, to explain what you want and how to get it.

The emphasis throughout is on functional explanations using straightforward grammatical examples. You will begin with individual words and phrases and gradually you will be introduced to the patterns of the language that govern their usage. This is, after all, what we mean by grammar. These patterns are given as demonstrations of how you can build your own sentences to use in other situations in which you might find yourself. Do not worry if you have not studied a language before or for some time or if you feel that your last attempt was not as successful as you had hoped it would be. This book offers you units containing graded dialogues and exercises accompanied by a recording to take you through the stages of listening to, speaking, reading and writing Croatian.

How to use the book

You will find that each unit is organized in the same way. Each has seven sections:

Dialogue: the dialogue shows you the langugage in operation in an everyday context; it is followed by a list of the new words and expressions used in the dialogue.

Insight: this section has notes that explain points about everyday life relevant to the dialogue.

True or false?: this gives statements about the dialogue that are either true or false for you to check that you have understood it.

Key phrases: this is a summary of the most important words and expressions used in the dialogue.

How it works: this section is full of notes that explain why phrases mean what they do and which show you how to create your own sentences.

Practice: these are for you to practise the new information about the language and new words as you acquire them.

Comprehension: this is either another dialogue or a dialogue and a text, with questions, designed to extend your comprehension of the language.

The last two units are slightly different as they give you exercises to revise phrases and language patterns studied earlier.

Complete Croatian follows the story of an English couple, Mark and Sandra Bryant, who come to Zagreb. Mark is working for a company wanting to expand its business contacts in the region. Mark and Sandra become friends with Mark's business contact, Rudolf Šimunić, and his girlfriend, Jasna Kušan. You will trace their outings together, their conversations and their holiday together and see them in different practical situations: in restaurants, shopping, arranging accommodation, changing money, contacting a doctor, conducting business, and so on. You will also find other situations and characters in the **Comprehension** section of each unit.

There is no one way of learning a language. We all have our favourite techniques. As you progress through the book you will discover which methods suit you best. Exploit these as your strengths.

The first steps in learning a language are always important. They provide essential and basic information that you will continue to need. It is also better to look at the book every day rather than try to cram all your study in to one day at the weekend.

Go through each section of each unit in turn. Read the dialogue and, if you have the recording accompanying this course, listen to the dialogue and repeat each phrase until you feel that you have mastered the pronunciation. Study the section and then test your knowledge of the **Dialogue** by attempting the **True or false?** questions. Once you have understood the passage learn the **Key phrases** and the **How it works** sections before moving to the **Practice** section. The **Comprehension** towards the end of each unit develops the vocabulary and phrases that you have learnt in the unit to help reinforce your knowledge of them and to extend your stock of words and expressions.

Give yourself time for revision and don't give up at the first sign of difficulty. What may seem complicated the first time you see it will become second nature to you by the end of the course.

Pronunciation and reading

◄)) **CD1, TR 1, 00:44**

Croatian is an easy language to spell and pronounce. Each letter is pronounced separately and each word is spelt as it is pronounced. The alphabet has 30 letters. Here the capital letters are listed and their lower case letters are in brackets:

A	(a)	G	(g)	O	(o)
B	(b)	H	(h)	P	(p)
C	(c)	I	(i)	R	(r)
Č	(č)	J	(j)	S	(s)
Ć	(ć)	K	(k)	Š	(š)
D	(d)	L	(l)	T	(t)
Dž	(dž)	Lj	(lj)	U	(u)
Đ	(đ)	M	(m)	V	(v)
E	(e)	N	(n)	Z	(z)
F	(f)	Nj	(nj)	Ž	(ž)

Dž, **lj** and **nj** are combinations of other letters but are regarded as single letters for pronunciation and dictionary purposes. Some letters are formed with the help of accents and other markings.

These are č, ć, đ, š and ž. As you will see this gives Croatian the advantage of having each letter represent one sound:

č   like the 'ch' in *church* but raise your tongue towards the roof of your mouth

ć   like the 'ch' in *church* but put your tongue behind your top front teeth

dž like the 'j' in *judge* but raise your tongue towards the roof of your mouth

đ   like the 'j' in *judge* but put your tongue behind your top front teeth

š   like the 'sh' in *shoe*

ž   like the 's' in *pleasure*

Others to watch for are:

c   always pronounced like 'ts' in *cats* (never as 'k' or 's')

g   always pronounced like 'g' in *goat*

h   pronounced in the throat like the 'ch' in *Scottish* loch

j   always pronounced like 'y' in *you*

lj sounds like 'll' in the middle of *million*

nj sounds like 'ni' in the middle of *onion*

r   is always trilled as is sometimes found in Scotland and commonly in other languages such as German or Spanish; it is never pronounced in the throat as in French. The letter 'r' is sometimes sandwiched between two consonants and used as a vowel, e.g. **hr**vatski *Croatian*.

The pronunciation of the remaining consonants is similar to their English equivalents: **b d f k l m n p s t v z**

Vowel sounds are pure and tend to be shorter than in English:

a   as in *hat* but shorter

e   as in *bell*

i   like the 'ea' in *meat* but shorter

o   as in northern English *not* but with rounder lips

u   like the 'oo' in English *moon* but shorter and with rounder lips

Finally, take care with the following combinations:

aj   as the vowel sound in *night*
ej   as the vowel sound in *late*
oj   as the vowel sound in *boy*

Other letters: you meet foreign letters such as **x** and **y** in the spelling of foreign names, place names and so on.

Read, or listen to, these words, which exemplify Croatian pronunciation:

adresa	*address*	limun	*lemon*
banka	*bank*	ljeto	*summer*
centar	*centre*	marka	*stamp*
čaj	*tea*	noć	*night*
ići	*to go*	Njemačka	*Germany*
da	*yes*	oprostite	*excuse me*
džep	*pocket*	park	*park*
do viđenja	*goodbye*	restoran	*restaurant*
Engleska	*England*	sala	*hall*
funta	*pound*	šuma	*forest*
govorite	*you speak*	taksi	*taxi*
hotel	*hotel*	učitelj	*teacher*
ili	*or*	valuta	*currency*
ja	*I*	zima	*winter*
karta	*ticket*	žena	*woman*

Stress in Croatian

In Croatian, as in English, one part of a longer word is pronounced more heavily than the others. This part is called the stressed syllable. So you say *lighting* and *concern* where the underlined syllable is pronounced more forcefully than the rest. Also, as in English, there are no rules to govern which part of a word is stressed, except that it is never the last syllable. So, in a word of two syllables, the first one is always stressed. The stressed syllable is not usually marked in Croatian, but by listening carefully to the recording that accompanies this course you will be able to acquire a good pronunciation. Remember that each part of a word is pronounced without reducing or contracting sounds as often happens at the ends of words in English.

Stress in Croatian is also accompanied by tonal lengths. There are four tones in all, two rising and two falling. However, few speakers these days distinguish between all four tones. There are some instances where a tone difference indicates a different meaning of the word. These are rare occasions. You will master the tones by imitating the sounds as you hear them on the recording. Also, vowels are sometimes pronounced longer than usual. They are not necessarily the stressed syllable, but you will be able to hear them on the recording.

Abbreviations and symbols

◄) indicates material included on the recording.

Insight: indicates information about everyday life in Croatia or gives useful grammar pointers.

masc.	masculine	gen.	genitive case
fem.	feminine	nom.	nominative case
neut.	neuter	sing.	singular
acc.	accusative case	ins.	instrumental case
dat.	dative case	voc.	vocative case
lit.	literally (for a literal translation)	pron.	pronounced

1

U hotelu
In the hotel

In this unit you will learn how to
- *Form basic statements and questions*
- *Introduce yourself and others*
- *Identify yourself and ask others their identity*
- *Say which languages you speak*
- *Use words and expressions in greeting*

Dialogue

Rudolf Šimunić is looking for Mark Bryant and his wife Sandra in their hotel in Zagreb. The Bryants have just arrived. Rudolf is Mark's business contact but they have not met before.

Rudolf	Oprostite, jeste li vi gospodin Bryant?
Mark	Da, jesam. A tko ste vi, gospodine?
Rudolf	Ja sam Rudolf Šimunić. Drago mi je.
Mark	Drago mi je. Ja sam Mark Bryant.
Rudolf	Jeste li vi Englez?
Mark	Jesam.
Rudolf	Dobro govorite hrvatski.
Mark	Hvala. Jeste li vi Hrvat?
Rudolf	Jesam.
Mark	Govorite li engleski?

◀ CD1, TR 1, 06:23

(Contd)

Rudolf	Govorim malo. Učim engleski.
Mark	Da vas upoznam. Ovo je moja žena, Sandra.
Rudolf	Drago mi je. Ja sam Rudolf Šimunić.
Sandra	Drago mi je. Ja sam Sandra.
Rudolf	I vi govorite hrvatski?
Sandra	Govorim malo. Učim jezik.

oprostite *excuse me (attracting attention)*
Jeste li vi ...? *Are you ...?*
gospodin Bryant *Mr Bryant*
da *yes*
jesam *I am*
A tko ste vi, gospodine? *And who are you, sir?*
a *and, but*
drago mi je *pleased to meet you*
ja sam ... *I am ...*
Englez/Hrvat *Englishman/Croat*
Dobro govorite hrvatski. *You speak Croatian well.*
hvala *thank you*
Govorite li engleski/hrvatski? *Do you speak English/Croatian?*
Govorim malo. *I speak a little.*
Učim engleski. *I am learning English.*
Da vas upoznam. *Let me introduce you.*
Ovo je moja žena. *This is my wife.*
i *and*
I vi govorite hrvatski? *And you speak Croatian (too)?*
Učim jezik. *I am studying the language.*

Rudolf arranges to meet Mark and Sandra that evening and he brings along his friend, Jasna.

Mark	Dobra večer, Rudolf. Kako ste?
Rudolf	Dobra večer. Ja sam dobro, hvala. A kako ste vi?
Sandra	Dobro, hvala.
Rudolf	Da vas upoznam. Ovo je moja prijateljica, Jasna.
Sandra	Drago mi je. Ja sam Sandra Bryant. Ovo je moj muž, Mark.
Jasna	Drago mi je. Ja sam Jasna Kušan.
Mark	Drago mi je, gospođice.

Dobra večer. *Good evening.*
Kako ste? *How are you?*
Dobro. *Fine.*
Ovo je moja prijateljica. *This is my (female) friend.*
Ovo je moj muž. *This is my husband.*
gospođice *Miss*
Jeste li vi Engleskinja? *Are you (an) English(woman)?*
A vi ste Hrvatica? *And you're a Croat(ian woman)?*
Razumijete li ...? *Do you understand ...?*
Razumijem dosta. *I understand a lot.*
ali *but*
slabo *not much* (lit. *weakly*)

QUICK VOCAB

True or false?

a Mark speaks Croatian well.
b Rudolf is studying English.
c Jasna is Rudolf's wife.

Insight

The word **gospodin** *Mr* is spelt with a small letter except at the beginning of a sentence. Other common titles are **gospođa** *Mrs* and **gospođica** *Miss*. They are abbreviated in writing to **g.**, **gđa** and **gđica**. In the dialogue, when **gospodin** and **gospođica** are used to address someone directly, they change slightly at the end of the word and you have the forms **gospodine** and **gospođice**. There are a number of patterns that affect the ends of words.

In these early stages be aware that you will come across a few examples where a word will appear with a slight variation. You will gradually learn the rules that govern these changes.

(Contd)

When greeting people the following formulas are used, depending on the time of day:

dobro jutro *good morning* until about 10 a.m.
dobar dan *good day* until late afternoon
dobra večer *good evening*

The word **večer** is used to refer to the time until midnight.
The phrases used when parting are:

do viđenja *goodbye*   **laku noć** *good night*

These are somewhat formal and polite expressions. In more
colloquial circumstances, people use **zdravo** when both
greeting and parting from people. In Zagreb, **bog** is said as a
very colloquial expression meaning *'bye* or *cheerio*.

Key phrases

◀)) **CD1, TR 1, 08:29**

How to:

▶ ask who people are	Tko ste vi?
	Jeste li vi …?
▶ say who you are	Ja sam …
▶ ask how someone is	Kako ste?
▶ reply that you are fine	Ja sam dobro.
▶ ask what language people speak or understand	Govorite li …
	Razumijete li …
▶ say what languages you speak or understand	Govorim …
	Razumijem …
▶ respond when being introduced	Drago mi je. Ja sam …
▶ introduce others	Da vas upoznam. Ove je …
▶ respond when meeting people –	
… in the morning	Dobro jutro.
… in the afternoon	Dobar dan.
… in the evening	Dobra večer.
▶ say goodbye	do viđenja/laku noć.

How it works

The, a **or** *an*

Croatian does not have separate words for *the* and *a*. So, the title of the unit, **U hotelu**, may mean either *'In the hotel'* or *'In a hotel'*, depending on the context. The lack of such words strikes the English ear as odd at first, but you soon get used to speaking without them.

I **and** *you*

The words **ja** *I* and **vi** *you* are rarely used. They tend to be omitted unless asking a direct, personal question or if emphasis is required.

I am **and** *you are*

In Croatian, there are two forms for saying *I am* and *you are*:

ja sam	*I am*
ja jesam	
vi ste	*you are*
vi jeste	

The first one in both examples is called the 'short form' and the other is called the 'long form'. The main difference is that the short form (**sam, ste**) is never used as the first word of a sentence or phrase. The long form is used for:

  a emphasis
  b giving one-word answers to questions
  c asking questions.

Compare the following:

Ja sam Mark Bryant.	*I am Mark Bryant.*
Ja sam Englez.	*I am English.*
Jeste li vi Mark Bryant?	*Are you Mark Bryant?*
Jesam.	*I am.*

When **ja** or **vi** are omitted word order is affected. Compare the following:

Kako ste?	*How are you?*
Ja sam dobro, hvala.	*I am well, thank you.*
or	
Dobro sam, hvala.	*I am well, thank you.*

I speak/you speak

Ja and **vi** are largely unnecessary because the end of each verb (verbs are words that express actions) tells you who is performing the action. These verbs form regular patterns. Note the difference at the ends of the verbs:

govori**m**	*I speak*
govori**te**	*you speak*

You can see and hear the same differences at the ends of the other verbs used in the dialogue:

razumije**m**	*I understand*
razumije**te**	*you understand*
uči**m**	*I study*
uči**te**	*you study*

There is only one form of each verb in the present tense, so that **govorim** means *I speak*, *I am speaking* and *I do speak*.

Statements and questions

Compare the following constructions to see the difference between a statement and a question:

Statement
Govorim hrvatski.	*I speak Croatian.*
Razumijem engleski.	*I understand English.*

Question
Govorite li hrvatski?   *Do you speak Croatian?*
Razumijete li engleski?   *Do you understand English?*

If you include the word **vi** in the question, then the word order is as follows:

Govorite li **vi** hrvatski?
Razumijete li **vi** engleski?

A question is made by putting **li** after the verb and before **vi**.
A question can also be made by putting **da li** in front of the verb:

Da li **govorite hrvatski?**   *Do you speak Croatian?*
Da li **razumijete engleski?**   *Do you understand English?*

Another type of question involves the use of an interrogative word, for example:

Tko ste vi?   *Who are you?*

Categories of nouns (gender)

All nouns (words which name things) in Croatian belong to one of three categories called genders: masculine, feminine and neuter. The gender of a noun can usually be recognized by its ending.

Masculine nouns end in consonants:

Englez   *Englishman*
jezik   *language*
muž   *husband*

Feminine nouns end in **-a**:

Engleskinja   *Englishwoman*
žena   *wife*
prijateljica   *friend (female)*

Neuter nouns end in -o or -e:

pero   *pen*
more   *sea*

There are some smaller groups that do not conform to these patterns, such as **večer** *evening*, which is a feminine noun although it ends in a consonant. The names of the categories are not always associated with biological gender (what is masculine about a language?) but where they are you will usually find that words are paired: e.g. **prijateljica** (*female friend*, fem. gender), **prijatelj** (*male friend*, masc. gender).

There are two other words to mean 'husband' and 'wife' that are more formal terms than the ones used in the dialogue. These are: **suprug** (*husband*, masc. gender); **supruga** (*wife*, fem. gender).

My **and** *your*

My and *your* are called possessive adjectives because they describe the possession of an object. In common with all adjectives (words that describe objects) in Croatian and in many other languages, too, their ending changes according to the gender of the noun. We say that the adjective agrees with the noun.

Masculine adjectives end in a consonant and feminine adjectives add -a:

Ovo je moj **muž.**   *This is my husband.*
Ovo je moja **žena.**   *This is my wife.*

The corresponding word for *your* is **vaš**:

Ovo je vaš **hotel.**   *This is your hotel.*
Ovo je vaša **sekretarica.**   *This is your secretary.*

◀) **CD1, TR 1, 09:37**

Languages and nationalities

Languages are spelt with a small letter: **hrvatski** *Croatian language.*

Nationalities and inhabitants of countries take a capital letter: **Hrvat** *Croatian man*, **Hrvatica** *Croatian woman*.

There are two different forms to denote a person by their nationality, one for men and one for women. Other examples of language and nationality are:

Language		Nationality
srpski	*Serbian*	Srbin/Srpkinja
slovenski	*Slovenian*	Slovenac/Slovenka
makedonski	*Macedonian*	Makedonac/Makedonka
engleski	*English*	Englez/Engleskinja
francuski	*French*	Francuz/Francuskinja
njemački	*German*	Nijemac/Njemica
ruski	*Russian*	Rus/Ruskinja

Insight

It is important to remember that Croatian distinguishes between male and female names for nationalities:

Hrvat	*Croat(man)*	**Hrvatica**	*Croat(woman)*
Englez	*English(man)*	**Engleskinja**	*English(woman)*

The names of languages are different and are written with a small letter:

hrvatski	*Croatian*
engleski	*English*

Practice

1 Unscramble the following letters to form words:
   a etajipricalj
   b bardo reveč
   c stroopite

2 Look at the information that Mark gives about himself:
Ja sam Mark Bryant. Ja sam Englez. Govorim engleski.
Make up similar sentences for:

   a Jasna
   b Rudolf
   c Sandra
   d yourself

3 Look at the following dialogue.

Jasna	Tko ste vi?
Metka	Ja sam Metka. Ja sam Slovenka.
Jasna	Govorite li slovenski?
Metka	Da, govorim slovenski.

Repeat the dialogue using the following names (say what you
think their likely nationalities and languages are):

   a Hans
   b Pierre
   c Ivan

4 You are introduced to someone. Ask them if they speak:

   a English
   b French
   c Croatian
   d Serbian

◀) **CD1, TR 1, 10:31**

5 What would you say to greet someone:

   a in the early part of the morning?
   b in the afternoon?
   c in the evening?
   d How would you say goodbye?

6 Fill in the missing part of the following dialogue:
Dobra večer.
Good evening. How are you?
Dobro, hvala. Da vas upoznam. Ovo je moj muž.
Pleased to meet you. I am …
Drago mi je. Ja sam Velimir.
Good night.
Laku noć.

7 Rudolf introduces Jasna:
Da vas upoznam. Ovo je Jasna. Jasna je moja prijateljica.
Make up introductions such as:
 a Sandra introduces Mark.
 b Mark introduces Sandra.

Comprehension

Earlier that day Jasna went to work. She met her boss, g. Kovač, in the corridor as she arrived. She met him again later in the day as he was showing a friend of his from another company around the office. Jasna works as a secretary (**sekretarica**).

Ujutro *In the morning*

G. Kovač	Dobro jutro. Kako ste gospođice Kušan?
Jasna	Dobro sam, hvala gospodine. A kako ste vi?
G. Kovač	I ja sam dobro, hvala. Do viđenja.
Jasna	Do viđenja, gospodine Kovaču.

Kasnije poslije podne *Later that afternoon*

G. Kovač	Ah, ovo je Jasna Kušan, moja sekretarica. Dobar dan Jasna. Da vas upoznam. Ovo je moj prijatelj, gospodin Marinković.

| Jasna | Drago mi je, gospodine Marinkoviću. Ja sam Jasna Kušan. |
| G. Marinković | Drago mi je. |

True or false?

a Jasna does not feel well in the morning.
b Jasna is Mr Kovač's secretary.
c Mr Kovač introduces Jasna to his friend.

[Note that the surnames of Mr Kovač and Mr Marinković change when they are addressed directly as does the word **gospodin** (see Insight earlier on in this unit)].

Test yourself

Here you can check some of the things you have learnt in this unit. Look at the questions that follow and choose the right answer:

1 How do you say *Good morning* in Croatian?
   a Dobar dan
   b Dobra večer
   c Dobro jutro

2 Which expression would you use to greet someone at 12 a.m.?
   a Dobar dan
   b Dobro jutro
   c Laku noć

3 What is the Croatian for *Goodbye*?
   a Laku noć
   b Do viđenja
   c Dobra večer

4 When do you use the greeting *Zdravo*?
  a when meeting and parting from friends
  b to greet people formally
  c only when parting from friends

5 Which of the following titles is the equivalent to *Mrs* in English?
  a gospođica
  b gospođa
  c gospodin

6 Which of the following nouns is masculine?
  a jezik
  b more
  c žena

7 What is the word **jutro** by gender?
  a masculine
  b feminine
  c neuter

8 Which word would you use to fill the gap in the phrase ... **žena**?
  a moja
  b moj

9 How would you ask someone *Do you speak English*?
  a Učite li engleski?
  b Govorite li engleski?
  c Razumijete li engleski?

10 How would you tell someone that you understand Croatian?
  a Razumijem hrvatski.
  b Govorim hrvatski.
  c Učim hrvatski.

2

U kavani
In the café

In this unit you will learn how to
- *Say what you want or like*
- *Ask others what they want or like*
- *Ask what others want to drink*
- *Give and ask for personal information*
- *Say* in *and* to
- *Make negative statements*

Dialogue

Now that Rudolf and Jasna have met the Bryants, they invite Mark and Sandra for a drink in the hotel.

Rudolf	Gdje živite, vi i Sandra?	CD1, TR 2
Mark	Živimo u Londonu.	
Rudolf	Da li volite živjeti u Londonu?	
Mark	Da, volimo tamo živjeti. Volimo London.	
Rudolf	Što želite popiti?	
Mark	Žedan sam. Ja bih pivo, hvala.	
Rudolf	Jasna, da li si žedna?	
Jasna	Nisam. Što želite popiti, Sandra?	
Sandra	Ja bih kavu, hvala.	

(Contd)

Jasna	Da ... kava je ovdje veoma dobra. I vino je dobro. Ja bih vino, Rudolf.
Rudolf	U redu. Ti želiš vino, Jasna, a vi želite kavu, Sandra.

Gdje živite? *Where do you live?*
živimo *we live*
u Londonu *in London*
Da li volite ...? *Do you like ...?*
živjeti *to live*
volimo *we like* (or *love*)
tamo *there*
Što želite ... *What do you want ...*
popiti *to drink*
Žedan sam. *I am thirsty.* (male speaking)
Ja bih ... *I would like ...*
pivo *beer*
Da li si žedna? *Are you thirsty?* (to a female)
Nisam. *I am not.*
Ja bih kavu. *I would like a coffee.*
Kava je veoma dobra. *The coffee is very good.*
ovdje *here*
Vino je dobro. *The wine is good.*
u redu *OK, all right*
ti želiš *you want*
vi želite *you want*

They order their drinks from the waiter and continue chatting.

Jasna	Volite li živjeti u Londonu, Sandra?
Sandra	Ne, ne volim živjeti u Londonu, ali radim tamo.
Jasna	Što radite?
Sandra	Radim u školi. Ja sam učiteljica. Radim kao učiteljica.
Jasna	Ja radim kao sekretarica u Zagrebu.
Sandra	Živite li u gradu?
Jasna	Ne, ne živim u gradu. Živim u predgrađu. Idem u grad na posao. Kamo vi idete?
Sandra	Idem u školu. Moja škola je u gradu.

Jasna	Rudolf, ideš li sutra u grad?
Rudolf	Da, idem.

ne *no*
ne volim ... *I do not like ...*
radim *I work, I do*
Što radite? *What do you do?*
u školi *in school*
učiteljica *teacher* (female)
kao *as*
u gradu *in town*
u predgrađu *in a suburb*
idem u grad *I go to town*
na posao *to work* (to my job)
Kamo vi idete? *Where do you go?*
u školu *to school*
moja škola je ... *my school is ...*
Ideš li ...? *Are you going ...?*
sutra *tomorrow*

True or false?

a Mark does not like living in London.
b Jasna is thirsty.
c Rudolf is going to town tomorrow.

Insight

In common with many other European languages, Croatian has two words for *you*: **ti** and **vi**. The **ti** form is used among friends, relations, to children and is generally recognized as an informal mode of address. It is only used when referring to one person. The **vi** form is always used when referring to more than one person. It is also a more formal and polite form, used to a boss at work or to a stranger.

Do not try to use **ti** to someone thinking that you are just being friendly. The conventions for choosing the correct form

(Contd)

depend on social factors that you might not recognize. You could cause great offence. Rudolf uses **ti** when he speaks to Jasna, but **vi** when he speaks to Mark or Sandra. Always let the Croat to whom you are speaking be the first to use the **ti** form. It is, however, common for teenagers and students to use the **ti** form within their own age group.

Insight

People might drop in at a **kavana** for a drink. The usual system is to find a table and wait for the waiter to come and take your order – which might be **kava, pivo, vino, sok** *fruit juice* or a **rakija** *brandy*. You could try asking for **čaj** *tea*, but you might get the herbal variety. In some of the trendy cafés in Zagreb and on the coast, you might find a bar with something like counter service as in a pub. These are usually small places, called a **kafić**. You can also buy snacks in some and even proper meals. The usual place for a meal would be a **restoran** *restaurant*, in many of which a small area is often set aside for customers who only want a drink. On a train or at a station look for the **bife** *buffet*.

Key phrases

◀ CD1, TR 2, 01:34

How to:

▶ ask what someone wants to drink	Što želite popiti?
▶ respond when offered a drink	Ja bih kavu.
	Ja bih pivo.
	Ja bih vino.
▶ ask where someone lives	Gdje živite?
▶ respond when asked where you live	Živim/Živimo u Londonu.
	(u Zagrebu, u gradu, u predgrađu)

▶ ask if someone likes to do something	**Da li volite ...** (or **Volite li ...**)
▶ respond that you do like something or that you do not like something	**Da, volim ...** **Ne, ne volim.**
▶ ask what someone does for a living	**Što radite?**
▶ say what you do for a living	**Radim kao ...**
▶ ask where someone is going	**Kamo ideš?**
▶ respond when asked where you are going	**Idem u grad.** (**u školu, na posao**)
▶ say that something is here or there	**Kava je ovdje dobra.** **Ne volim tamo živjeti.**

How it works

You **and** *we*

The two new words for referring to people in this unit are **ti** *you* and **mi** *we*. They are rarely used except for emphasis. The ending of the verb changes according to the following pattern:

ti voliš	*you like/love*
mi volimo	*we like/love*
ti ideš	*you go*
mi idemo	*we go*

These endings can be added to the other verbs that you have met so far:

ti govoriš	*you speak*
mi razumijemo	*we understand*

Here is the exception:

ti si (jesi – long form)	*you are*
mi smo (jesmo – long form)	*we are*

I like to live in ... **(infinitive)**

You have met verbs in one of two ways, either with a person
(*I like, you work*, etc.) or as an infinitive (*to live, to drink*, etc.).
The infinitive usually follows a verb with a person (I like *to live* in
London). In English, the infinitive is two words, but, in Croatian,
it is one word:

živjeti	*to live*
popiti	*to drink*

Once you know both the infinitive and the **ja** parts of the verb, you
will be able to produce any form of a verb. You can recognize the
other infinitives from the parts of the verb you already know:

govorim	**govoriti**	*to speak*
razumijem	**razumjeti**	*to understand*
učim	**učiti**	*to study*
radim	**raditi**	*to do, work*
volim	**voljeti**	*to like, love*
želim	**željeti**	*to want*

There are one or two exceptions: e.g. **ja sam** – biti *to be*. Most
infinitives end in **-ti** but some end in – **ći**: e.g. **idem** – **ići** (*to go*).
You can find more verbs in the lists of new words following the
Dialogue with their infinitives and **ja** forms.

I do not like **(negation)**

To say that you are not doing something (to negate a verb) simply
place **ne** before the verb:

Ne **volim živjeti u Londonu.**	*I do not like to live in London.*
Ne **želimo popiti pivo.**	*We do not want a drink of beer.*

The verb **biti** as usual provides an exception. The pattern that
means *I am not*, etc. is all one word:

nisam	*I am not*	**nismo**	*we are not*
nisi	*you are not*	**niste**	*you are not* (plural)

Thirsty/hungry **(adjectives)**

Adjectives change their endings like nouns: e.g. Mark says **žedan sam** *I am thirsty* while Sandra says **žedna sam**.

Masculine adjectives end in a consonant.
Feminine adjectives end in -a.
Neuter adjectives end in -o.

There is a rule of spelling and pronunciation that after certain consonants you write and say **e** instead of **o**. These are called soft consonants and they are **c, č, ć, dž, đ, j, lj, nj, š** and **ž**.

If there is the letter **a** between the final two consonants it is omitted when you add the ending for feminine and neuter:

Masc.	**Fem.**	**Neut.**
dobar	dobra	dobro
žedan	žedna	žedno
gladan (*hungry*)	gladna	gladno
moj	moja	moje

Possessive adjectives

The two possessive adjectives relevant to this unit are:

tvoj	*your* (corresponds to **ti**)
naš	*our* (corresponds to **mi**)

Ovo je moja kava.	*This is my coffee.*
Ovo je tvoje pivo.	*This is your beer.*
Ovo je naš grad.	*This is our town.*
Ovo je vaša žena.	*This is your wife.* (someone to whom you would normally use the **vi** form)

···

Insight

Croatian uses the same word to mean both *in* and *to*: **u**.

The difference between the two meanings is indicated at the end of the noun. Compare the following two sentences:

Idem u grad.	*I go to town.* (motion)
Ja sam u gradu.	*I am in town.* (stationary)
Idem u školu.	*I go to school.*
Ja sam u školi.	*I am in school.*

···

Words like **u**, which relate two things together often in a spatial way as in these examples, are called prepositions. Different prepositions require different endings. The endings indicate what are called the cases of the noun. Here there are examples of two cases: the accusative (acc.) and the dative (dat.) case. (In some grammar books this use of the dative after **u** is sometimes referred to as the locative case. However, given that the locative and dative case endings are always the same we have continued them under the dative heading in this book.) They follow these patterns:

Masc. (e.g. **grad**)
acc.   **grad** (no change)
dat.   **gradu** (add -**u**)

Fem. (e.g. **škola**)
acc.   **školu** (change -**a** to -**u**)
dat.   **školi** (change -**a** to -**i**)

Neut. (e.g. **predgrađe**)
acc.   **predgrađe** (no change)
dat.   **predgrađu** (change -**e**/-**o** to -**u**)

The acc. after **u** indicates being in motion.
The dat. after **u** indicates being stationary.

Study the following examples:

Da li živiš u Londonu?	*Do you live in London?*
Idemo u London.	*We are going to London.*
Ne idem u kavanu.	*I am not going to the café.*
Mi smo u kavani.	*We are in the café.*
Idete li u predgrađe?	*Are you going to the suburb?*
Nisam u predgrađu.	*I am not in the suburb.*

Croatian has two ways of asking *where?*:

Gdje živite?	*Where do you live?*
Kamo idete?	*Where are you going?*

Gdje asks where something is (being stationary).
Kamo asks to where something is going (being in motion).
In answering a question with **gdje**, you use dat.
In answering a question with **kamo**, you use acc.

Other ways of saying *to*

You have seen that **na** can also mean *to* in the expression:

Idem na posao.	*I am to going to work.*

The word **na** usually means *on* but is also used with certain nouns where you would not say *on* in English, such as with the word **pošta** *post office* and **kolodvor** *station* and in some idioms:

Ja sam na pošti.	*I am in the post office.*
Idem na kolodvor.	*I am going to the station.*
Idemo na kavu.	*We are going for a coffee.*
Ideš li na pivo?	*Are you going for a beer?*

The acc. after **na** indicates being in motion.
The dat. after **na** indicates being stationary.

Unusual noun categories

Somewhere and somehow, there are always words in any language that do not behave like most of the others. For example, most masculine nouns end in a consonant. **Posao** *job*, *work*, however, is a masculine noun. Centuries ago the -o at the end was an -l, but with time its pronunciation was softened into this vowel sound. When you add case endings, the old 'l' returns to replace the 'o'.

Posao also has that -a before the last letter that disappears as soon as you add a different ending to the word (think of **dobar dan** and the change to **dobro jutro**). The pattern of its changes looks like this:

acc. posao
dat. poslu

Practice

◀) CD1, TR 2, 03:02

1 Answer the following questions: positively, negatively.
   e.g. Volite li pivo?
         Volim. Ne volim.
   a Volite li kavu?
   b Govorite li engleski?
   c Jeste li vi Englez?
   d Volite li London?
   e Želite li živjeti u Londonu?
   f Želite li ići u grad?
   g Volite li ići na posao?
   h Idete li na kavu?

2 Change all the questions in Question 1 to the **ti** form of the verb.

3 Find the two correct forms of the verbs in the lists on the right to match the personal pronouns on the left:
   a ja   si, sam, razumijete, govorimo, učim
   b ti   želiš, želite, ideš, razumijem
   c mi   živim, razumijemo, učimo, volite
   d vi   ste, smo, učite, učimo

4 Put the noun in brackets into the correct case.
   Kamo ideš, Rudolf?   Gdje je Jasna?
   a Idem u (grad).   **g** Jasna je u (grad).
   b Idem u (kavana).   **h** Jasna je u (London).
   c Idem u (škola).   **i** Jasna je u (škola).
   d Idem u (Zagreb).   **j** Jasna je na (posao).
   e Idem na (posao).   **k** Jasna je u (kavana).
   f Idem na (kava).   **l** Jasna je u (predgrađe).

5 Put the verbs and nouns in brackets into the correct forms:
   e.g. (ići – ti)   u (grad)
       Ideš   u grad.
   a (željeti – mi) živjeti u (London).
   b (željeti – ja) živjeti u (Zagreb).
   c (ići – ti) na (kava).
   d (živjeti – ja) u (grad).
   e (živjeti – mi) u (predgrađe).
   f (voljeti – vi) biti na (posao).

6 Match the following questions with the appropriate responses:
   a Kamo idete?   **i** Ja bih kavu.
   b Gdje želite živjeti?   **ii** Idem u grad.
   c Što želite popiti?   **iii** Radim kao učiteljica.
   d Što radite?   **iv** Želim živjeti u Londonu.

7 Put the adjectives in brackets into the correct form:
   e.g. Jasna je (gladan).
       Jasna je gladna.
   a (dobar) večer.
   b Sandra je (žedan).

c Ovo je (naš) predgrađe.
d Mark je (vaš) muž.
e Ovo je (moj) (dobar) prijateljica.
f Ovo je (tvoj) kavana.
g Rudolf je (gladan).

Comprehension

Two friends, Velimir and Zvonko, are chatting about Velimir's new flat.

CD1, TR 2 04:28

Zvonko	Gdje živiš?
Velimir	Živim u gradu.
Zvonko	Kako to? Imaš stan u predgrađu.
Velimir	Imam nov stan u gradu.
Zvonko	Voliš li živjeti u gradu?
Velimir	Volim. Moj posao je u gradu.
Zvonko	Ideš li sutra na posao?
Velimir	Idem. Volim ići na posao.
Zvonko	Gdje radiš?
Velimir	Radim u školi.
Zvonko	Što radiš?
Velimir	Sada radim kao učitelj.

QV

Kako to? *How come?*	**posao** *job* (work)
imaš *you have*	**sada** *now*
imam *I have*	**učitelj** *teacher* (masc.)
nov stan *a new flat*	

True or false?

a Velimir has a new flat.
b Velimir has a job in the suburbs.
c Velimir has a new job as a bus conductor.

Test yourself

Here you can check some of the things you have learnt in this unit. Look at the questions that follow and choose the right answer:

1 How would you ask someone what they want u to drink?
  a Što želite raditi?
  b Što želite učiti?
  c Što želite popiti?

2 How would you say that you are working in a school
  Radim u ...?
  a školi
  b škola
  c školu

3 How would Mark say that he is hungry?
  a Žedan sam.
  b Gladna sam.
  c Gladan sam.

4 What does Jasna mean when she says *Nisam žedna*?
  a she is not hungry
  b she is not thirsty
  c she is not tired

5 How would you say that you would like a coffee?
  a Ja bih kavu.
  b Ja bih pivo.
  c Ja bih vino.

6 Match the question on the left with the correct answer on the right:
  a Kamo ideš sutra?   **i** Da, jesam.
  b Da li si žedna?   **ii** Ja bih pivo.
  c Volite li živjeti u Londonu? **iii** Radim kao učitelj.
  d Što želite popiti?   **iv** Idem na posao.
  e Što radiš u školi?   **v** Ne, ne volim tamo živjeti.

3

U gradu
In town

In this unit you will learn how to
- *Express basic directions*
- *Ask where something is*
- *Say where something is in relation to something else*
- *Say other expressions useful in getting about a town*
- *Express* can *and* have to

Dialogue

Rudolf and Jasna have invited the Bryants to join them for a trip into the town. This is the first time the Bryants have had the opportunity to see something of Zagreb. Their Croatian friends call at their hotel.

CD1, TR 3

Rudolf	Dobar dan, Mark. Dobar dan, Sandra. Kako ste?
Mark	Dobro smo, hvala. A, kako ste vi?
Rudolf	I ja sam dobro.
Mark	Gdje je Jasna?
Rudolf	Ona dolazi. Parkira auto ispred hotela. Evo Jasne, sada možemo ići u grad.

QV

Ona dolazi. (dolaziti, dolazim) *She is coming.*
Parkira auto. (parkirati, parkiram) *She (or he) is parking the car.*

28

ispred hotela *in front of the hotel*
Evo Jasne. *Here is Jasna.*
sada *now*
možemo (moći, mogu – irregular verb) *we can, we may,*
  we are able

From here onwards you will find both the infinitive and **ja** forms of
  new verbs. (You can recognize the infinitive by the ending, and it is
  followed by the **ja** form.)

Sandra and Jasna walk and chat together. Rudolf and Mark walk
ahead.

Sandra	Gdje smo sada?
Jasna	Na desno je Esplanade. To je dobar hotel. Na lijevo je glavni kolodvor. Sada idemo ravno u centar grada. Vidite li tamo veliku zgradu? Da … Rudolf tamo radi. Njegov ured je u zgradi.
Sandra	A što je tamo ispred kolodvora?
Jasna	To je park. U parku je spomenik. Ovo je lijep kraj grada.
Sandra	Da, lijep je. Gdje su Mark i Rudolf?
Jasna	Vidim Rudolfa blizu spomenika. I Mark je tamo ispod drveta.
Sandra	Što rade?
Jasna	Gledaju spomenik.

QUICK VOCAB

na desno *on the right*
To je Hotel Esplanade. *That is the Esplanade hotel.*
na lijevo *on the left*
glavni kolodvor *main station*
ići ravno *to go straight on*
centar grada *the centre of town*
vidite (vidjeti, vidim) *you see* (**vi** form)
veliku zgradu *large building* (acc.)
njegov ured *his office*
ispred kolodvora *in front of the station*
park *park*

spomenik *monument*
lijep kraj grada *a nice part of town*
Gdje su ...? *Where are ...?*
Vidim Rudolfa. *I see Rudolf.*
blizu spomenika *near the monument*
ispod drveta *under the tree*
Što rade? *What are they doing?*
Gledaju spomenik. (gledati, gledam) *They are looking at the monument.*

Mark	Kamo idemo sada?
Rudolf	Idemo na Jelačićev trg, a onda u Gornji grad.
Mark	Gdje je pošta? Moram kupiti marke i koverte. Jesu li skupe?
Rudolf	Ne, nisu skupe. Pošta nije daleko od trga. Možemo tamo otići kasnije.

QUICK VOCAB

Jelačićev trg *Jelačić Square*
a onda *and then, next*
Gornji grad *Upper Town*
pošta *post office*
moram ... (morati) *I have to ...*
kupiti (kupim) *to buy*
marke *stamps* (acc. plural)
koverte *envelopes* (acc. plural)
Jesu li skupe? *Are they expensive?*
nisu *they are not*
Nije daleko od trga. *It is not far from the square.*
otići *to go on to, to go away*
kasnije *later*

True or false?

a Jasna is coming to the hotel by bus.
b The Esplanade is a good hotel.
c The post office is near the main square.

Insight

Zagreb is the capital city of Croatia. It is the cultural, political and industrial centre of the region. Parts of **Gornji grad** *Upper Town* date from the medieval period. **Gornji grad** is aptly named as it sits on top of a hill overlooking the modern centre, much of which was constructed in the last century when Zagreb was a provincial capital in the Hapsburg Empire. After the Second World War the city was the capital of the Republic of Croatia within the Yugoslav Federation and from the beginning of 1992 has been the capital of the independent state of Croatia. It has a population of about one million.

Insight

The Upper Town has no bus or tram services as the streets are too narrow and such modern conveniences would spoil this old part of town. The area is well known for its small squares with their restaurants and cafés. It can be reached on foot from **Jelačićev trg** through the old streets that twist their way uphill. There is also a funicular railway that can be found not far from **Jelačićev trg** along one of the main streets called **Ilica**.

Key phrases

◀) **CD1, TR 3, 01:49**

How to:

▶ say that something is on the left or on the right	Ovo je na lijevo. Ovo je na desno.
▶ say 'We're going straight on'	Idemo ravno.
▶ say where things are –	
in front of (the hotel)	ispred (hotela)
near (the monument)	blizu (spomenika)
under (the tree)	ispod (drveta)
not far from (the square)	nije daleko od (trga)

- ▶ say this is (a nice part of town) **Ovo je (lijep kraj grada).**
  or that is (a good hotel) **To je (dobar hotel).**
- ▶ express (we) can (go now) **sada možemo (ići)**
  and (I) must (buy) **moram (kupiti)…**
  (both verbs are followed by the infinitive of what can or
  must be done)
- ▶ announce that someone is here **Evo Jasne.**

How it works

*He/she/it **and** they*

In this unit, you have learnt the final parts of the verb in the
present tense. They express *he/she/it does* or *they do*. The words
for the pronouns (*he*, etc.) are as follows:

	Masc.	Fem.	Neut.
singular	on	ona	ono
plural	oni	one	ona

Unlike in English, there are three forms of the plural (*they*) and
the pronouns may be used to refer to both people and things
depending on the gender of the noun they are replacing, e.g.:

Spomenik (masc.) je u parku. *The monument is in the park.*
On je u parku. *It is in the park.*
Oni su u parku. *They* (monuments) *are in in the park.*

Zgrada (fem.) je na trgu. *The building is on the square.*
Ona je na trgu. *It is on the square.*
One su na trgu. *They* (buildings) *are on the square.*
Kazalište (neut.) je u gradu. *The theatre is in the town.*
Ono je u gradu. *It is in the town.*
Ona su u gradu. *They* (theatres) *are in the town.*
Rudolf je ovdje a Jasna je tamo. *Rudolf is here and Jasna is there.*

On je ovdje a ona je tamo.   *He is here and she is there.*
Oni su na lijevo a one su na   *They (men) are on the left*
desno.   *and they (women) are on*
   the right.

When you are talking about two things, one masculine and one feminine, the masculine forms are used:

Spomenik i zgrada su u parku.   *The monument and the building*
   are in the park.
Oni su u parku.   *They are in the park.*

Verbal forms and categories

Now that you have all the parts of the verb you can see the complete pattern of endings in the present tense. There are just three standard types of ending depending on the vowel that occurs immediately before the -m of the ja form:

  a i type (dolazim)
  b e type (idem)
  c a type (gledam)

dolaziti *to come*

ja	dolazim	mi	dolazimo
ti	dolaziš	vi	dolazite
on/a/o	dolazi	oni/e/a	dolaze

ići *to go*

ja	idem	mi	idemo
ti	ideš	vi	idete
on/a/o	ide	oni/e/a	idu

gledati *to look at*

ja	gledam	mi	gledamo
ti	gledaš	vi	gledate
on/a/o	gleda	oni/e/a	gledaju

These three verbs represent the three patterns of the verb in the present tense in Croatian.

There are a small number of irregular verbs that do not follow this plan. The ones which you have met so far are:

moći *may, can, able to do something*

ja	mogu	mi	možemo
ti	možeš	vi	možete
on/a/o	može	oni/e/a	mogu

biti *to be*

short form				*long form*	
ja	sam	mi	smo	jesam	jesmo
ti	si	vi	ste	jesi	jeste
on/a/o	je	oni/e/a	su	jest	jesu
				(**jest** also has form **jeste**)	

The negative form is spelt as one word:

nisam	nismo
nisi	niste
nije	nisu

There is one exception to the use of the short form of **biti** and that is when asking a question with **je**. In this instance, the short form may come at the beginning of the question. Compare the following:

Je li Sandra u hotelu?   *Is Sandra in the hotel?*
Jesu li Sandra i Mark u hotelu?   *Are Sandra and Mark in the hotel?*

Where things are

New expressions are used in this unit that tell you where things are:

ispred hotela	*in front of the hotel*
Evo Jasne.	*Here is Jasna.*
blizu spomenika	*near the monument*
ispod drveta	*under the tree*

Nije daleko od trga.	*It is not far from the square.*
Daleko je od trga.	*It is far from the square.*

Each position word is followed by the genitive case (gen.). This is another of the cases in Croatian. You can see the pattern of changes from the following examples:

Masc. (e.g. hotel)
gen.   **hotela** (add -a)

Fem. (e.g. škola)
gen.   **škole** (change -a to -e)

Neut. (e.g. predgrađe)
gen.   **predgrađa** (change -e/-o to -a)

How to say *of*

The genitive is not only used after certain place words. It has another important use to mean *of*.

u centru grada – *in the centre of town*
where **grada** actually means *of town*

Cases are often used when, in English, we would have to use one of those small words like *of*, *to*, *by*, etc. They give a greater economy to the language, although it takes a little while for the English speaker to become used to thinking about the ends of words in this way.

Other uses of cases

Look at these examples taken from the dialogues in this and the previous unit:

Kava je dobra.	*The coffee is good.*
Ja bih kavu.	*I would like a coffee.*
Vidite li tamo veliku zgradu?	*Do you see the big building there?*
Vidim Rudolfa **blizu spomenika.**	*I see Rudolf near the monument.*

The words **kava**, **zgrada** and **Rudolf** all change at the end. To understand why these words change here, look at these two English sentences:

I see him.
He sees me.

When *I* comes before the verb, it is called the subject because it is the one who is performing the action of the verb. When it comes after the verb, it changes to *me* and is called the object because the action of the verb is carried out on it. This is the pattern of the English language and you would be unlikely to confuse *I* and *me* (or *he* and *him*). The same principle operates in Croatian with all nouns.

In Croatian, nouns that are the object of the sentence are put into the accusative case. The accusative case of masculine nouns is the same as the nominative except when masculine nouns in the singular refer to people or animals when the accusative case is the same as the genitive. Study the following examples:

Volim kavu.	*I like coffee.*
Volim pivo.	*I like beer.*
Volim London.	*I like London.*
Vidim Rudolfa.	*I see Rudolf.*
Vidim Marka.	*I see Mark.*
Vidim Jasnu.	*I see Jasna.*

The case that identifies the gender of a noun is the nominative (nom.), and is used to express the subject of a sentence. Study the following examples:

Sandra (nom.) vidi Jasnu (acc.).	*Sandra sees Jasna.*
Mark (nom.) vidi Rudolfa (acc.).	*Mark sees Rudolf.*

Insight
You have now met the three most important uses of cases in Croatian.

in front of words to indicate position, movement or similar (called prepositions):

Idem u školu.	*I go to school.*
Rudolf je blizu spomenika.	*Rudolf is near the monument.*
Sandra je u hotelu.	*Sandra is in the hotel.*

to replace small linking words in English like *of*:

centar grada	*the centre of town*

to show the grammatical function of a word such as the subject and object of a sentence:

Jasna vidi Rudolfa.	*Jasna sees Rudolf.*
Rudolf vidi Jasnu.	*Rudolf sees Jasna.*

His/her/its/their **(possessive adjectives)**

Jasna points out to Sandra the building where Rudolf has his office and says **Tamo je njegov ured**. The words for *his*, *her*, *its* and *their* are adjectives like **moj**, **tvoj**, **naš** and **vaš**:

njegov	*his*
njen (or **njezin**)	*her*
njihov	*their*

Njegov also substitutes for neuter nouns as in:

Ovo je kazalište.	*This is the theatre.*
Njegova fasada je ...	*Its facade is ...*

The ending of the word changes to match in gender (agreement) with the thing being owned. Examples:

Ovo je njegov ured.	*This is his office.*
Ovo je njihov hotel.	*This is their hotel.*

Ovo je njena kava.   *This is her coffee.*
Ovo je njegovo pivo.   *This is his beer.*

Unusual noun categories

You have seen how nouns and verbs change their form and how all these changes fall into certain patterns; and how some words do not follow the standard patterns, like **posao**, which is a masculine noun although it ends in -o.

Drvo *tree* is a neuter noun, but with a slight difference to the usual pattern. Before case endings it adds -et- as in **ispod drveta**. A small group of such nouns follows this pattern:

nom.	drvo		gen.	drveta
acc.	drvo		dat.	drvetu

Practice

1 There are two correct and two incorrect verb endings given for each personal pronoun. Choose the two correct ones:
    a ja   moram, moramo, mogu, možemo
    b ti   govoriš, razumiješ, idete, morate
    c on   idu, dolazi, radi, moraju
    d mi   vidimo, idemo, uči, radi
    e vi   ste, smo, govorite, razumiješ
    f oni   idu, rade, razumije, vidi

2 Put the nouns in brackets into the correct case for the preposition:
    a Spomenik je u (park).
    b Naš hotel nije daleko od (kavana).
    c Pošta je na (trg).
    d Rudolf je blizu (drvo).
    e Mark ide u (grad).
    f Sandra ide na (pošta).

3 Put the nouns in brackets into the correct case for the object of the sentence:

    a Rudolf vidi (Jasna) ispod drveta.
    b Gledamo (spomenik) u parku.
    c Sandra mora kupiti (kava) i (sok).
    d Žele piti (vino).
    e Učiteljica voli (škola) u gradu.
    f Sekretarica vidi (gospodin) u uredu.

4 Supply the correct form of **njegov**, **njen** or **njihov** as required:

    e.g. Mark je u kavani.   Ovo je _____ kava.
                               Ovo je njegova kava.

    a Jasna je u kavani.   Ovo je _____ sok.
    b Rudolf je u kavani.   Ovo je _____ vino.
    c Sandra radi u školi.   Ovo je _____ škola.
    d Mark i Rudolf rade u uredu. Ovo je _____ ured.
    e Jasna i Sandra su u kavani. Ovo je _____ vino.
    f Mark i Sandra su u Zagrebu. Ovo je _____ hotel.

◀) **CD1, TR 3, 03:19**

5 Fill in your part of the dialogues:

    a Gdje je hotel?
       It is on the left in front of the station.
       A gdje je kolodvor?
       It is not far from the post office.
    b *Where can I buy stamps and envelopes?*
       Na pošti.
       Where is the post office?
       Idete ravno. Pošta je na desno.
    c *Where is Rudolf going?*
       Ide na posao.
       Where does he work?
    d Da li Mark gleda Sandru?
       Yes, he is looking at Sandra.
       Gdje je Sandra?
       Sandra is near the building.

6 Substitute the noun or nouns in brackets for **on/ona/ono** or **oni/one/ona**:

a (Zgrada) je velika.
b (Mark) je u hotelu.
c (Rudolf i njegova prijateljica) su na trgu.
d (Pošta) je u centru grada, blizu parka.
e (Sandra i Jasna) su ispred kolodvora.
f (Drvo) nije daleko od spomenika.
g (Rudolf i Mark) idu u centar grada.
h (Spomenik) je u parku.

Comprehension 1

Marija Marinković is a tour guide in Zagreb. She is showing a group of tourists around the centre of Zagreb.

◆ CD1, TR 3, 04:54

Marija	Sada smo u centru grada. Zagreb je lijep grad. To je kulturni i politički centar Hrvatske. Mi smo ispred hotela. Tamo je Glavni kolodvor. Na desno je hotel Esplanade. Idemo ravno prema trgu.
Turist	Oprostite, što je ono u parku?
Marija	To je spomenik. On se nalazi u parku.
Turist	Gdje je kazalište?
Marija	Kazalište nije daleko. Idete ravno, a ono je na desno. Zgrada je velika i lijepa. Sada dolazimo na Jelačićev trg. Velika zgrada na desno je Gradska kavana. Sada idemo u Gornji grad. On je vrlo star.

QUICK VOCAB

kulturni i politički centar *cultural and political centre*
Hrvatske *of Croatia*
prema trgu *towards the square*
ono *that* (over there)
On se nalazi u parku. *It is situated in the park.* (lit. *finds itself in the park.*)
star *old*

True or false?

a Zagreb is the cultural and political centre of Croatia.
b To get to the theatre, you go straight on and it is on the left.
c The café on the square is called **Gradska kavana**.

Comprehension 2

Read the following short passage about Velimir and Zvonko and answer the questions that follow:

Velimir ide u grad. Na ulici vidi Zvonka. Idu zajedno kroz park i razgovaraju. Dolaze do spomenika. Onda idu na desno, prema trgu.

Zvonko	Želiš li ići na kavu, Velimire?
Velimir	Možemo ići na kavu, ali prvo moram ići na poštu. Želim kupiti marke.
Zvonko	Gradska kavana nije daleko od pošte. Idemo tamo. *Idu zajedno na poštu. Velimir ulazi u zgradu. Zgrada je velika. Velimir izlazi i idu na desno. Ulaze u kavanu.*
Zvonko	Što želiš popiti?
Velimir	Ja bih kavu, hvala.
Zvonko	I ja bih kavu.

QUICK VOCAB

na ulici *on the street*
Vidi Zvonka. *He* (i.e. Velimir) *sees Zvonko.* (Zvonka is acc.)
kroz *through* (+ acc.)
zajedno *together*
razgovarati, razgovaram *to chat, have a conversation*
do *up to, as far as* (+ gen.)
prvo *first*
ulaziti, ulazim *to enter* (followed by **u zgradu**)
izlaziti, izlazim *to go out, come out*

Select the correct answer from **a**, **b** and **c** for each of the questions that follow.

1 Kamo idu Zvonko i Velimir?
  a Idu kroz park.
  b Idu u kazalište.
  c Idu u Gornji grad.

2 Što Velimir želi kupiti?
  a Želi kupiti koverte.
  b Želi kupiti kavu.
  c Želi kupiti marke.

3 Što žele Zvonko i Velimir popiti?
  a Žele popiti pivo.
  b Žele popiti kavu.
  c Žele popiti vino.

Test yourself

Here you can check some of the things you have learnt in this unit. Look at the questions that follow and choose the right answer:

1 If someone says that something is **na desno**, where is it?
  a on the right
  b on the left

2 What does **ispred** mean?
  a in front of
  b not far from
  c under

3 If you were looking for the theatre in a town, what would you ask?
  a Gdje je park?
  b Gdje je kazalište?
  c Gdje je kolodvor?

4 How would you say that you want to buy stamps in the post office?
   a Moram kupiti marke na pošti.
   b Mogu kupiti marke na pošti.
   c Želim kupiti marke na pošti.

5 Which case follows the word **blizu**?
   a nominative
   b accusative
   c genitive

6 Which form of the verb means *he is working*?
   a ja radim
   b on radi
   c mi radimo

7 What does **oni gledaju** mean?
   a I am looking
   b you are looking
   c they are looking

8 Which is the correct answer to the question **Da li su u hotelu?**
   a Jesam.
   b Jesu.
   c Jesmo.

9 Complete the following sentence by supplying the missing verb **Sada Rudolf i Jasna ... ići**:
   a mogu
   b možemo
   c može

10 Which form of the word meaning *they* would you use to talk about Jasna and Sandra?
   a oni
   b one
   c ona

4

Želim kupiti ...

I want to buy ...

In this unit you will learn how to

- ***Use phrases and expressions when shopping for basic items and when in the post office***
- ***Say numbers 1–20***
- ***Use words for handling money***
- ***Use expressions relating to need or desire***

Dialogue

Sandra treba kupiti neke stvari.

CD1, TR 4

Sandra Želim kupiti razglednicu, Jasna. Moram pisati mami. Gdje mogu kupiti razglednicu?

Jasna Razglednice možete kupiti u kiosku. Tamo je kiosk. Ali u svim kioscima ne prodaju razglednice.

QUICK VOCAB

trebati, trebam *to need, require*
neke stvari *some things*
razglednica *postcard*
pisati, pišem *to write*
mama *Mum*
kiosk *kiosk*
u svim kioscima *in all kiosks*
prodavati, prodajem *to sell*

From now onwards you will find more nouns in the nominative case, although they might appear in another case in the **Dialogue**.

Adjectives are given in the masculine nominative case. The forms are as they appear in the **Dialogue** where confusion might otherwise occur.

Sandra	Molim vas, imate li razglednice?
Prodavačica	Imam i velike i male razglednice. Kakve želite?
Sandra	Trebam veliku razglednicu. Koliko košta velika razglednica?
Prodavačica	Velika razglednica košta četiri kune, a mala tri kune.
Sandra	Dajte mi, molim vas, jednu veliku razglednicu, i jednu malu.
Prodavačica	Sedam kuna. Još nešto?
Sandra	Ne, hvala. *(Daje novac ženi.)*
Prodavačica	Molim.
Jasna	Hoćete li još nešto, Sandra?
Sandra	Znate, trebam sapun, šampon i zubnu pastu.
Jasna	Idemo u samoposlugu.

prodavačica *saleswoman*
imati, imam *to have*
molim vas *please* (lit. *I beg you*)
i ... i ... *both ... and ...*
male razglednice *small postcards*
Kakve želite? *What kind do you want?*
Koliko košta velika razglednica? *How much does a large postcard cost?*
velika razglednica košta *a large postcard costs*
četiri kune *4 kuna*
tri kune *3 kuna*
(**kuna** currency of Croatia abbreviated to **Kn**: divided into 100 **lipa**)
dajte mi *give to me*
jednu veliku razglednicu *one large postcard* (acc.)
sedam kuna *7 kuna*
Hoćete li još nešto? *Do you want anything else?*
htjeti, hoću (irregular verb) *to want*
davati, dajem *to give*
novac *money*

QUICK VOCAB

žena *woman*
hvala *thank you*
molim response to **hvala,** *please*
sapun *soap*
šampon *shampoo*
zubna pasta *toothpaste*
samoposluga *self-service shop*

Mark i Rudolf ulaze u poštu.

Mark	Molim vas, dajte mi tri koverte i marke za Englesku.
Čovjek	Ne prodajem koverte i nemam marke. Ovo je pogrešan šalter. Trebate šalter broj sedam.
Mark	Molim vas, mogu li ovdje kupiti marke i koverte?
Čovjek	Kako da ne, gospodine. Ovo je pošta!

čovjek *person, man*
tri koverte *three envelopes*
marke za Englesku *stamps for England*
nemam *I have not*
pogrešan šalter *the wrong counter*
šalter broj sedam *counter number seven*
kako da ne *of course*

True or false?

a Small postcards cost 4 kuna at the kiosk.
b Mark wants to buy four envelopes.
c Mark goes straightaway to the correct counter.

Insight

Kiosks are dotted along the streets of towns in the whole region. They sell newspapers, cigarettes, postcards, stamps, and often other small items. When handing over change or your purchases the shopkeeper might say **izvolite** (*here you are*). When asking for something it sounds a little harsh in English to say the equivalent of *give to me* (**dajte mi**), but it is said.

Insight

In addition to selling stamps and other items obvious to a visitor from England, you can also make telephone calls from a post office. This is particularly important if making a call overseas, as the rates tend to be much higher in hotels than in a post office. Simply go to the main desk in the post office, say where you want to call, you will then be told which booth (**kabina**) to use, make your call and pay on your way out.

Insight

It is polite to reply with **molim** when someone says **hvala** to you. You have met these words before. **Molim** also has other meanings. It is the equivalent of *please* when making a polite request or, if said with a questioning intonation, it means that you are asking that someone repeat what they have just said (very useful!).

Key phrases

◄» CD1, TR 4, 01:42

How to:

▶ express need or desire to different degrees

I need	**trebam**
I may, can	**mogu**
I must	**moram**
I want	**želim**
Do you want …?	**Hoćete li …?**

▶ request something in a shop

Molim vas, imate li …?
Molim vas, dajte mi …

▶ ask how much something costs **Koliko košta …?**
▶ use some numbers **jedna razglednica**
tri kune
tri koverte

▶ name basic items for purchase

postcard	**razglednica**
envelope	**koverta**
stamp	**marka**
soap	**sapun**
shampoo	**šampon**
toothpaste	**zubna pasta**

▶ say thank you   **hvala**

    and to reply politely   **molim**

How it works

Htjeti, hoću

Another common word meaning *want* is used in this unit. It follows an irregular pattern:

ja	**hoću**	**mi**	**hoćemo**
ti	**hoćeš**	**vi**	**hoćete**
on/a/o	**hoće**	**oni/e/a**	**hoće**

Like **biti** this verb also has a negative form that is all one word:

ja	**neću**	**mi**	**nećemo**
ti	**nećeš**	**vi**	**nećete**
on/a/o	**neće**	**oni/e/a**	**neće**

Hoću razglednicu.	*I want a postcard.*
Neću kupiti razglednicu.	*I do not want to buy a postcard.*
Hoćemo kavu.	*We want coffee.*
Nećete velike razglednice.	*You don't want the big postcards.*

Htjeti (**hoću**, *I want*) is an alternative to the verb **željeti** (**želim**) which was used in Unit 2. Željeti is a verb which follows the regular patterns which you know, but **htjeti** is also commonly used.

Nemam ... *I have not* ...

The words meaning *I have not* ..., etc. are also a single word:

ja	nemam
ti	nemaš
on/a/o	nema
mi	nemamo
vi	nemate
oni/e/a	nemaju

You have now met the only three verbs that form their negative as a single word (**nisam, neću, nemam**). As you know, all the others put **ne** in front of the verb:

Ne pišem.	*I'm not writing.*
Ne govore.	*They're not speaking.*

How to say *to*

As seen in the previous unit, little words in English such as *of* are conveyed in Croatian by the use of cases. The dative case is used in such phrases as *to write to*, *to give to* and *to say to*, so Sandra remarks **Moram pisati mami** *I must write to Mum*.

There is no separate word for *to* in the Croatian sentence. It is implied by the use of the dative case. Similarly, the word *for* is implied by the use of the dative case in the sentence **Moram kupiti sapun mami** *I must buy the soap for Mum*. Look at these other examples:

Jasna mora pisati Rudolfu.	*Jasna must write to Rudolf.*
Mi pišemo prijateljici.	*We are writing to our* friend.* (female)
Konobar daje salatu ženi.	*The waiter gives the salad to the woman.*

*Words such as *my*, *your*, etc. are often omitted in Croatian if it is clear from the context which word is implied.

Look at the way the last example is built up of nouns with different endings (cases):

Subject	Verb	Object	To ...
nominative		accusative	dative
konobar	**daje**	**salatu**	**ženi**

Compare with the following sentence:

žena	**daje**	**salatu**	**konobaru**

It is important to use the correct case ending in Croatian, since to use the wrong one could make you imply that the woman did not like her salad and she was returning it!

Plurals

To say more than one of something in the nominative and accusative cases:

Masc. (e.g. hotel, grad)
nom.	**hoteli** (add -i)
acc.	**hotele** (add -e)

Masc. nouns of one syllable usually add **-ov-** before the case ending:

nom.	**gradovi** (add -ovi)
acc.	**gradove** (add -ove)
	after a soft consonant (**c, č, ć, dž, đ, j, lj, nj, š, ž**) add **-evi** and **-eve** (e.g. **muž – muževi**) (see spelling rule in the How it works section in Unit 2)

Fem. (e.g. škola)
nom.	**škole** (change -a to -e)
acc.	**škole** (change -a to -e)

Neut. (e.g. kazalište)
nom.	**kazališta** (change -e/-o to -a)
acc.	**kazališta** (change -e/-o to -a)

Examples

Masc.

Hoteli su tamo.	*The hotels are there.*
Vidim hotele tamo.	*I see the hotels there.*

Fem.

Razglednice su na šalteru.	*The postcards are on the counter.*
Imam razglednice.	*I have the postcards.*

Neut.

Kazališta su ispred parka.	*The theatres are in front of the park.*
Vidim kazališta.	*I see the theatres.*

Spelling rules

There are certain rules for spelling that affect nouns. When **-i** is added after **k, g, h**, these letters change to **c, z, s**. Study the following examples:

Kiosk **je na ulici.**	*The kiosk is on the street.*
Kiosci **su na ulici.**	*The kiosks are on the street.*
Idemo u samoposlugu.	*We are going to the self-service shop.*
Sada smo u samoposluzi.	*Now we are in the self-service shop.*

Exceptions are made for people's proper names: **Branka** (a girl's name) becomes **Branki**.

Unusual noun categories

1 stvar

The word **stvar** *thing* is a feminine noun although it ends in a consonant (like **večer**). There is a small subcategory of these nouns with the following endings:

	singular	plural
nom.	stvar	stvari
acc.	stvar	stvari
gen.	stvari	
dat.	stvari	

2 čovjek

The word **čovjek** refers to a person regardless of sex. It has an unusual plural in the form **ljudi** *people, men*. Both words are masculine:

	singular	plural
nom.	čovjek	ljudi
acc.	čovjeka	ljude
gen.	čovjeka	
dat.	čovjeku	

Čovjek je na ulici.   *A person is in the street.*
Ljudi su na ulici.   *People are in the street.*

◀ CD1, TR 4, 03:02

Numbers 1–20

jedan, jedna, jedno	1	**jedanaest**	11
dva/dvije	2	**dvanaest**	12
tri	3	**trinaest**	13
četiri	4	**četrnaest**	14
pet	5	**petnaest**	15
šest	6	**šesnaest**	16
sedam	7	**sedamnaest**	17
osam	8	**osamnaest**	18
devet	9	**devetnaest**	19
deset	10	**dvadeset**	20

The number *one* behaves like an adjective. This means that its ending changes according to the word that follows:

Masc.
jedan **stol**   *one table*

Fem.
jedna **žena**   *one woman*

Neut.
jedno **kazalište**   *one theatre*

The number *two* has different forms when it refers to masculine or neuter nouns (**dva**) and when it refers to feminine (**dvije**). Like the numbers *three* (**tri**) and *four* (**četiri**) they are followed by words in the genitive singular:

dva stola	*two tables*
dva piva	*two beers*
dvije kave	*two coffees*
tri kune	*three kuna*
četiri koverte	*four envelopes*

The numbers 5–20 are followed by the genitive plural. The most frequent ending for the genitive plural is **a** for all genders:

Masc.
pet sapuna
šest gradova

Fem.
sedam kuna
osam razglednica

Neut.
devet piva

However, when there are one or more consonants at the end, they are separated by an extra **a**:
marka (add case ending to **mark-**)   deset maraka

Some nouns take **i** at the end:
stvar   stvari
čovjek   ljudi

···

Insight

Numbers in Croatian do not behave as they do in English. Number 1 is an adjective:

jedan Englez	*one Englishman*
jedna Engleskinja	*one Englishwoman*

(Contd)

Numbers 2, 3 and 4 are followed by the genitive singular:

dva piva *two beers*
četiri kune *four kunas*

Numbers 5 to 20 are followed by the genitive plural:

pet ljudi *five people*
dvanaest maraka *twelve stamps*
dvadeset stolova *twenty tables*

Practice

1 Write out the following prices and then add them up:

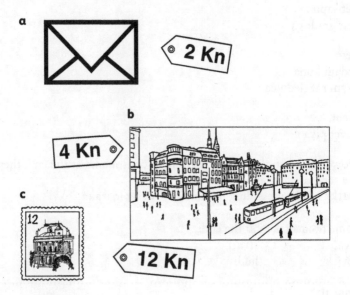

a **2 Kn**

b **4 Kn**

c **12 Kn**

Koliko košta ..?
  a koverta
  b razglednica
  c marka

2 Look at this table and make up sentences similar to this:
Rudolf hoće kavu. Koliko košta kava? Kava košta deset kuna.

a Rudolf	kava	10 Kn
b Sandra	razglednica	4 Kn
c Mark	pivo	15 Kn
d Jasna	šampon	20 Kn
e Zvonko	marka	2 Kn
f Velimir	marka za Englesku	12 Kn

3 Put the nouns in brackets into the plural *and* the correct case:
   a Moram kupiti (marka i razglednica).
   b Vidim (park) gdje su (spomenik).
   c (Hotel) su u centru grada.
   d (Čovjek) vole živjeti u gradu.
   e U centru grada su velike (zgrada).
   f Prodajete li (koverta)?

◆) CD1, TR 4, 03:51

4 Complete the missing part of the dialogue:
   Hello. Do you have any postcards?
   Dobar dan. Imamo razglednice.
   May I see the large postcards?
   Izvolite.
   How much does one large postcard cost?
   Četiri kune.
   Give me three, please.
   To je dvanaest kuna.
   Thank you. Goodbye.
   Molim. Do viđenja.

5 Make up sentences according to the following model using the information that follows:
   e.g. Sandra davati novac žena.
      Sandra daje novac ženi.

a Mark	davati	kava	Rudolf
b Čovjek	davati	marka	Jasna
c Mi	davati	sapun	mama
d Žena	davati	pivo	Velimir

e Oni	davati	novac	čovjek
f Konobar	davati	vino	Branka

6 Match the question on the left to the correct answer on the right:

a Trebam marke i koverte.		**i**	Gdje je Jasna?
b Idem na kavu.		**ii**	Što trebate?
c Evo Jasne.		**iii**	Imate li marke?
d Nemamo.		**iv**	Kamo ideš?

7 Complete the sentences with the most appropriate verbs chosen from the box. If necessary the required form of the verb is indicated by **ja**, etc. in brackets, where it would not normally be included in such a sentence or question:

a _____ li (ja) kupiti razglednice u kiosku?
b _____ li vi engleski?
c Mark i Sandra _____ u hotelu u Zagrebu.
d Oprostite, _____ li vi gospođa Bryant?
e Kamo _____ Rudolf i Mark?
f Ja _____ živjeti u centru grada.

> živjeti   ići   voljeti   govoriti   moći   biti

Comprehension 1

U samoposluzi Sandra traži neke stvari.

Sandra	Molim vas, gdje su sapuni i šamponi?
Prodavač	Tamo lijevo.
Sandra	Koji sapun je dobar, Jasna?
Jasna	Ja koristim ovaj sapun. Kažu da je i taj dobar. Ovdje su šamponi.
Sandra	Dobro, gdje je zubna pasta?
Jasna	Ovdje negdje. Ovo je odlična pasta.
Sandra	Hvala. Imam sve. Gdje mogu platiti?
Jasna	Na blagajni kod izlaza.

Na blagajni

Sandra traži ... *Sandra looks for ...*
tražiti, tražim *to look for* (also in the sense of *to ask for*)
prodavač *salesman*
koji sapun? *which soap?*
koristiti, koristim *to use*
ovaj sapun *this soap*
kažu da ... *they say that ...*
taj *that, that one*
negdje *somewhere*
odličan *excellent*
sve *everything*
platiti, platim *to pay*
na blagajni *at the checkout*
kod izlaza *by the exit*
blagajnica *checkout operator* (female)
gospođo *madam* (from **gospođa**)

QUICK VOCAB

True or false?

a Sandra traži sapune i šampone.
b Blagajna je kod izlaza.
c Sandra treba još nešto na blagajni.

Comprehension 2

◄ **CD1, TR 4, 04:59**

Read or listen to the following passage and answer the questions that follow.

Sandra i Mark dolaze u hotel. Idu na recepciju.

Sandra	Molim vas, dajte mi ključ od sobe broj 20. To je naša soba.
Recepcija	Evo ga, gospođo. Izvolite.
Sandra	Hvala.
Recepcija	Molim.
Sandra	Oprostite, gdje se u hotelu mogu kupiti novine?
Recepcija	Novine prodajemo tamo blizu lifta.

Mark i Sandra idu tamo.

Mark	Molim vas, imate li engleske novine?
Prodavač	Imamo *Guardian* i *The Economist*.
Mark	Imate li možda *Financial Times*?
Prodavač	Nemamo.
Mark	Dajte mi, molim vas, *Guardian*. A prodajete li cigarete?
Prodavač	Ovdje ne prodajemo cigarete. Morate ići u bar.
Mark	Hvala.
Prodavač	Molim.

QUICK VOCAB

recepcija *reception*
ključ od sobe *key to the room*
soba *room*
Gdje se u hotelu mogu kupiti novine? *Where can one buy newspapers in the hotel?*
broj *number*
novine *newspaper(s)*
lift *lift*
možda *perhaps*
cigareta *cigarette*
bar *bar*

Select the correct answer from **a**, **b** and **c** for each of the questions that follow.

1 Što Sandra traži na recepciji?
  a Traži sapun.
  b Traži ključ od njihove sobe.
  c Želi kupiti cigarete.

2 Gdje se u hotelu mogu kupiti novine?
  a Kod izlaza.
  b Ispred bara.
  c Blizu lifta.

3 Gdje se u hotelu mogu kupiti cigarete?
  a Na recepciji.
  b U restoranu.
  c U baru.

Test yourself

Here you can check some of the things you have learnt in this unit. Look at the questions that follow and choose the right answer:

1 What do you say as a polite reply to someone who says **hvala** to you?
  a oprostite
  b kako da ne
  c molim

2 How do you ask in a shop how much some soap costs?
  a Koliko košta sapun?
  b Imate li sapun?
  c Gdje je sapun?

3 What kind of a place is a **samoposluga**?
  a bank where you change money
  b supermarket where you buy groceries
  c post office where you buy stamps

4 Which word would you use to say that you must do something?

   a mogu

   b trebam

   c moram

5 How does your friend say that she does not want a coffee?

   a Neće kavu, hvala.

   b Neću kavu, hvala.

   b Nećemo kavu, hvala.

6 How do you say that you and your friend do not have any stamps?

   a Nemam marke.

   b Nemaš marke.

   c Nemamo marke.

7 If Jasna is telling Sandra that she is buying a present *for Rudolf*, which word (i.e. which case) will she use?

   a Rudolfu

   b Rudolf

   c Rudolfa

8 If Rudolf is telling Mark that he is writing a letter *to Jasna*, which word (i.e. case) will he use?

   a Jasni

   b Jasna

   c Jasnu

9 What is the correct form of the word for coffee to use after the number **dvije**?

   a kava

   b kave

   c kavu

10 What is the correct form of the word **kuna** to use after the number **dvadeset**?

   a kuni

   b kunu

   c kuna

5

U restoranu
In the restaurant

In this unit you will learn how to
* *Order a meal*
* *Ask for and state opinions, preferences, advice*
* *Express agreement*
* *Attract the attention of others*
* *Say there is/are and there is/are not*

Dialogue

Mark i Sandra idu s Rudolfom i Jasnom u restoran. Idu na večeru. U restoranu sjede za stolom u uglu. Za drugim stolovima ima mnogo ljudi. Rudolf zove konobara.

Rudolf	Konobaru, molim vas, imate li jelovnik?
Konobar	Imamo. Izvolite, gospodine.
Rudolf	Hvala.
Konobar	Molim.
Rudolf	Konobaru, što nam preporučujete za večeru?
Konobar	Naša riba je uvijek svježa, a i meso je odlično. Preporučujem vam nacionalne specijalitete. Imamo zagrebački odrezak i lignje na ribarski način.
Rudolf	Ja znam da je sve ovdje vrlo svježe. Sandra, što ćete jesti?

(Contd)

♦ CD1, TR 5

Sandra	Volim meso, ali više volim ribu.
Jasna	Onda vam savjetujem lignje na ribarski način.
Mark	A što meni savjetujete, Jasna? Mislite li da je roštilj dobar?
Jasna	Pretpostavljam da jest, ali zagrebački odrezak je nacionalni specijalitet.
Mark	Dobro. Čini mi se da moram probati zagrebački odrezak. Slažete li se?
Jasna	Slažem se. I ja bih isto.
Rudolf	Možemo naručiti večeru. Hoćemo li vino?
Jasna	Naravno. Volite li više crno ili bijelo vino, Sandra?
Sandra	Više volim crno.
Jasna	Dobro, i hoćemo juhu i tri salate, Rudolf.
Sandra	Prvo, mogu li dobiti čašu vode? Žedna sam.
Jasna	I ja sam žedna. Nema vode na stolu. Konobaru, molim vas, dvije čaše vode.

QUICK VOCAB

jesti, jedem *to eat*
s (preposition with instrumental) *with*
večera *dinner*
ići na večeru *to go to dinner*
sjediti, sjedim *to be sitting*
za stolom (stol nom.) *at a table*
u uglu (**ugao** masc. like **posao**) *in the corner*
za drugim stolovima *at other tables*
Ima mnogo ljudi. *There are many people.*
zvati, zovem *to call*
konobar *waiter*
jelovnik *menu*
Što nam preporučujete? (preporučivati, preporučujem)
   What do you recommend to us?
za večeru *for dinner*
riba *fish*
svjež *fresh*
meso *meat*
odličan *excellent*
... vam *... to you*

nacionalni specijalitet *national speciality* (dish)
zagrebački odrezak *Zagreb schnitzel*
lignje na ribarski način *squid in the fisherman's way*
Što ćete jesti? *What will you eat?*
više volim *I prefer* (lit. *I like more*)
savjetovati, savjetujem *to advise*
Mislite li da ...? *Do you think that ...?*
roštilj *barbecue*
pretpostavljati, pretpostavljam *to suppose*
Čini mi se da ... *It seems to me that ...*
probati, probam *to try*
Slažete li se? (slagati se, slažem se) *Do you agree?*
I ja bih isto. *I would like the same too.*
naručiti *to order*
naravno *of course*
juha *soup*
salata *salad*
crno ili bijelo vino *red* (lit. *black*) *or white wine*
Volite li više ...? *Do you prefer ...?*
Mogu li dobiti čašu vode? *May I have a glass of water?*
Nema vode. *There is no water.*
dvije čaše vode *two glasses of water*

Their conversation turns to meals and food.

Jasna	Sandra, što jedete za doručak u Londonu?
Sandra	Jedem kruh i džem, i pijem čaj s mlijekom.
Jasna	A što volite za ručak? Da li je ručak vaš glavni obrok?
Sandra	Ručak nije naš glavni obrok. Na poslu jedem sendvič.
Jasna	Što vi jedete, Mark?
Mark	Za ručak i ja jedem malo.

Što jedete? *What do you eat?*
za doručak *for breakfast*
Jedem kruh i džem. *I eat bread and jam.*
Pijem čaj s mlijekom. *I drink tea with milk.*
piti, pijem *to drink*

za ručak *for lunch*
vaš glavni obrok *your main meal*
na poslu *at work*
sendvič *sandwich*
malo *a little*

True or false?

a The restaurant has fish and meat.
b Sandra prefers meat.
c Sandra drinks coffee for breakfast.

Insight

The words for meals are **doručak** *breakfast*, **ručak** *lunch* and **večera** *dinner*. Breakfast is usually eaten at about 9 a.m. or 10 a.m. and often eaten at work. Many people begin work earlier than in England, e.g. at 6 a.m., and return home from work in the middle of the afternoon. Lunch is then taken as the main meal of the day, after which follows a nap. The evening meal is usually a light supper. However, this pattern of starting the day early and having a nap in the afternoon is slowly being replaced in urban areas by a more nine to five routine as found commonly elsewhere in Europe.

Insight

There are many types of eatery, from a local **kavana** to hotels that serve international cuisine. But one of the delights of visiting a country is to try local specialities. Eating out is not expensive and each region offers different specialities. In most restaurants, you will find various first courses (**predjelo**), followed by main courses (**gotova jela, specijaliteti**) and sweets (**slatko**) with ice cream (**sladoled**), filled pancakes (**palačinke**) or cakes (**kolači**). You may be asked if you would like an aperitif (**aperitiv**) of a local brandy such as grape brandy (**lozovača**). There are many types of wine vary greatly in quality and price.

Key phrases

◆ CD1, TR 5, 02:30

How to:

▶ ask for a recommendation	Što nam preporučujete?
▶ suggest something	Preporučujem vam ...
▶ ask for	Što mi savjetujete?
and give advice	Savjetujem vam ...
▶ ask for	Slažete li se?
and give agreement	Slažem se.
▶ ask for	Što volite više ...?
and give your own preference	Volite li više ...?
	Više volim ...
▶ ask for another person's opinion	Mislite li da ...?
▶ state what you think	Znam da ...
	Čini mi se da ...
	Pretpostavljam da ...
▶ ask for the menu	Imate li jelovnik?
▶ request a glass of water	Mogu li dobiti čašu vode?
▶ say *there is* or *there are*	Ima mnogo ljudi.
▶ say *there is not* or *there are not*	Nema vode na stolu.

How it works

Cases

You have now met the last of the cases and the standard endings for nouns.

a Instrumental singular

The two prepositions **s** *with* and **za** *behind* (but used in the phrase *at a table*) are followed by the instrumental case (although **za** may also be followed by the accusative when it will mean *for*). The endings are as follows:

Masc. (e.g. grad, muž)

ins.	**gradom** (add -om)
ins.	**mužem** (add -em before a soft consonant c, č, ć, dž, đ, j, lj, nj, š, ž)

Fem. (e.g. prijateljica, stvar)

ins.	**prijateljicom** (change -a to -om; -om does not change before a soft consonant for fem. nouns)
ins.	**stvari/stvarju** (add -i or -ju to fem. nouns which end in a consonant)

Neut. (e.g. pivo, predgrađe)

ins.	**pivom** (change -o to -om)
ins.	**predgrađem** (change -e to -em)

b Instrumental and dative plural

You can learn these two together as they are the same:

Masc. (e.g. prijatelj, grad, kiosk)

ins. + dat.	**prijateljima** (add -ima)
ins. + dat.	**gradovima** (add -ov- before the case endings for masc. nouns with one syllable)
ins. + dat.	**kioscima** (the k changes to c before -i)

Fem. (e.g. žena, stvar)

ins. + dat.	**ženama** (change -a to -ama)
ins. + dat.	**stvarima** (add -ima to fem. nouns which end in a consonant)

Neut. (e.g. predgrađe)

ins. + dat.	**predgrađima** (change -e/-o to -ima)

c Vocative singular and plural

This case is used when addressing people directly in speech or in a letter. It is the case used when you want to call someone (vocative). The endings in the singular are:

Masc. (e.g. **prijatelj, gospodin**)

voc.   **gospodine** (add -e)

voc.   **prijatelju** (add -u after a soft consonant and sometimes after -r)

Fem. (e.g. **žena, gospođica**)

voc.   **ženo** (change -a to -o)

voc.   **gospođice** (change -a to -e if ending is -ica)
            However, in practice, few fem. nouns change:
            voc. of **Jasna** is **Jasna**.

Neut. (e.g. **dijete** *child*)

voc.   **dijete** (no change)

There are few occasions when you would use the vocative with the neuter as most words refer to inanimate objects. Theoretically, there is a vocative ending for all nouns, but there are not many occasions in life when you want to address something like a house (**kućo!**). The endings in the plural are the same as the nominative in all genders.

There is a spelling rule for masculine nouns in the vocative singular; -g will change to -ž, -k will change to -č, -h will change to -š, and you add the ending -e. Look at the example:

Bog *God*   **Bože!** (used as a mild expletive)

To me/to you, **etc. (dative)**

You already know the words for *I, you*, etc. (the personal pronouns):

ja	*I*	**mi**	*we*
ti	*you*	**vi**	*you*
on/ona	*he/she*	**oni/one**	*they* (masc. and fem.)

(there are also neut. forms **ono** and **ona**)

As you also know in certain circumstances you use the dative to mean *to someone*:

Konobar daje salatu ženi.   *The waiter gives the salad to the woman.*

So there are also words which mean *to me, to you,* etc.

Look at the examples given so far:

Što nam preporučujete?   *What do you recommend to us?*
Preporučujem vam ...   *I recommend to you ...*
Čini mi se ...   *It seems to me ...*

nam   *to us*
vam   *to you*   (equivalent to **vi**)
mi   *to me*

Here are all the forms together, both long and short forms:

	short	long		short	long
ja	mi	meni	mi	nam	nama
ti	ti	tebi	vi	vam	vama
on	mu	njemu	oni	im	njima
ona	joj	njoj	one	im	njima

(the forms for **ono** and **ona** are the same as for **on** and **oni**)

You can use these words in other phrases and expressions which you know:

Konobar joj daje salatu.   *The waiter gives the salad to her.*
Moram mu pisati.   *I must write to him.*
Pišemo joj.   *We are writing to her.*

Look at these examples carefully and you will notice how the short forms come in second place. This is the normal word order. They behave in the same way as the short forms of **biti**.

The long forms have two basic functions.

a They may come at the beginning to stress the person involved:

Meni se čini ...   (lit.) *To me it seems ...*
Tebi preporučujem ...   (lit.) *It is to you that I'm recommending ...*

b They are used after prepositions:

u zgradi   *in the building*
u njoj   *in it*

Otherwise, use the short forms.

Ima/nema

Croatian has just one word to express *there is ...* and *there are ...*: **ima**. It is the same form as the word that means *he/she has*. When it means *there is/are*, it is followed by the genitive case to mean *some*:

Ima **vode**.	*There is some water.*
Ima **kruha**.	*There is some bread.*
Ovdje ima **Engleza**.	*There are English people here.*

The negative form is **nema** (*there is not/there are not*):

Nema **vode**.	*There is no water.*
Nema **kruha**.	*There is no bread.*
Ovdje nema **Engleza**.	*There are no English people here.*

You use the genitive singular or the plural as required by the sense of the sentence, as you use either singular or plural in English.

Mnogo **and words of quantity**

Mnogo *many, much, a lot of* is followed by the genitive case. Most words which indicate a quantity are followed by the genitive case, such as **čaša vode** *a glass of water* or **mnogo ljudi** *many people*.

Unusual noun categories

The word **ugao** *corner* is masculine and it follows the same pattern as **posao**. When adding an ending the **a** is lost and the **o** changes to **l**:

	singular	plural
nom.	**ugao**	**uglovi** (**ugl-** is one syllable)
acc.	**ugao**	**uglove**
gen.	**ugla**	**uglova**
dat.	**uglu**	**uglovima**
ins.	**uglom**	**uglovima**

Practice

1 Replace the pronoun in brackets with the corresponding form meaning *to me, to you,* etc.:

   a Čini (on) se da Rudolf sjedi za stolom.
   b Što (mi) preporučujete?
   c Preporučujem (vi) crno vino.
   d Što (ona) savjetujete?
   e Čini (oni) se da je riba svježa.
   f Sandra (ja) želi savjetovati.
   g Moram (ti) pisati.
   h Konobar (ona) daje salatu.
   i Čovjek (ja) daje marke na pošti.
   j Daje li (mi) bijelo vino?

2 Add the appropriate case ending to the nouns in brackets (note that some nouns are in the plural):

   a (Jasna) se čini da je roštilj dobar.
   b Što savjetuješ (konobari)?
   c Vidim (čovjek) na ulici.
   d Sandra vidi (zgrada) gdje radi Rudolf.
   e Idemo li sada na (kava)?

f Idemo s (prijatelji) u grad.
g Rudolf sjedi za (stol) s (Jasna).
h Gledamo (konobari) u uglu restorana.
i Mark hoće (cigarete) i (novine).
j Volimo učiti (jezici).

◀) **CD1, TR 5, 03:50**

3 Fill in the missing part of the dialogue.
Waiter! Hello. Do you have a menu?
Izvolite, gospodice.
Thank you.
Molim. Želite li naručiti?
What do you recommend to me?
Preporučujem naše lignje i salatu.
I prefer meat. I would like meat and a salad, please.
Hoćete li vino? Što više volite, crno ili bijelo?
I prefer red, and may I have a glass of water?

JELOVNIK

PREDJELO

GOTOVA JELA

SLATKO

4 Match the answers to the questions:

- **a** Slažem se.
- **b** Na stolu je.
- **c** Kako da ne.
- **d** Naše lignje su uvijek dobre.

- **i** Gdje je kruh?
- **ii** Mogu li dobiti čašu vode?
- **iii** Slažete li se s Jasnom?
- **iv** Što nam preporučujete?

5 Imagine that you have invited some friends to a restaurant. How would you ask the waiter the following:

- **a** if he has the menu.
- **b** for fish and salad.
- **c** for two beers.
- **d** for a glass of water.

6 Look at the following advertisements:

Which one sells fish?

7 Make up questions for the following responses:

- **a** Da, volim pivo.
- **b** Ne, ne volim pivo.
- **c** Sutra idem u grad.
- **d** Želim piti crno vino.
- **e** Volimo ići u grad.
- **f** Ne, ne možeš dobiti čašu vode.

8 In the following sentences, the noun in brackets is being used with either **mnogo** or **ima/nema**. Put the noun into the genitive case and either singular or plural as appropriate (all the nouns are given here in the nominative singular):

   a Ima li (kruh) na stolu?
   b Vidim mnogo (park) u centru grada.
   c Konobar daje mnogo (salata) ženi.
   d Nema (čovjek) na ulici.
   e Mislite li da Rudolf ima mnogo (prijatelj)?
   f Nema (vino) na stolu.
   g Čini joj se da ima (čovjek) za stolovima.
   h Ima li (Englez) ovdje u hotelu?
   i Nema (kava).
   j Tamo ima (razglednica).

Comprehension 1

Zvonko i Velimir ulaze u kavanu.

Zvonko	Je li slobodno, gospodine?
Gospodin	Jest, izvolite.

♦ CD1, TR 5, 05:03

Sjede za stolom.

Zvonko	Voliš li više pivo ili vino, Velimire?
Velimir	Više volim vino. Ali znam da nije dobro piti alkohol. Dobro je piti vodu ili sok.
Zvonko	Imaš pravo. Što mi preporučuješ danas? Hoćemo li piti crno ili bijelo vino?
Velimir	Konobaru, što nam preporučujete danas?
Konobar	Imamo dobru svježu ribu, a i meso je odlično.
Velimir	Ja hoću ribu, a ti Zvonko?
Zvonko	Znaš da ne volim ribu. Ja hoću meso.
Konobar	Dobro. A želite li vino?
Velimir	Želimo jedno bijelo, i jedno crno vino.

Je li slobodno? *Is it* (this place) *free?* (i.e. *vacant*)
Imaš pravo. *You are right.*
Znaš da ... *You know that ...*

True or false?

a Velimir prefers beer to wine.
b Zvonko likes fish.
c Velimir orders two red wines.

_____

Comprehension 2

Read the passage and answer the questions that follow.

Sandra voli doručak. Svako jutro jede kruh s džemom i pije
čaj. Njen muž, Mark, ne voli čaj, više voli piti bijelu kavu ili
mlijeko. Sandra ruča u školi. Ne jede mnogo za ručak. Sjedi i
jede sendvič. U sendviču je salata ili meso. Mark ponekad ruča
s prijateljima u gradu, ali također ne voli jesti mnogo za ručak.
Navečer, kod kuće, Sandra i Mark večeraju. Spremaju ribu ili
dobro meso sa salatom. Vole jesti i kolače.

svako jutro *every morning*
ili *or*
ručati, ručam *to have lunch*
sendvič *sandwich*
također *also*
navečer *in the evening*
kod kuće *at home*
večerati, večeram *to have dinner*
spremati, spremam *to prepare*

1 Što Mark više voli piti za doručak?
  a Više voli piti mlijeko.
  b Više voli piti sok.
  c Više voli piti bijelu kavu ili mlijeko.

2 Gdje Sandra ruča?
  a Ruča u gradu s mužem.
  b Ruča kod kuće.
  c Ruča na poslu.

3 Što vole Mark i Sandra jesti za večeru?
  a Vole jesti palačinke.
  b Vole jesti kolače.
  c Vole jesti lignje na ribarski način.

Test yourself

Here you can check some of the things you have learnt in this unit.
Look at the questions that follow and choose the right answer:

1 How would you say *I prefer* …?
  a Više volim …
  b Želim …
  c Preporučujem …

2 What does **Slažem se** mean?
  a I think
  b I agree
  c I know

3 Which is the correct ending for the word **prijatelj** after the preposition **s** to mean *with*?
  a prijatelja
  b prijatelju
  c prijateljem

4 Which is the correct ending for the word **kiosk** after the preposition **za** to mean *behind the kiosks*?
  a kiosci
  b kioske
  c kioscima

5 Which is the missing personal pronoun in the phrase **Čini ... se** to mean *It seems to us*?

 a nam
 b mi
 c vam

6 Match the question on the left with the correct answer on the right:

a	Imate li jelovnik?	**i**	Da. Pijem kavu s mnogo mlijeka.
b	Ima li kruha na stolu?	**ii**	Imamo. Izvolite.
c	Da li volite crno vino?	**iii**	Mislim da je riba odlična.
d	Što nam preporučujete?	**iv**	Nema.
e	Da li pijete kavu s mlijekom?	**v**	Više volim bijelo.

6

Dođite k meni
Come to my place

In this unit you will learn how to
- *Give an invitation*
- *Accept or decline an invitation*
- *Give and ask for directions*
- *Give your address and telephone number*
- *Express degrees of certainty and uncertainty*

Dialogue

Rudolf poziva Sandru i Marka.

◆ CD1, TR 6

Rudolf	Sandra i Mark, molim vas, hoću vas pozvati k meni sutra navečer.
Mark	Žao mi je, ali ne možemo doći. Moram raditi kod nas u hotelu.
Sandra	Mark, ne možeš stalno raditi. Vrlo rado prihvaćamo poziv. Gdje stanujete?
Rudolf	Stanujem blizu centra. Moja adresa je Heinzlova ulica šezdeset šest, a moj stan je na petom katu. Od hotela idite pješice do Glavnog kolodvora. Tamo uzmite ili tramvaj dvadeset, ili autobus sedamnaest. Voze prema Autobusnom kolodvoru. Siđite na osmoj stanici. Moj blok

(Contd)

se nalazi odmah preko puta te stanice. To je Heinzlova ulica. Je li jasno? Za svaki slučaj, moj telefonski broj je dva šest sedam – sedam osam pet.

Sandra Da, u redu, imam sve podatke. Kada trebamo doći?

Rudolf Dođite sutra u sedam sati. I nemojte doći taksijem. Morate naučiti putovati gradskim prijevozom.

Dođite k meni. *Come to my place* (house/flat).
Rudolf poziva ... *Rudolf is inviting ...*
k njemu *to his place*
Hoću vas pozvati k meni. *I want to invite you to my place.*
Žao mi je. *I'm sorry.*
kod nas u hotelu *at our place* (room) *in the hotel*
stalno *continuously*
vrlo rado *very gladly*
Prihvaćamo poziv. *We accept the invitation.*
stanovati, stanujem *to live, reside*
blizu (preposition with gen.) *near*
adresa *address*
ulica *street*
šezdeset šest *66*
stan *flat*
na petom katu *on the fifth floor*
idite pješice *go on foot*
uzmite (uzeti, uzmem) *take* (a bus)
tramvaj *tram*
autobus *bus*
Voze prema Autobusnom kolodvoru. *They drive towards the bus station.*
siđite (sići, siđem) *get down/off* (bus)
na osmoj stanici *at the eighth stop*
blok *block* (of flats)
preko puta (preposition with gen.) *opposite*
Je li jasno? *Is that clear?*
za svaki slučaj *in any event/case*
telefonski broj *telephone number*
u redu *all right, OK*

Imam sve podatke. *I have all the information.*
kada *when*
u sedam sati *at seven o'clock*
Nemojte doći taksijem. *Don't come by taxi.*
naučiti putovati gradskim prijevozom *to learn to travel by city transport*

Sandra i Mark idu autobusom i silaze na osmoj stanici. (*Unfortunately, they have taken the wrong bus.*)

Mark	Da li si sigurna da je ovdje pravo mjesto? Ne vidim blok preko puta.
Sandra	Sigurna sam. Ovo je osma stanica. Dolazi jedan gospodin. Pitaj njega.
Mark	Oprostite, gospodine, možete li mi reći gdje je Heinzlova šezdeset šest?
Gospodin	Ovo nije Heinzlova ulica.
Mark	Možete li mi reći kako možemo tamo doći?
Gospodin	Nije teško. Idite ravno i skrenite u drugu ulicu lijevo, onda skrenite u prvu ulicu desno i opet idite ravno do glavne ceste. To je Heinzlova.
Mark	Hvala lijepo, gospodine.
Gospodin	Nema na čemu. Do viđenja i laku noć.

silaze (silaziti, silazim) *they get off* (the bus)
siguran (masc.) **sigurna** (fem.) *sure, certain*
da *that*
pravo mjesto *the right place*
pitaj njega *ask him*
pitati, pitam *to ask*
Možete li mi reći ...? *Can you tell me ...?*
... kako možemo tamo doći? *... how we can get there?*
Nije teško. *It's not difficult.*
idite ravno *go straight on*
skrenite u drugu ulicu (skrenuti, skrenem) *turn into the second street*
... u prvu ulicu *... into the first street*

opet *again*
do glavne ceste *as far as the main road*
Hvala lijepo. *Thanks very much.*
Nema na čemu. *Don't mention it.*

True or false?

a Mark ne prihvaća poziv.
b Rudolf stanuje daleko od centra grada.
c Mark i Sandra idu taksijem.

Insight

When writing an address you usually indicate the floor
on which the addressee lives by roman numerals after
the number of the house or block of flats. So Rudolf would
write:

Heinzlova 66/v

Key phrases

◀》 CD1, TR 6, 02:15

How to:

▶ extend an invitation	Želim vas pozvati ...
▶ decline politely an invitation	Žao mi je ...
▶ accept an invitation	Vrlo rado prihvaćamo poziv.
▶ give an address	Moja adresa je ...
and a telephone number	Moj telefonski broj je ...
▶ ask for directions	Možete li mi reći gdje je ...?
▶ ask how to get somewhere	Kako možemo tamo doći?
▶ give directions	idite ravno
	idite ravno do glavne ceste
	skrenite u prvu ulicu desno
	skrenite u drugu ulicu lijevo

- ▶ ask if someone is sure
  of something

  Da li si sigurna?
  (**ti** form asking female)
  Jeste li sigurni? (**vi** form
  asking a stranger)

- ▶ reply that you are sure

  Siguran sam. (male speaking)
  Sigurna sam. (female speaking)

- ▶ say thank you very much
  and reply
  (alternative reply)

  hvala lijepo
  nema na čemu
  molim lijepo

How it works

Giving commands

There is a special form of the verb that is used when you want
to tell someone what to do or what not to do. It is called the
imperative. There are a number of examples in this unit:

Dođite k meni.   *Come to my place (home).*
Siđite na osmoj stanici. *Get off at the eighth stop.*
Nemojte doći taksijem.   *Don't come by taxi.*
Pitaj ga.   *Ask him.*

There are, as you would expect, two forms. One corresponds to the
ti form and one to the **vi** form.

Ti form
Take the **ja** form of the verb:

a if it ends in **-am** replace the **-m** by **-j**
  pitam → pitaj;
b if it ends in **-jem** remove the ending **-em**
  pijem → pij;
c for all other verbs replace **-em/-im** by **-i**
  idem → idi
  uzmem   uzmi
  radim   radi

Vi form

To form the more formal or polite way of giving a command simply add -te to the ti form:

pitam	→	pitajte
pijem		pijte
idem		idite
uzmem		uzmite
radim		radite

Do not do ...

The negative imperative is a command not to do something. It is formed by placing **nemoj** (for the **ti** form) and **nemojte** (for the **vi** form) in front of the infinitive. Look at these examples:

Nemojte doći taksijem.	*Don't come by taxi.*
Nemojte sići na osmoj stanici.	*Don't get off at the eighth stop.*
Nemoj pitati.	*Don't ask.*

There is an alternative way of forming the negative imperative made by putting **ne** in front of the imperative. However, this form sounds quite brusque and is best used sparingly. It is only made from the imperfective form of the imperative (see following section on completed and uncompleted actions):

| **Ne dolazi!** | *Don't come!* |

A completed and uncompleted action

There have been a few occasions when you have been given two different verbs to mean the same thing:

dolaziti, doći	*to come*
silaziti, sići	*to get off*
piti, popiti	*to drink*
davati, dati	*to give*
uzimati, uzeti	*to take*

These pairs of verbs are important to using the system of verbs in Croatian. The differences between them can be described like this:

a the first verb of the pair is used to express an action that is, was or will be continuous, repeated or incomplete

b the second verb of the pair is used to express an action that was or will be completed, which happened or will happen once only or is of a momentary nature.

Most often when you are talking in the present tense, you use the first verb in the pair. If an action is still in progress then it is not yet complete. You have used the second verb of the pair in its infinitive form and in its imperative form. Look at the following examples and the differences between the pairs of verbs:

Pijem vodu kad* sam žedan.   *I drink water when I'm thirsty.*
(i.e. on each occasion when thirsty I drink water)

Moram popiti čašu vode.   *I must drink a glass of water.*
(i.e. I must drink a glass and finish it, as in the sense of 'drink up')

*Some words may be used with or without **-a** at the end depending on how easy it is to pronounce with the following word; **kada, kad** *when*, **sada, sad** *now*, **s, sa** *with*:

Sandra daje novac ženi.   *Sandra is giving the money to the woman.* (i.e. the action is still incomplete)

Dajte mi, molim vas ...   *Give me, please ...* (i.e. a single action that you expect to be momentary)

These pairs of verbs are called aspects. The first verb is the imperfective aspect and the second one is the perfective aspect.

Not all verbs come in pairs like this. **Vidjeti** is both imperfective and perfective.

Uses of cases (instrumental)

The instrumental case is so called because it is used to name an instrument by means of which an action is carried out. So you use it in the following phrases:

Idem taksijem.   *I am going by taxi.*
Idem autobusom.   *I am going by bus.*

(That is, the means of transport is the instrument by which the action is being carried out.)

Taksi (masc.) is slightly unusual in that is adds j before the case ending:

	singular
	singular
nom.	taksi
acc.	taksi
gen.	taksija
dat.	taksiju
ins.	taksijem

I see him …

The words for *me*, *him* and *us*, etc. are also pronouns like the words mi *to me* or mu *to him* except that they are in the accusative case. There is an example in the first line of the **Dialogue** in this unit **Hoću vas pozvati …** (*I want to invite you …*).

Consider the following sentence:

Vidim Rudolfa i Jasnu   *I see Rudolf and Jasna in*
  na ulici.   *the street.*

The endings of the words have changed to indicate that Rudolf and Jasna are the object of the verb. Separate forms are also needed to indicate *him* and *her*.

Here is the full list of the words for *me, him*, etc. These are the accusative case of the pronouns. They have both long and short forms like the dative pronouns:

	short	long		short	long
ja	me	mene	mi	nas	nas
ti	te	tebe	vi	vas	vas
on	ga	njega	oni	ih	njih
ona	ju	nju	one	ih	njih

The forms for **ono** and **ona** (neut.) are the same as for **on** and **oni**.

The same forms are used for the genitive case of the pronouns with the following exception for **ona**: **je** (short form), **nje** (long form). However, there is a preference for using **je** as the short form in the accusative.

The rules for the use of long and short forms are the same as when we looked at the dative. The long form is used for emphasis and after prepositions. The short form cannot stand at the beginning of a sentence. If you have an accusative or genitive pronoun used with a dative pronoun, the dative always comes first. Study the following examples:

Vidim Rudolfa.	*I see Rudolf.*
Vidim ga.	*I see him.*
Gledamo Jasnu.	*We are watching Jasna.*
Gledamo je.	*We are watching her.*
Dajem novac ženi.	*I am giving the money to the woman.*
Dajem joj ga.	*I am giving it to her.*
Konobar daje salatu ljudima.	*The waiter is giving the salad to the people.*
Konobar im je daje.	*The waiter is giving it to them.*

Note that the pronouns, like the short forms of **biti**, tend to come in second place after the first word.

New prepositions

You have met a number of new words to indicate position or
direction in this unit:

Dođite k meni.	*Come to my place.* (Come and see me.)
Dođite k njemu.	*Come to his place.* (Come and see him.)
Radim kod nas.	*I am working at our place.*

These two words distinguish between going to someone or being
at someone's: **k** (followed by the dative) indicates going round
to see someone; **kod** (followed by the genitive) indicates being at
someone's house.

Idem k Rudolfu.	*I am going round to Rudolf's.* (i.e. to see him)
Sad sam kod Rudolfa.	*Now I am at Rudolf's.*

The expression **kod nas** may also mean *in our country*.

Note the difference between the following two expressions (**kuća** =
house, home):

Rudolf je kod kuće.	*Rudolf is at home.* (stationary)
Rudolf ide kući.	*Rudolf is going home.* (movement)

Other prepositions followed by the genitive are:

bez	*without*
blizu	*near*
do	*to, as far as*
iz	*out of, from*
preko puta	*opposite*

Another preposition that is followed by the dative is:

prema	*towards*

◀) **CD1, TR 6, 03:27**

First, second, **etc.**

In addition to the numbers discussed before, there are others that are not used in counting but in ordering things (*first*, *second*, etc.). They are called ordinal numbers. In Croatian, they are all adjectives and so agree in number, case and gender with the noun they describe:

Masc.	Fem.	Neut.	
prvi	prva	prvo	*first*
drugi	druga	drugo	*second*
treći	treća	treće	*third*
četvrti	četvrta	četvrto	*fourth*
peti	peta	peto	*fifth*
šesti	-a	-o	*sixth*
sedmi	-a	-o	*seventh*
osmi	-a	-o	*eighth*
deveti	-a	-o	*ninth*
deseti	-a	-o	*tenth*

The pattern is then repeated by simply adding an adjective ending on the following numbers (**jedanaesti, dvanaesti, trinaesti,** etc.).

Practice

1 Choose the correct command from the pair given (the first verb is always the imperfective):
- **a** Pij/popij mlijeko svaki dan.
- **b** Pijte/popijte čašu vode odmah.
- **c** Dolazi/dođi k meni danas.
- **d** Uzimajte/uzmite tramvaj dvadeset četiri.

2 Choose the correct form of the infinitive:
- **a** Moraš silaziti/sići na trećoj stanici.
- **b** Volim piti/popiti mlijeko.
- **c** Želim dolaziti/doći k tebi sutra.
- **d** Hoćete li mi davati/dati čašu vina?

3 Put the noun or nouns in the brackets in the correct case after the preposition:
- **a** Sutra smo kod (Mark i Sandra).
- **b** Autobus ide prema (centar) grada.
- **c** Autobus ide u (centar) grada.
- **d** Autobus je u (centar) grada.
- **e** Idite ravno do (trg).
- **f** Gradska kavana se nalazi na (trg).
- **g** Dođite iz (hotel) do (restoran).
- **h** On sutra ide na (večera).
- **i** Njegov stan je blizu (kolodvor).
- **j** Rudolf stoji ispod (drvo) u (park) preko puta (stanica).

4 Put the noun or nouns in the brackets in the correct case according to the uses of cases:
- **a** Konobar daje (Jasna) (salata).
- **b** Idemo u Zagreb (autobus).
- **c** Trafalgar Square se nalazi u centru (London).
- **d** (Konobar)! Želimo naručiti večeru.
- **e** Sandra mora pisati (Mark).

5 Look at the diagram. You are at the spot marked X.

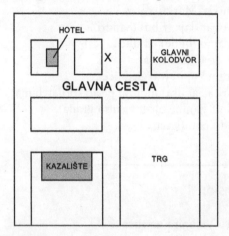

You see a man walking towards you. Stop him and ask if he knows the way to the theatre. How would he describe to you:

a the way to the theatre?
b the way to the main station?
c the way to the hotel?
d the way to the square?

◀ CD1, TR 6, 05:58

6 Fill in the missing parts of the dialogue:
> *I want to invite you to my place today.*
> Ne mogu. Moram danas ići k mami.
> *I am sorry. Can you come tomorrow?*
> Dobro. Kada?
> *At eight o'clock.*
> Kako mogu doći k vama?
> *Take the bus number 14 or the tram number 6 opposite the park and get out at the seventh stop. My flat is in the block opposite the theatre.*
> Dajte mi, molim vas, vašu adresu i telefonski broj.
> *My address is ... My telephone number is ...*

7 Replace the nouns in brackets with the appropriate pronoun. Take care to use the long or short form as appropriate and to use the correct word order:

   a Idemo k (Marku).
   b Konobar daje (ribu) (Sandri).
   c Gledamo (ljude) na ulici.
   d Idite do (kolodvora).
   e Moram kupiti (razglednice).
   f (Mark i Sandra) moraju pisati (prijateljima).
   g Rudolf stanuje blizu (centra grada).
   h (Ljudi) piju (kavu).

Comprehension 1

Zvonko poziva Velimira na ručak.

CD1, TR 6, 07:29

Zvonko	Velimire, dođi sutra k meni na ručak.
Velimir	Na žalost, ne mogu. Moram sa ženom ići u grad. Moramo kupiti poklon za njenu mamu.
Zvonko	Dovedi i ženu na ručak.
Velimir	Ne znam. Ona uvijek kaže da je teško doći do tebe. Ti stanuješ daleko od glavne ceste.
Zvonko	Žao mi je. Možete li doći taksijem?
Velimir	Možemo. Znaš, kad idemo k tebi, moramo ići u centar tramvajem, onda uzeti autobus. Možemo doći taksijem direktno iz centra grada.
Zvonko	Dobro. Drago mi je, dođite onda u tri.
Velimir	Hvala lijepo.
Zvonko	Molim lijepo. Do viđenja.
Velimir	Do viđenja, do sutra.

na žalost *unfortunately*
poklon *present*
Dovedi i ženu. *Bring your wife too.*
uvijek *always*

teško *difficult*
kaže da ... (kazati, kažem) *he/she says that ...*
direktno *directly*
u tri *at three* (o'clock)
do sutra *until tomorrow*

True or false?

a Zvonko poziva Velimira na večeru.
b Velimir ide sutra na posao.
c Velimir i njegova žena mogu doći taksijem.

Comprehension 2

Read the following passage and answer the questions that follow.

U gradovima u Europi čovjek danas vidi tramvaje i autobuse na ulicama. Tramvaji i autobusi voze svugdje. Tramvajem ili autobusom ljudi idu na posao i k prijateljima. Gradski transport je jedan veliki sistem. Spaja jednu stranu grada s drugom. Spaja ljude s poslom, s prijateljima, s centrom grada i s mjestima gdje se ljudi skupljaju. Naravno, nije uvijek lako putovati po gradu. Neki ljudi stanuju daleko od centra. Živjeti tamo nije lako. Teško je doći u grad. Ali neki ljudi vole stanovati daleko od grada. Život je miran kada čovjek ne gleda stalno ljude na ulicama.

Europa *Europe*
svugdje *everywhere*
sistem *system*
spaja *it links*
jednu stranu (acc.) *one side*
gdje se ljudi skupljaju *where people gather together*
naravno *of course*
po gradu *around the town*
život *life*
miran *quiet, peaceful*

1 Što vidi čovjek u gradovima danas?
  a Vidi taksije.
  b Vidi tramvaje i autobuse.
  c Vidi samoposluge.

2 Kamo idu ljudi tramvajem ili autobusom?
  a U hotel.
  b Na posao i k prijateljima.
  c Na poštu.

3 Gdje je život miran?
  a U predgrađu.
  b Na Glavnom kolodvoru.
  c U centru grada.

Test yourself

Here you can check some of the things you have learnt in this unit.
Look at the questions that follow and choose the right answer:

1 The dialling code for Croatia is 385. Which number is that?
  a tri pet osam
  b tri osam pet
  c osam tri pet

2 You want to ask someone where they live. Which question
would you use?
  a Gdje stanujete?
  b Gdje radite?
  c Gdje gledate?

3 You are looking for someone who lives in flat 18 on the fourth
floor. Which of the following is the correct address?
  a stan osamnaest na četvrtom katu
  b stan osamnaest na trećem katu
  c stan osam na četvrtom katu

4 Someone tells you that they live *opposite the theatre*. What would they say?
  a pored kazališta
  b nedaleko od kazališta
  c preko puta kazališta

5 You are asking for directions and someone tells you **Idite ovdje desno i skrenite u drugu ulicu lijevo.** What are you to do?
  a go left and turn into the second street on the right
  b go straight on and turn into the second street on the left
  c go right here and turn into the second street on the left

6 You are asking for directions and someone tells you **Idite ravno i skrenite u treću ulicu desno.** What are you to do?
  a go right and turn into the third street on the left
  b go straight on and turn into the third street on the right
  c go straight on and turn into the third street on the left

7 Which word would you use to attract someone's attention?
  a Hvala
  b Izvolite
  c Oprostite

8 You want to tell someone that it is not difficult to get somewhere by bus. Which form of the word would you use: **Nije teško ići …?**
  a autobusu
  b autobusom
  c autobusa

9 You are in a bus and not sure where to get off. Which question should you ask?
  a Kada trebam doći?
  b Gdje trebam sići?
  c Što trebam pitati?

10 You are going to see Jasna. How would you say that you are going *to her place*?
  a k njoj
  b k njemu
  c k tebi

Koliko imate godina?
How old are you?

In this unit you will learn how to
* **Give and ask for more personal information concerning age,
  marital status, occupation, where you are from, and about
  other members of your family**

Dialogue

Rudolf ulazi u stan s Markom i Sandrom. Njegova majka je u sobi.

Rudolf	Da vas upoznam. Ovo je moja majka. Mama, ovo su moji prijatelji. Zovu se Sandra i Mark.
Sandra	Drago mi je. Ja sam Sandra.
Mark	Drago mi je, gospođo. Ja sam Mark Bryant.
Majka	Drago mi je, gospođo i gospodine. Sjednite, molim vas.

Mark i Rudolf izlaze iz sobe. Majka i Sandra razgovaraju.

Majka	Odakle ste vi, Sandra?
Sandra	Ja sam iz Engleske.
Majka	A gdje žive vaši roditelji?
Sandra	Žive u Londonu.
Majka	Imate li brata ili sestru?
Sandra	Imam sestru. Ona živi s roditeljima. Cijela moja obitelj živi u Londonu. Mark ima brata.

Majka	Gdje on živi?
Sandra	Njegov brat živi u Njemačkoj, u Berlinu. Radi tamo i oženjen je Njemicom.
Majka	Koliko dugo ste vi u braku?
Sandra	U braku smo već osam godina.
Majka	Moj Rudolf je još uvijek samac. Vrijeme je da se oženi, ali se Jasna neće udati… Sandra, koliko imate godina?
Sandra	Imam trideset pet godina.
Majka	A koliko ima vaš muž?
Sandra	Ima trideset sedam godina.
Majka	Moj Rudolf ima trideset devet godina. Radi već deset godina u istoj firmi. Imate li posao?
Sandra	Imam. Radim kao učiteljica u školi kod nas. Mark prodaje opremu za kompjutore i urede. On je predstavnik svoje firme u Zagrebu. Moja mama je računovođa, a tata radi u banci. Markov otac je mehaničar.

majka *mother*
soba *room*
zovu se *they are called*
sjednite (sjesti, sjednem) *sit down*
razgovaraju (razgovarati, razgovaram) *they talk, chat*
Odakle ste vi? *Where are you from?*
roditelj *parent*
brat *brother*
sestra *sister*
cijeli, cijela, cijelo *whole*
obitelj (fem.) *family*
u Njemačkoj *in Germany*
Oženjen je Njemicom. *He is married to a German* (woman).
koliko dugo … *(for) how long …*
u braku *married* (lit. *in marriage*)
već *already*
godina *year*
još uvijek *still*
samac *bachelor*
Vrijeme je da … *It is time that …*
oženiti se *to get married* (of male)

QUICK VOCAB

udati se *to get married* (of female)
u istoj firmi *in the same firm*
Koliko imate godina? *How old are you?*
Imam trideset pet godina. *I am 35.*
oprema za kompjutore *equipment for computers*
predstavnik *a representative*
firma *firm, company*
računovođa *accountant*
tata *Dad*
u banci (nom. banka) *in a bank*
Markov otac *Mark's father*
mehaničar *mechanic*

True or false?

a Sandra ima trideset jednu godinu.
b Markov brat živi u Njemačkoj.
c Markov tata je računovođa.

Insight

To be invited as a guest (**gost**) in a family home is to be treated with all the hospitality you could wish for. The problem is often how to refuse the excessive zeal with which food is put on plates. There are a number of phrases that can be repeated like, **Ne, hvala, ne mogu više** *No, thank you, I can't any more.* Perhaps you could add a little later **stvarno, ne mogu više** *really, I can't any more.* As for drink, if you don't want any more simply keep your glass full. Although the word **gost** is monosyllabic its plural form is **gosti** (without the **-ov-** typical of other such words like **grad/gradovi**).

Obitelj

The names of the members of the family which you have met so far are:

muž *husband*	**žena** *wife*
otac *father*	**majka** *mother*

tata *Dad*   **mama** *Mum*
brat *brother*   **sestra** *sister*

You will find more in the last section of this unit. The word **obitelj** is slightly unusual in that although it ends in a consonant it is a feminine word (like **stvar**).

Key phrases

🔊 **CD1, TR 7, 02:06**

How to:

- ask where someone is from and   **Odakle ste vi?**
  say where you are from   **Ja sam iz …**
- ask how long someone has   **Koliko dugo ste u braku?**
  been married
- say if you are married   **Već smo osam godina u braku.**
- say *to get married* (of a man)   **oženiti se**
  and *he is married*   **oženjen je**
- say *to get married* (of a woman)   **udati se**
  and *she is married*   **udata je**
- say that you are married   **Oženjen sam.**
  (man speaking)   **Nisam oženjen.**
  or not married
- say that you are married   **Udata sam.**
  (woman speaking)
  or not married   **Nisam udata.**
- ask if someone is married   **Jeste li oženjeni?**
     Jeste li udati?

There are two ways of saying you are married depending on whether you are a man or a woman. A man would use the verb **oženiti se** and a woman the verb **udati se**. Do not mix them up!

How to:

▶ ask about age:
How old are you?	**Koliko imate godina?**
I am ...	**Imam ...**
How old is your husband?	**Koliko ima godina vaš muž?**
My husband is ...	**Moj muž ima ...**

How it works

Adjectives

You have already seen a variety of adjective endings in previous units. Your attention has not been drawn to them because we were concentrating on nouns and verbs.

There is a basic similarity in adjective and noun endings, but there are things to watch for. Look at the following patterns for the nominative singular:

Masc.
Hotel je star.   *The hotel is old.*

Fem.
Kava je vruća.   *The coffee is hot.*

Neut.
Kazalište je lijepo.   *The theatre is beautiful.*

However, notice that the masculine ending is not always a consonant, but may be -i:

Ovo je dobar hotel.	*This is a good hotel.*
Ovo je taj stari čovjek.	*This is the old man.*

You add **-i** to the masculine nominative case in order to add the meaning of *the*. This is the only instance in which this happens.

Several adjectives only exist in this **-i** form. For example, **prvi** and other ordinal numbers.

There are a number of adjectives to which you may not add **-i**. For example, **moj, njegov** (and the other possessive adjectives), **jedan**, etc.

The ending without **-i** is always used in the following pattern:

Hotel je star.   *The hotel is old.* ('something' *is* 'something')

So far you have mainly seen the nominative and accusative adjective case endings. These endings in both the singular and the plural are similar to the endings for the nouns:

Singular	Masc.	Fem.	Neut.
nom.	**star(i)**	**stara**	**staro**
acc.	**star(i)**	**staru**	**staro**
nom.	**vruć(i)**	**vruća**	**vruće**
acc.	**vruć(i)**	**vruću**	**vruće**

Plural	Masc.	Fem.	Neut.
nom.	**stari**	**stare**	**stara**
acc.	**stare**	**stare**	**stara**
nom.	**vrući**	**vruće**	**vruća**
acc.	**vruće**	**vruće**	**vruća**

U Njemačkoj (dative case of adjectives)

When Sandra says that Mark's brother lives in Germany (**u Njemačkoj**), she uses the dative case of the word for Germany. In principle, it is no different from saying that he works in a school (**u školi**). However, the word for Germany is an adjective

Njemačka. It behaves like an adjective with feminine endings.
There are a number of names for countries that behave similarly:

Engleska	*England*	**u Engleskoj**
Francuska	*France*	**u Francuskoj**
Poljska	*Poland*	**u Poljskoj**
Danska	*Denmark*	**u Danskoj**
Hrvatska	*Croatia*	**u Hrvatskoj**
Škotska	*Scotland*	**u Škotskoj**
Irska	*Ireland*	**u Irskoj**

Not all the names of countries behave in this way, for example:

Italija	*Italy*	**u Italiji**
Rusija	*Russia*	**u Rusiji**
Amerika	*America*	**u Americi**
Srbija	*Serbia*	**u Srbiji**

The endings for dative adjectives are:

Masc. add -om (or -em to a word ending in a soft consonant)

dobar	dobrom
lijep	lijepom
vruć	vrućem

Fem. add -oj

dobra	dobroj
lijepa	lijepoj
vruća	vrućoj

Neut. add -om (or -em to a word ending in a soft consonant)

dobro	dobrom
lijepo	lijepom
vruće	vrućem

The plural ending is -im in all genders:

dobri	dobrim
lijepi	lijepim
vrući	vrućim

Look at the following examples:

Masc.

lijep grad	*a beautiful town*
u lijepom gradu	*in a beautiful town*

Fem.

vruća kava	*hot coffee*
u vrućoj kavi	*in hot coffee*

Neut.

dobro kazalište	*a good theatre*
u dobrom kazalištu	*in a good theatre*

Plural

lijepi gradovi	*beautiful towns*
u lijepim gradovima	*in beautiful towns*

Iz Engleske (genitive case of adjectives)

In answer to the question **Odakle ste vi?** you say **Ja sam iz Engleske.** You are using the preposition iz *from* followed by the genitive case of the name of the country, which is an adjective:

The endings for genitive adjectives are:

Masc.   add -og (or -eg to a word ending in a soft consonant)

dobar	dobrog
lijep	lijepog
vruć	vrućeg

Fem.   add -e

dobra	dobre
lijepa	lijepe
vruća	vruće

Neut.   add **-og** (or **-eg** to a word ending in a soft consonant)

dobro	dobrog
lijepo	lijepog
vruće	vrućeg

The plural ending is **-ih** in all genders:

dobri	dobrih
lijepi	lijepih
vrući	vrućih

Study the following examples:

Ja sam iz Njemačke.	*I am from Germany.*
Rudolf izlazi iz visoke zgrade.	*Rudolf is coming out of the tall building.*
Mark izlazi iz starog kazališta.	*Mark is coming out of the old theatre.*
U Zagrebu ima lijepih parkova.	*There are some nice parks in Zagreb.*

Remember that the accusative case for masculine nouns denoting persons or animals is the same as the genitive. Adjectives that agree with these nouns also have an accusative case that is *the same as the genitive*. Compare the following:

Vidim lijepi park.	*I see the nice park.*
Vidim starog čovjeka.	*I see the old man.*

Mark's father (**possession**)

You can make adjectives from personal names. For a man's name add **-ov**:

Mark	Markov
Rudolf	Rudolfov
Zvonko	Zvonkov

For a woman's name replace -a with -in:

Sandra   Sandrin
Jasna   Jasnin

These adjectives never take the -i ending in the masculine.
These words are just like other adjectives:

Ovo je Markova majka.	*This is Mark's mother.*
Izlaze iz Jasnine kuće.	*They are coming out of Jasna's house.*
Ovo je Rudolfovo pivo.	*This is Rudolf's beer.*

Use of *svoj*

Look at the following sentence in English:

He is taking his money.

There is a possibility here of ambiguity, because the word *his* may refer to *his own* or to *somebody else's* money. In Croatian, you distinguish between these two meanings of his:

On uzima svoj novac. (his own)
On uzima njegov novac. (somebody else's)

When the person who possesses the object is the same as the one who also performs the action you use the possessive adjective **svoj.** Look at the following examples:

On daje jelo svojoj ženi.	*He gives the dish to his (own) wife.*
On daje jelo njegovoj ženi.	*He gives the dish to his* (i.e. not his own) *wife.*
Oni gledaju svoju kuću.	*They are looking at their (own) house.*
Oni gledaju njihovu kuću.	*They are looking at their* (i.e. not their own) *house.*
On uzima svoj kaput.	*He takes his coat.*
Njegov kaput je tamo.	*His coat is there* (i.e. the coat is his own but the subject of the sentence is his coat).

kaput *coat*

Svoj follows the same pattern as **moj** and other adjectives that end in a soft consonant.

....

Insight

Note that **svoj** always refers back to the subject of the sentence and, therefore, cannot be used as part of the subject:

Rudolf ima svoj novac. | *Rudolf has his money.*
Njegov novac je na stolu. | *His money is on the table.*

In the first sentence, it is absolutely clear that Rudolf is in possession of his own money. In the second sentence, we would only know whose money is in question because of the context.

....

◀) **CD1, TR 7, 03:25**

Numbers (20–99)

For numbers above 20, simply combine the numerals:

dvadeset jedan	21	pedeset	50
dvadeset dva/dvije	22	pedeset pet	55
dvadeset tri	23	šezdeset	60
dvadeset pet	25	šezdeset tri	63
dvadeset osam	28	sedamdeset	70
sedamdeset	29	sedamdeset šest	76
trideset	30	osamdeset	80
trideset jedan	31	osamdeset jedan	81
trideset četiri	34	devedeset	90
trideset šest	36	devedeset devet	99
trideset sedam	37		
četrdeset	40		

The word which follows the number follows the same pattern as for the earlier numbers:

... jedan (singular)
dvadeset jedan čovjek   *21 people*

The word after **jedan** is always singular even when used in combination with other numbers, and **jedan** behaves like an adjective:

dvadeset jedna kuća   *21 houses*

... dva/dvije, tri, četiri (genitive singular)
trideset dva čovjeka   *32 people*
trideset dvije žene   *32 women*
osamdeset četiri godine   *84 years*

... pet, šest, sedam, etc. (genitive plural)
pedeset sedam stolova   *57 tables*
devedeset devet ljudi   *99 people*

The ordinal numbers (*twentieth*, etc.) are adjectives:

dvadeseti, dvadeseta,   *twentieth*
  dvadeseto
trideseti, trideseta, trideseto   *thirtieth*

In compound numbers, only the last number is treated as an adjective:

dvadeset prvi   *twenty-first*
trideset deveti   *thirty-ninth*

Use of *već*

When in English you use the past tense to ask *How long have you been married?*, in Croatian, you use the present tense and include the word **već** *already*: **Koliko dugo ste već u braku?**:

Koliko dugo ste u braku?   *How long have you been married?*
U braku smo već osam godina.   *We have been married for eight years.*

Unusual noun categories

a Look at the pattern of case endings for **otac**:

	singular	plural
nom.	otac	očevi
voc.	oče	očevi
acc.	oca	očeve
gen.	oca	očeva
dat.	ocu	očevima
ins.	ocem	očevima

It is affected by the spelling rules of Croatian.

The penultimate **a** between two consonants drops out when case endings are added.

The letter **t** is the same sound as the beginning of **c** (**ts**) and this is treated as a double consonant. Double consonants are rarely tolerated and so the first **t** is also omitted.

It has a plural that is regular in its case pattern but with a stem of **očev-**.

b Nijemac: the penultimate **a**, normally lost from masculine nouns with their case endings, returns in the genitive plural form:
dva Nijemca   *two Germans* (gen. singular)
pet Nijemaca   *five Germans* (gen. plural)

The **a** returns in the genitive plural form only with all such nouns.

c Tata is unusual in that the word looks feminine (like **kava** or **žena**) and it changes according to the regular pattern for such nouns. However, adjectives take the corresponding masculine endings because the word refers to a masculine person. Study the following examples:
Naš stari tata je u sobi.   *Our old dad is in the room.*
Vidim starog tatu.   *I see the old dad.*

Koliko imate godina?

The word **koliko** means *how much* or *how many*. It is followed by the genitive case like other words of quantity (such as **mnogo**). Remember the word order in the question *How old are you?*:

Koliko imate godina?

Practice

1 Fill in the missing adjective from the box (all the adjectives are given with the correct case ending and each is therefore appropriate to just one sentence):

  a Hotel je _____.
  b Dan je _____.
  c Riba je _____.
  d Meso je _____.
  e Jasna je _____.
  f Razglednica je _____.
  g Vino je _____.
  h Zgrada je _____.

> star velika žedna bijelo svježa vruć odlično skupa

2 Add the correct case ending to the adjectives in the sentences that follow:

  a Spomenik je u lijep _____ parku.
  b Čovjek izlazi iz velik _____ pošte.
  c Koverte nisu skup _____.
  d Skrenite u treć _____ ulicu desno.
  e Izlazi iz star_____ hotela.
  f Jasna hoće kupiti velik _____ razglednice.
  g Idemo na Glavn _____ Kolodvor.
  h Pijemo dobr _____ kavu u Gradsk _____ kavani.

3 Make up sentences from the information given as indicated in the examples:

John   Englez   Engleska   banka
John je Englez.
Živi u Engleskoj.
Radi u banci.

a Pierre	Francuz	Francuska	ured
b Vjekoslav	Hrvat	Hrvatska	restoran
c Branka	Srpkinja	Srbija	hotel
d Maša	Ruskinja	Rusija	škola

4 Change the name in brackets into an adjective and supply the correct case ending:
   a Milivoj živi u (Branka) stanu.
   b On izlazi iz (Mark) sobe.
   c Gledamo (Sandra) sestru.
   d (Mark) brat živi u Njemačkoj.
   e (Rudolf) ured je u centru grada.
   f Ulazimo u (Velimir) školu.

◄》 CD1, TR 7, 04:34

5 Complete the missing part of the dialogue:
   Are you married, Rudolf?
   Ne, nisam oženjen.
   Is Jasna married?
   Ne, nije udata.

6 Match the question on the left to the correct answer on the right:
   a Da li je ovo vaša kava?   **i** Vidim ga.
   b Da li je Jasna udata?   **ii** Ne, to je moja.
   c Gdje je Rudolfova majka?   **iii** Sjedi u svojoj sobi.
   d Da li vidite Marka?   **iv** Nije.

◄》 CD1, TR 7, 05:05

7 Supply in words the numbers given in numerals:
   22, 47, 64, 29, 17, 11, 43, 38, 77, 58, 90, 61.

Comprehension 1

Sandrina sestra živi u Londonu s roditeljima. Ima dvadeset jednu godinu. Studira medicinu na sveučilištu u Londonu. Želi postati liječnica.

Markov brat živi u Berlinu. On je vojnik. Njegova žena je Njemica iz Frankfurta. Markov brat ima trideset godina, a njegova žena dvadeset devet. Imaju sina i kćerku. Sin ima pet godina, a kćerka tri.

studirati, studiram *study*
medicina *medicine*
sveučilište *university*
postati *become*
liječnica *doctor* (woman)
vojnik *soldier*
sin *son*
kćerka *daughter*

True or false?

a Sandrina sestra ima dvadeset dvije godine.
b Žena Markovog brata je Njemica.
c Njihov sin ima pet godina.

Comprehension 2

Read the following passage and answer the questions that follow:

Rudolf govori Marku o svojoj obitelji. Brat njegove majke je njegov ujak. Njegova žena je Rudolfova ujna. Brat njegovog tate je njegov stric. Njegova žena je Rudolfova strina. Rudolfovi roditelji imaju i sestre. Sestre majke i oca su Rudolfove tetke. Njihovi muževi su Rudolfovi teci – to znači da ako je tetka udata, njen muž je Rudolfov tetak. Dijete jednog ujaka, strica ili tetke je Rudolfov brat ili sestra. Kaže se da je brat od strica, ili sestra od tetke. Koliko Mark razumije obiteljske odnose?

QUICK VOCAB

ujak *uncle*
ujna *aunt* (his wife)
stric *uncle*
strina *aunt* (his wife)
tetka *aunt*
tetak *uncle* (her husband)
to znači *that means*
ako *if*
kaže se *it is said, one says*
obiteljski odnosi *family relations*

1 Brat Rudolfovog oca je …
   a Rudolfov stric.
   b Rudolfov ujak.
   c Rudolfov brat od tetke.

2 Sestra Rudolfove majke je …
   a Rudolfova tetka.
   b Rudolfova strina.
   c Rudolfova ujna.

3 Žena Rudolfovog strica je …
   a Rudolfova strina.
   b Rudolfova sestra.
   c sestra Rudolfove majke.

Test yourself

Here you can check some of the things you have learnt in this unit. Look at the questions that follow and choose the right answer:

1 Mark's wife, Sandra, is English. Which of these statements is not true?

a Markova žena je Engleskinja.
b Mark je oženjen Engleskinjom.
c Markova žena je iz Hrvatske.

2 What is the correct Croatian word for a *brother*?
a brat
b tata
c stric

3 What relation is Sandra's mother's sister to her?
a sestra
b mama
c tetka

4 If someone asks **Jasna Odakle ste vi?** what is the correct response?
a Iz Rusije.
b Iz Hrvatske.
c U Hrvatskoj.

5 How would you ask someone *How old are you?*
a Koliko imate godina?
b Koliko imaju godina?
c Koliko dugo ste već u braku?

6 How would Jasna say that she is single?
a Nisam oženjen.
b Ja sam u braku.
c Nisam udata.

7 Which number comes after **pedeset devet**?
a pedeset osam
b šezdeset
c sedamdeset

8 There are 21 people in a room. What form of the word for people is correct here: **dvadeset jedan ...**?
a čovjek
b čovjeka
c ljudi

9 There are 25 people in a room. What form of the word for people is correct here: **dvadeset pet** …?

   a čovjek

   b čovjeka

   c ljudi

10 In what kind of institution in Croatia would you study to become a doctor?

   a škola

   b sveučilište

   c kazalište

8

Kakav stan imate?
What kind of flat do you have?

In this unit you will learn how to
- *Describe a room, your house or flat*
- *Describe your day's routine*
- *Use more question words*
- *Tell the time*
- *Use expressions for the divisions of the day*

Dialogue

Sandra i Mark su na večeri kod Rudolfa. Rudolf pokazuje Marku stan. U dnevnoj sobi su dva naslonjača, veliki kauč i dva stolića za kavu. Namještaj je udoban. U uglu je televizor. Oni izlaze iz dnevne sobe, dok Sandra razgovara s Rudolfovom majkom.

Mark	Kakav stan imate? Koliko imate u stanu soba?
Rudolf	Imamo četiri sobe, kupaonicu i kuhinju. Ovo je blagovaonica. Vidite da u sredini stoji veliki stol. Oko njega su stolice. Kroz vrata vidite kuhinju gdje su frižider, zamrzivač i ormari. U ormarima su tanjuri, šalice, vilice, noževi, žlice i tave.
Mark	Koliko spavaćih soba imate?
Rudolf	Imamo dvije. Ovo je mamina soba, a to je moja. Moja soba je velika. To je i moja radna soba. Tamo imam kompjutor, radni stol i police s knjigama.

◆ CD1, TR 8

pokazuje Marku (pokazivati, pokazuje) *he shows (to) Mark*
dnevna soba *living room*
naslonjač *armchair*
kauč *couch*
stolić *little table*
namještaj *furniture*
udoban *comfortable*
dok *while*
Kakav imate stan? *What kind of flat do you have?*
Koliko imate soba? *How many rooms do you have?*
kupaonica *bathroom*
kuhinja *kitchen*
blagovaonica *dining room*
u sredini *in the middle*
stoji (stojati, stojim) *he/she/it is standing*
oko njega *around it*
stolica *chair*
kroz vrata *through the door*
frižider *fridge*
zamrzivač *freezer*
ormar *cupboard*
tanjur *plate*
šalica *cup*
vilica *fork*
nož *knife*
žlica *spoon*
tava *saucepan*
spavaća soba *bedroom*
radna soba *study* (workroom)
radni stol *desk*
polica s knjigama *bookshelf*
knjiga *book*

Sandra i Rudolfova majka razgovaraju. Majka je pita o njenom životu u Londonu.

Majka	U koliko sati počinje vaš radni dan?
Sandra	Počinje u sedam sati kad obično ustajem. Stižem u školu oko osam i pol i radim od deset do devet do podne.

Majka	Imate li pauzu?
Sandra	Imamo pauzu prije podne. Ta pauza traje dvadeset minuta. Imamo i pauzu za ručak. Poslije ručka škola počinje u jedan i petnaest. Kao i prije podne, učenici imaju četiri sata sa pauzom poslije drugog sata.
Majka	To znači da se škola završava oko četiri sata.
Sandra	Da, onda idem kući. Kod kuće obično večeram s Markom oko pola osam.

o *about* (preposition followed by dat.)
u koliko sati *at what time*
počinjati, počinjem *to begin*
obično *usually*
ustajati, ustajem *to get up*
stizati, stižem *to arrive*
oko osam i pol *about half past eight*
deset do devet *ten to nine*
podne *midday*
pauza *pause, break*
trajati, traje *to last*
prije podne *in the morning* (before noon)
poslije ručka *after lunch*
poslije (preposition followed by gen.) *after*
jedan i petnaest *quarter past one*
učenik *pupil*
sat *hour, o'clock, class, lesson*
završavati se *to finish*
oko četiri sata *about four o'clock*
oko pola osam *about half past seven*

QUICK VOCAB

True or false?

a Rudolf i njegova majka imaju dvije spavaće sobe.
b Veliki stol je u kuhinji.
c Poslije ručka Sandrina škola počinje u jedan i pet.

Key phrases

◀) **CD1, TR 8, 02:12**

How to:

▶ describe rooms in your house/flat	kupaonica
	kuhinja
	dnevna soba
	blagovaonica
	spavaća soba
	radna soba
▶ show someone round your house/flat	pokazivati stan Marku (dat.)
▶ name some divisions of the day	prije podne
	podne
▶ ask/say at what time something happens	U koliko sati?/U sedam sati.
▶ give an approximate time	Oko pola osam.

How it works

Adjectives (instrumental case)

Look at this example of an adjective used in the instrumental case
after the preposition **s**:

Sandra govori s njegovom majkom.   *Sandra speaks with her mother.*

The endings for adjectives in the instrumental are:

Masc.   add -im
dobar   dobrim
lijep   lijepim
moj   mojim

Fem.   add -om
dobra   dobrom
lijepa   lijepom
moja   mojom

Neut.   add -im
dobro   dobrim
lijepo   lijepim
moje   mojim

The plural ending is -**im** in all genders:
dobri   dobrim
lijepi   lijepim
moji   mojim

◀) **CD1, TR 8, 02:58**

Telling the time

In official contexts, such as railway timetables, the 24-hour clock is
used. Thus,

dva sata i pet minuta

pet sati i petnaest minuta

deset sati i dvadeset minuta

četrnaest sati i četrdeset minuta

dvadeset sati i pedeset pet minuta

In most everyday circumstances, a different system is used.

Minutes past the hour:
Here the pattern resembles the 24-hour clock:

jedan (sat) i pet (minuta)

dva (sata) i deset (minuta)	tri (sata) i petnaest (minuta)	pet (sati) i dvadeset pet (minuta)	šest (sati) i trideset (minuta)

The words for hours and minutes are usually omitted. Here, they
have been put in brackets. After **jedan** the word for hour is in the
nominative (**sat**), after **dva**, **tri** and **četiri** in the genitive singular

(**sata**) and after the other numbers in the genitive plural (**sati**). The word for *minute* is **minuta**.

Alternative ways of expressing *half past the hour*:

a   4.30   četiri i pol
        9.30   devet i pol
b   5.30   pola šest
        11.30   pola dvanaest
        (Here, you are saying: *it is now half of the sixth, twelfth hour*)

Minutes to the hour:

dvadeset pet do osam   dvadeset do devet

petnaest do deset   deset do jedanaest   pet do dvanaest

◀) CD1, TR 8, 05:16

What time is it now?

Koliko je sada sati?   *What time is it now?*

To state the time simply put **Sada je ...** in front of the time:

Sada je jedan sat.	*It is now one o'clock.*
Sada je tri i petnaest.	*It is now quarter past three.*
Sada je šest i pol.	*It is now half past six.*
Sada je pola sedam.	*It is now half past six.*
Sada je deset do dvanaest.	*It is now ten to twelve.*

To give an approximate time add **oko**:

Sada je oko šest.   *It's about six. (It's sixish.)*
Sada je oko pola jedanaest.   *It's about half ten.*

◀》 CD1, TR 8, 06:21

At what time?

U koliko sati ...   *At what time ...*

To say *at what time* ... put **u** before the time:

u pet sati   *at five o'clock*
u šest i pol   *at six thirty*
u deset do dvanaest   *at ten to twelve*
u dvanaest   *at twelve o'clock*
u podne   *at noon*

To give an approximate time, again use **oko**, but without **u**:

oko osam sati   *at about eight o'clock*
oko tri i dvadeset   *at about twenty past three*
oko petnaest do pet   *at about quarter to five*

To say *from ... to ...* use **od ... do ...**:

od pet do šest   *from five to six o'clock*
od petnaest do sedam do   *from quarter to seven to*
osam sati   *eight o'clock*

Insight

Telling the time is not difficult in Croatian. The simplest method is as follows:

Whole hours	**dva sata**	2.00
Minutes past the hour	**dva i petnaest**	2.15
Half past the hour	**dva i pol**	2.30
Minutes to the hour	**petnaest do tri**	2.45

jutro *morning*	**večer** *evening*
jutros *this morning*	**večeras** *this evening*
ujutro *in the morning*	**uvečer** (or **navečer**) *in the evening*
prije podne *morning*	**poslije podne** *afternoon*
dan *day*	**noć** *night*
danas *today*	**noćas** *tonight*
danju *during the day*	**noću** *at night*
podne (u podne) *noon*	**ponoć** (u ponoć) *midnight*

Divisions of the day

Po podne is often used instead of poslije podne.

The following are approximate times:
  jutro: *6 a.m. to 10 a.m.* dan: *10 a.m. to 6 p.m.*
  večer: *6 p.m. to 12 p.m.* noć: *12 p.m. to 6 a.m.*

Take care not to invite someone to meet you **noćas**, when you really mean **večeras**!

The divisions of the day are used to clarify time by the clock:

osam sati ujutro	*eight o'clock in the morning*
deset sati prije podne	*nine o'clock in the morning*
u četiri poslije podne	*at four in the afternoon*
u šest i pol večeras	*at half past six this evening*

You can add to these divisions of the day with the following:

prekjučer *day before yesterday*
jučer *yesterday*
sinoć *last night*
sutra *tomorrow*
prekosutra *day after tomorrow*

u šest sati sutra ujutro	*at six o'clock tomorrow morning*
u sedam i petnaest sinoć	*at quarter past seven last night*
oko tri poslije podne	*at about three in the afternoon*
prekjučer	*the day before yesterday*

More prepositions

1 Followed by the accusative:
kroz *through*

Idem kroz kuću	*I'm going through the house.*

2 Followed by the genitive:
oko *around, about*

Gosti sjede oko stola.	*The guests are sitting around the table.*

poslije *after*

Škola počinje poslije ručka.	*School begins after lunch.*

3 Followed by the dative:
o *about*

Govore o školi.	*They are speaking about school.*

Kakav

Kakav is an adjective, so it changes its ending according to the
noun. It has two meanings:

a *What kind of ...?*

Kakav naslonjač stoji u dnevnoj sobi?	*What kind of an armchair stands in the living room?*
Kakvu juhu više volite?	*What kind of soup do you prefer?*
Kakve knjige su na stolu?	*What kind of books are on the table?*

b *What a ...!*

Kakav čovjek!	*What a person!*
Kakva kuća!	*What a house!*

This/that

Sandra says: Ta pauza traje dvadeset minuta. *That break lasts
for 20 minutes.*

The adjectives meaning *this* and *that* are **ovaj**, **taj** and **onaj**. They
do not have the masculine nominative ending with -i. Add endings
for other genders and cases on to **ov-**, **t-** and **on-**:

Ulaze u ovu **zgradu.**	*They are entering this building.*
Vidite li tog **čovjeka?**	*Do you see that man?*
Novine se mogu kupiti u onoj	*One can buy newspapers in that*
prodavaonici na uglu.	*shop on the corner.*

Both **taj** and **onaj** mean *that*, with the difference that **onaj** refers to an object that is further away.

Unusual noun categories (*vrata*)

Vrata is one of the words in Croatian that only exists in a plural form. It ends in **-a** and it is neuter plural.

All adjectives and verbs agree with the neuter plural form of the word:

Vrata **su lijepa.**	*The door is beautiful.*
Ideš kroz crna vrata **u hodnik.**	*You go through the black door into the corridor.*

Novine also exists only in this feminine plural form, although it may refer to one, or more than one, newspaper:

To su dobre novine.	*That is a good newspaper.*

Practice

1 Choose the most appropriate adjective to fit the gaps in the following sentences. The adjectives are in the masculine nominative form, you will have to put them in the correct gender, case and number (i.e. singular or plural). You may use each adjective only once:

   a Nije daleko od _____ ceste do našeg bloka.

   b Ona govori sa _____ majkom u kuhinji.

   c Više volim _____ vino, ali mogu piti i bijelo.

   d Možemo ići pješice od hotela do _____ zgrada u centru grada.

e Danas idemo u _____ školu, a ne u moju školu.
f Gosti sjede na _____ stolicama u blagovaonici.

> udoban   tvoj   glavan   velik   crn   njegov

2 Choose the most appropriate preposition to fit the gaps in the following sentences. Make sure that you consider the case endings of the nouns and adjectives:

a Idem kući _____ škole.
b Radim od šest sati ujutro _____ tri poslije podne.
c Pošta se nalazi _____ trgu.
d Ideš _____ velika vrata tamo u njihov stan.
e Jasna govori sa Rudolfovom majkom _____ kuće.
f Oni izlazi _____ kavane u šest sati uvečer.

> do   iz   na   kroz   kod   poslije

3 Answer the questions that follow by referring to the drawings:
a Kakav namještaj imate u dnevnoj sobi?

I have three armchairs, one small table and a television set in the corner.

b Što imate u kuhinji?

In the kitchen I have a fridge, a freezer and cupboards.

c Radite li u spavaćoj sobi?
Da, moram raditi u spavoćoj sobi. Imam tamo...

A desk and two shelves for books.

d Kakav namještaj imate u blagovaonici?

I have a large table and six chairs for guests.

4 Match the question on the left to the correct answer on the right:
- **a** Kakvu dnevnu sobu imate?   **i** Počinje u sedam.
- **b** U koliko sati počinje film?   **ii** Idem k tetki.
- **c** Što radite sutra?   **iii** Jasna ne može doći.
- **d** Tko ne dolazi na ručak danas?   **iv** Velika je sa stolom.

5 Write out the times shown on the clock faces:

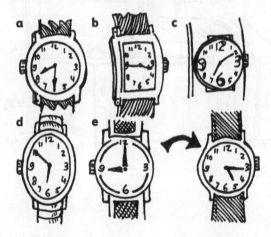

6 Fill in the gaps with the most appropriate divisions of the day from the box:

   a Učenici počinju raditi u školi _____.
   b Idemo _____ u kazalište.
   c Autobusi ne idu kroz grad _____.
   d Danas i _____ idem k bratu.

> sutra   večeras   prije podne   noću

Comprehension 1

◆ CD1, TR 8, 07:31

Jasna Kušan je sekretarica u velikoj zagrebačkoj firmi. Ovdje govori o svom tipičnom radnom danu.

Ustajem u pola sedam. Znam da je rano, ali moram se istuširati i popiti kavu prije posla. Na posao idem autobusom. Put traje oko dvadeset minuta. U uredu odmah počinjem raditi, uvijek me nešto čeka na radnom stolu. U devet i petnaest idem na doručak. Kupujem sendviče i pijem kavu. Radim do tri. Ponekad idem u grad kupiti nešto ili možda rezervirati karte za kazalište ili kino. Ručam kod kuće ili s prijateljicama u restoranu.

zagrebački *of Zagreb*
tipičan *typical*
radni dan *working day*
rano *early*
istuširati se, istuširam se *shower*
prije *before*
put *road, journey*
nešto *something*
čekati, čekam *wait*
kupovati, kupujem (imperfective; kupiti perfective) *to buy*
možda *perhaps*
rezervirati, rezerviram *reserve*

QUICK VOCAB

karta *ticket*
kino *cinema*

True or false?

a Jasnina firma je u Zagrebu.
b Put na posao traje oko dvadeset minuta.
c Jasna radi do tri po podne.

Comprehension 2

Read the passage and answer the questions that follow:

Poslije lijepe večere kod Rudolfa i njegove majke, Sandra razmišlja o svom i Markovom životu u Zagrebu. Sjeća se njihovog stana u Londonu. U tom stanu imaju dnevnu sobu sa zelenim tepihom i zavjesama iste boje. Stan nije velik, ali ima kuhinju i spavaću sobu za goste. Koliko dugo su već u Zagrebu? Hotel nije loš, ali je teško stanovati u jednoj sobi. Kaže mužu, "Moram priznati, sviđa mi se Rudolfov stan. Možemo li mi tražiti stan u Zagrebu? Ne volim živjeti stalno u hotelu." Mark sluša ženu i kaže, "Moramo čekati. Ne znam koliko dugo ostajemo u Zagrebu."

QUICK VOCAB

razmišljati, razmišljam *to consider, think about*
sjećati se, sjećam se (followed by gen.) *remember*
zelen *green*
tepih *carpet*
zavjesa *curtain*
iste boje *of the same colour*
Koliko dugo su već u Zagrebu? *How long have they been in Zagreb?*
loš *bad*
teško je *it is difficult*
kazati, kažem *to say, tell*
priznati *to confess, admit*
Sviđa mi se Rudolfov stan. *I like Rudolf's flat.*
slušati, slušam *to listen to*
Koliko dugo ostajemo u Zagrebu? *For how long are we staying in Zagreb?*

1 Kakve su zavjese u Rudolfovoj dnevnoj sobi?

    a Lijepe su.

    b Zelene su.

    c Loše su.

2 Gdje Sandra ne može stanovati?

    a Ne može stanovati u Zagrebu.

    b Ne može stanovati u Londonu.

    c Ne može stanovati u jednoj sobi.

3 Što misli Mark?

    a Misli da je to dobra ideja.

    b Ne zna koliko dugo ostaju u Zagrebu.

    c Misli da hotel nije udoban.

Test yourself

Here you can check some of the things you have learnt in this unit. Look at the questions that follow and choose the right answer:

1 In which room do you cook?

    a kuhinja

    b dnevna soba

    c spavaća soba

2 In which room do you sleep?

    a blagovaonica

    b kupaonica

    c spavaća soba

3 You are waiting for your train at Zagreb railway station which is due at quarter to five in the afternoon. What time will the station announcer say?

    a petnaest sati i četrdeset pet minuta

    b šesnaest sati i četrdeset pet minuta

    c sedamnaest sati i petnaest minuta

4 You arrange to meet your friend at 7.30 that evening. Which is the correct time?

    a u pola sedam večeras

    b u sedam i pol večeras

    c u sedam sati večeras

5 Which word means *the day after tomorrow*?

    a prekosutra

    b prekjučer

    c sutra

6 Which word means *last night*?

    a sutra

    b sinoć

    c jutros

7 Jasna is walking through the living room. Complete the sentence with the word for *living room* in the correct case **Jasna ide kroz ...?**

    a dnevnu sobu

    b dnevnoj sobi

    c dnevne sobe

8 Jasna wants to say that after her working day she goes home. Choose the phrase with the correct case ending to follow **poslije ...**

    a radni dan

    b radnog dana

    c radnom danu

9 What is **kino**?

    a cinema

    b theatre

    c kitchen

10 Which phrase means *For how long?*

    a Kakav sat?

    b Koliko je sati?

    c Koliko dugo?

9

Sviđa mi se plivanje
I like swimming

In this unit you will learn how to
* **Describe hobbies, sports and free time**
* **Use other expressions of time, days of the week and months of the year**

Dialogue

Mark govori sa Rudolfom o sportovima i o slobodnom vremenu.

Mark	Rudolf, bavite li se sportom?
Rudolf	Da, bavim se sportom. Volim igrati tenis i nogomet. Sviđa mi se plivanje. Idem na bazen svakog ponedjeljka.
Mark	I meni se sviđa plivanje. U Londonu idem dva-tri puta tjedno. Gdje je vaš bazen?
Rudolf	Idem u Sportsko-rekreacijski centar. Zatvoren bazen radi svaki dan i zimi i ljeti. Imaju i otvoren bazen, radi od početka lipnja do kraja rujna.
Mark	Što još ima tamo?
Rudolf	Ima terena za sve sportove. Imaju stadion za hokej na travi i stadion za hokej na ledu. Ljudi igraju košarku. Imaju rukometno igralište, i terene za tenis i za nogomet. Stadioni za hokej rade svaki dan, rukometno igralište radi subotom i nedjeljom.

(Contd)

● CD2, TR 1

Mark	Volim igrati badminton.
Rudolf	Imaju teren za igranje badmintona. Radi srijedom od devet sati do podne, i subotom po podne.
Mark	Da li se Jasna bavi sportom?
Rudolf	Igra badminton. A bavi li se Sandra sportom?
Mark	Sandri se sviđa plivanje.
Rudolf	Morate doći u Centar.
Mark	Kada idete?
Rudolf	Da vidim … Danas je četvrtak. Idem prekosutra.
Mark	Dobro. Ja sam u subotu slobodan.

QUICK VOCAB

sport *sport*

slobodno vrijeme (o **slobodnom vremenu** … without '**…ij…**')
 free time (leisure)

baviti se, bavim se (followed by instrumental case) *to be occupied
 with, take part in*

do kraja rujna *to the end of September*

teren *pitch, court* (for sports)

za sve sportove *for all sports*

stadion za hokej na travi *stadium for grass hockey*

hokej na ledu *ice hockey*

igrati, igram *to play*

tenis *tennis*

nogomet *football*

bazen *swimming pool*

svakog ponedjeljka *every Monday*

dva-tri puta *two or three times*

tjedno *weekly*

Sportsko-rekreacijski centar *sports centre*

zatvoren bazen *covered pool*

zimi *in winter*

ljeti *in summer*

otvoren bazen *open-air pool*

od početka lipnja *from the beginning of June*

košarka *basketball*

rukometno igralište *handball pitch*

rukomet *handball*

teren za tenis *tennis court*
svaki dan *every day*
subotom *on Saturdays*
nedjeljom *on Sundays*
igranje *playing*
srijedom *on Wednesdays*
Sandri se sviđa plivanje. *Sandra likes swimming.*
Da vidim ... *Let me see ...*
četvrtak *Thursday*
Ja sam slobodan. *I am free. (available)*
u subotu *on Saturday*

Mark čita informacije o Sportsko-rekreacijskom centru:

> ZATVORENI BAZENI (olimpijski i mali)
> **Radno vrijeme:** radnim danom od **12.00** do **19.00** sati,
> subotom od **10.00** do **20.00** sati. Nedjeljom ne radi.
>
> RUKOMETNO IGRALIŠTE
> **Radno vrijeme:** svake subote i nedelje od travnja do listopada.
>
> ATLETSKI STADION
> Tečaj atletike traje 15 sati (3 tjedna x 5 dana) od **15.30** do **16.30** sati.

čitati, čitam *to read*
informacija (usually used in plural **informacije**) *information*
radnim danom *on working days*
Nedjeljom ne radi. *It does not work on Sundays.* (i.e. it is not open)
svake subote *every Saturday*
od travnja do listopada *from April to October*
atletski stadion *athletics stadium, track*
tečaj *course*

True or false?

a Rudolf se bavi tenisom, nogometom i plivanjem.
b Mark voli igrati košarku.
c Zatvoreni bazeni rade svaki dan.

Key phrases

◆ CD2, TR 1, 02:36

How to:

▶ use more expressions of time

every day	svaki dan
every Monday	svakog ponedjeljka
every Saturday	svake subote
on Saturdays	subotom
on Sundays	nedjeljom
on Wednesdays	srijedom
weekly	tjedno
today is …	danas je …
on Saturday	u subotu
in winter	zimi
in summer	ljeti
from the beginning of June	od početka lipnja
to the end of September	do kraja rujna
from April to October	od travnja do listopada

▶ express involvement with sport   bavim se sportom
▶ say that you play a sport   igram tenis
▶ say that you like a sport   volim tenis
    or   sviđa mi se plivanje

How it works

Sviđa mi se plivanje

You have already met the phrase **volim …** to express that you like something. There is another common expression used: **sviđa mi se …** This expression literally means *It is pleasing to me* and is formed by using the dative case of the relevant person (i.e. *me*):

Sviđa mi se plivanje.	*I like swimming.*
Sviđa joj se Zagreb.	*She likes Zagreb.*
Marku se sviđa plivanje.	*Mark likes swimming.*
Sandri se sviđa Zagreb.	*Sandra likes Zagreb.*

The verbal part **sviđa** is an **-a** verb like **gledati**. Look what happens when more than one thing is liked, **sviđa** is transformed into a plural form **sviđaju**:

Sviđaju mi se te knjige.	*I like those books.*

Reflexive verbs

In this unit, you have met more verbs called reflexive verbs. These verbs include **se** when used: (**baviti se, sjećati se,** etc.). The short word **se** never changes.

Se is roughly equivalent to the English *oneself*, although it is not always immediately apparent in English that this word has to be used with the verb.

These verbs are never followed by the accusative case:

Bavim se sportom.	*I am engaged in sport.*
(instrumental – **sportom**)	(I involve *myself* in sport)
Sjećam se stana u Londonu.	*I remember the flat in London.*
(genitive – **stana**)	
Ženi se Njemicom. (ženiti se –	*He is getting married to a*
to be getting married)	*German.*
(followed by the instrumental –	
Njemicom)	

The word **se** is like the short forms of **biti** or of **ja, ti,** etc. It never comes as first word, but as second word in the sentence:

Kako se zovete?	*What is your name?* (lit. *How do you call yourself?*)
Zovem se Mark.	*My name is Mark.* (I call myself Mark)

Word order

Words like **se**, which never come at the beginning of the sentence, are called *enclitics*. There is a strict order for the enclitics when more than one occurs together. The order is **li**, dative enclitic, genitive enclitic, accusative enclitic, **se**. Study these examples:

Sjećam ga se.	*I remember him.*
Dajem joj ga.	*I give it to her.*
Sviđa mi se plivanje.	*I like swimming.*
Da li vam se sviđa plivanje?	*Do you like swimming?*
Sviđaju li vam se nogomet i košarka?	*Do you like football and basketball?*

In other instances, word order is fairly flexible in Croatian. The case endings mean that you cannot get the meaning wrong, whatever the order of words. Look at these examples, which all mean the same because Sandra is nominative case each time:

Sandra daje ženi novac.
Sandra daje novac ženi.   } *Sandra gives the money to the woman.*
Novac Sandra daje ženi.

◀ **CD2, TR 1, 03:40**

Days of the week

The days of the week are:

ponedjeljak *Monday*	**petak** *Friday*
utorak *Tuesday*	**subota** *Saturday*
srijeda *Wednesday*	**nedjelja** *Sunday*
četvrtak *Thursday*	

Days are always spelt with a small letter in Croatian.

To say *every* ... use the genitive case with the adjective **svaki** *every*:

| svakog ponedjeljka | *every Monday* |
| svake subote | *every Saturday* |

(Sometimes the accusative case is used with **dan: svaki dan**.)

To say *on Tuesdays*, etc. simply use the word in the instrumental case (singular):

| utorkom | *on Tuesdays* |
| četvrtkom | *on Thursdays* |

To say on a day use the preposition **u** followed by the name of the day in the accusative case:

| u utorak | *on Tuesday* |
| u subotu | *on Saturday* |

The word for *week* is **tjedan** and for *weekly* is **tjedno**.

🔊 **CD2, TR 1, 04:00**

Months of the year

The names of the months are as follows:

siječanj *January*	**srpanj** *July*
veljača *February*	**kolovoz** *August*
ožujak *March*	**rujan** *September*
travanj *April*	**listopad** *October*
svibanj *May*	**studeni** *November*
lipanj *June*	**prosinac** *December*

Months are always spelt with a small letter in Croatian. To say in a month use **u** followed by the name of the month in the dative case:

u siječnju	*in January*
u veljači	*in February*
u ožujku	*in March*

The word **studeni** is an adjective in form:

u studenom   *in November*

The word for *month* is **mjesec** and for *monthly* is **mjesečno**.

🔊 **CD2, TR 1, 04:27**

Seasons of the year

The seasons of the year are:

proljeće *spring*	**u proljeće** *in spring*
ljeto *summer*	**ljeti** *in summer*
jesen *autumn*	**u jesen** *in autumn*
zima *winter*	**zimi** *in winter*

Dva-tri puta

To say *two or three* in Croatian you join the two numbers together with a hyphen. Look at the following examples:

pet-šest ljudi	*five or six people*
sedam-osam terena za tenis	*seven or eight tennis courts*

....
Insight
Remember these patterns for useful expressions of time:

svake srijede   *every Wednesday*
(to say *every …* use genitive case)

subotom   *on Saturdays*
(to say *on Mondays* etc. use instrumental case)

u subotu   *on Saturday*
(to say *on a day* use **u** and accusative case)

u kolovozu   *in August*
(to say *in January* etc. use **u** and dative case)
....

138

Practice

1 Replace the verb **voljeti** with the corresponding phrase taken from **sviđati se** as in the example:

Examples: Mark voli nogomet. Marku se sviđa nogomet.

Take care to choose the correct person in the dative case and to choose the correct endings for both the verb (**sviđa** or **sviđaju**) and the thing which is liked.

  a Vole ove knjige.
  b Volim nogomet.
  c Da li volite plivanje?
  d Rudolf voli košarku.
  e Sandra i Jasna vole badminton.

2 Replace the noun or nouns in bold in the following sentences with the appropriate pronouns.

Example: Konobar daje **nož ženi**. Konobar joj ga daje.

Take care with choosing the correct case for each person and take care to position each short enclitic form correctly.

  a Čovjek daje **marke Marku**.
  b Da li žena daje **Sandri** novac?
  c Vidim **Rudolfa** blizu spomenika.
  d Ljudi piju **kavu** u kavani.
  e Mark gleda **ženu**.
  f Pišemo **mami**.
  g Dajem **knjige ljudima**.
  h Sjeća se **stana** u Londonu.

◀ CD2, TR 1, 04:54

3 Fill in the missing parts of the dialogue:

Do you like swimming?
Ne, ne sviđa mi se.

Do you involve yourself in a sport?
Da, bavim se rukometom.
I like to play handball too. Where is the handball court?
Ima rukometno igralište u Sportsko-rekreacijskom centru.
Do they have a covered swimming pool there?
Imaju. Zatvoren bazen radi svaki dan.
At what time does it work?
Radi od devet sati prije podne do dva sata po podne.
When are you going to the sports centre?
Idem u srijedu. Dođite u Centar u srijedu!

◀) CD2, TR 1, 06:19

4 Supply the expression of time as indicated in English in brackets to complete the sentences.

Example: Igram tenis. (*on Thursdays*) Četvrtkom.

   a Pijem kavu. (*every day*)
   b Volim igrati badminton. (*every Saturday*)
   c Idem u Zagreb. (*on Wednesday*)
   d Ljudi idu na skijanje. (*in winter*)
   e Otvoren bazen radi. (*from May to September*)
   f Jedemo ribu. (*on Fridays*)
   g Više vole igrati tenis. (*in spring*)
   h Mark i Sandra idu u grad. (*on Sunday*)
   i Jasna ide u London. (*in March*)
   j Zvonko se ženi Marijom. (*on Saturday*)

Comprehension 1

Dva dana kasnije Sandra i Jasna idu na kavu.

Sandra	Jasna, što radite kada niste na poslu?
Jasna	Kod kuće gledam televiziju ili čitam.
Sandra	Bavite li se sportom?

Jasna	Bavim se sportom.
Sandra	Kakav sport volite?
Jasna	Volim igrati badminton i tenis.
Sandra	Kada ih igrate?
Jasna	Ovaj tjedan idem u sportski centar u subotu. Igram tenis subotom.
Sandra	Kada igrate badminton?
Jasna	Teren za badminton radi utorkom i nedjeljom po podne. Tamo idem nedjeljom.
Sandra	A, imaju li tamo otvoren bazen?
Jasna	Imaju. Otvoren bazen radi ljeti, od početka srpnja do kraja kolovoza.
Sandra	Što radite zimi?
Jasna	Zimi idem na skijanje.
Sandra	Kamo idete na skijanje?
Jasna	Idem na Sljeme. To nije daleko od Zagreba. Možete ići tamo autobusom iz centra grada.

ići na skijanje *to go skiing*

QV

True or false?

a Jasna igra košarku.
b Ovaj tjedan Jasna ide u sportski centar u subotu.
c Zimi Jasna ide na skijanje.

Comprehension 2

Read the passage that follows and answer these questions.

1 Kada radi trim kabinet?
  a Od deset sati ujutro do šest sati navečer.
  b Od deset sati ujutro do osam sati navečer.
  c Od jedanaest sati ujutro do pola devet navečer.

2 Kada radi Noćni klub?

    a Od sedam sati navečer.

    b Od devet sati navečer.

    c Od jedanaest sati navečer.

3 Kada ne radi stolni tenis?

    a Ponedjeljkom.

    b Subotom.

    c Nedjeljom.

Velimir i njegova žena su na odmoru. Oni su u hotelu na moru. Na recepciji su informacije o sadržajima hotela. Velimir ih čita.

VAŠ HOTEL

PRIZEMLJE

Zatvoren bazen radi svaki dan od 8.00 do 21.30 sati.

Uz bazen gosti imaju trim kabinet, salon za masažu i saunu.

Radno vrijeme: Trim kabinet od 10.00 do 20.00 sati

                    Salon za masažu od 11.00 do 18.00 sati

                    Sauna od 10.00 do 20.30 sati.

(salon za masažu **ne radi** subotom i nedjeljom)

(sauna **ne radi** nedjeljom)

PRVI KAT

Četvorostazna automatska kuglana radi svaki dan od 10.00 do 21.00 sati.

Pored kuglane je Noćni klub vašeg hotela. Radno vrijeme: od 21.00

ČETVRTI KAT

Stolni tenis radi od 12.00 do 23.00 sati svaki dan osim ponedjeljka.

Ljeti gosti imaju i druge mogućnosti za sport u okolini hotela.

Mini-golf.

Badminton i tenis igrališta.

Sportovi na vodi.

QV

na odmoru *on holiday*

na moru *by the sea*

sadržaj *facility, content*

prizemlje *ground floor*

uz bazen *along with the pool*
trim kabinet *exercise room*
salon za masažu *massage salon*
četvorostazna automatska kuglana *four-lane automatic bowling alley*
pored (preposition followed by gen.) *next to*
noćni klub *night club*
stolni tenis *table tennis*
osim ponedjeljka (**osim** preposition with gen.) *except Monday*
druge mogućnosti *other possibilities*
u okolini hotela *in the vicinity of the hotel*
sportovi na vodi *water sports*

Test yourself

Here you can check some of the things you have learnt in this unit. Look at the questions that follow and choose the right answer:

1 If you want to say that you play football using the phrase **Bavim se ...**, which is the correct form of the word **nogomet**?
  a nogometa
  b nogometom
  c nogometu

2 Which of these phrases means *We like swimming*?
  a Sviđa mi se plivanje.
  b Sviđa joj se plivanje.
  c Sviđa nam se plivanje.

3 There is an announcement in your hotel that the swimming pool will be open every day **od deset sati do osamnaest sati.** When is it open?
  a from 10 a.m. to 8 p.m.
  b from 10 a.m. to 6 p.m.
  c from 9 a.m. to 6 p.m.

4 What is **košarka?**
- **a** handball
- **b** hockey
- **c** basketball

5 Which month is **svibanj?**
- **a** January
- **b** May
- **c** September

6 Match the question on the left with the correct answer on the right:

a Kada radi zatvoren bazen?	**i** Na recepciji.
b Gdje je sauna u hotelu?	**ii** Od deset ujutro do pet po podne.
c Što Jasna radi zimi?	**iii** Na drugom katu.
d Koji sport vam se sviđa?	**iv** Volim igrati tenis.
e Gdje su informacije o hotelu?	**v** Ide na skijanje.

10

Na izletu

On an excursion

In this unit you will learn how to
- *Use more phrases to express agreement and disagreement*
- *Express further degrees of certainty*
- *Express satisfaction*
- *Talk about travelling, the weather and the countryside*

Dialogue

Danas Sandra i Mark idu s prijateljima u planine. Putuju kolima. Jasna vozi kola.

Mark	Kako je dobro biti izvan grada u prirodi! Kako su lijepe ove planine!
Rudolf	U pravu ste. Planine su lijepe kad sunce sija.
Sandra	Da, slažem se. Vidimo planine, šumu, rijeku i polja.
Rudolf	Međutim, kad je loše vrijeme, kad pada kiša ili snijeg, nije lijepo biti na planinama.
Mark	Ali, danas je dobro vrijeme. Ja sam zadovoljan ovim pogledom na planine.
Jasna	Slažem se s vama. Pogled je zaista divan. Sada dolazimo u selo. Tko ima kartu?
Sandra	Ja je imam. Ne mogu naći selo.

(Contd)

♦ CD2, TR 2

Rudolf	Dajte mi kartu, mislim da znam gdje smo. Idemo prema Varaždinu.
Mark	Gdje je Varaždin?
Rudolf	Varaždin je grad u sjeverozapadnoj Hrvatskoj.
Mark	Znači, mi smo na sjeveru Hrvatske.
Rudolf	Idemo u tom pravcu, prema sjeveru. Ali, mislim da je već vrijeme da skrenemo na lijevo. Kako se zove ovo selo? Nije mi jasno gdje smo. Po mom mišljenju, autocesta je na lijevo. Mi smo na krivom putu.
Jasna	Nemaš pravo, Rudolf. Ovo je pravi put.
Rudolf	Nisam baš siguran.
Jasna	Ja jesam sigurna.
Rudolf	U pravu si. Slažem se s tobom. Nije daleko do autoceste. Je li to kavana pored ceste?
Jasna	Da. Ja sam žedna.
Rudolf	I ja sam žedan. Putujemo već dva sata. Možemo ovdje napraviti kratku pauzu.

planina *mountain*
putovati, putujem *to travel*
kola (neut. pl.) *car*
kolima *by car*
voziti, vozim *to drive*
Kako su lijepe ove planine! *How beautiful these mountains are!*
izvan (preposition with gen.) *outside*
priroda *nature, countryside*
U pravu ste. *You are right.*
sunce *sun*
sijati, sija *to shine*
šuma *forest*
rijeka *river*
polje *field*
međutim *however*
loše vrijeme *bad weather*
pada kiša *it rains, it is raining*
pada snijeg *it snows, it is snowing*
dobro vrijeme *good weather*
zadovoljan (with ins.) *pleased with, satisfied with*

pogled na (with acc.) *view of*
s vama *with you*
zaista *really*
divan *wonderful*
selo *village*
karta *map*
naći, nađem *to find*
u sjeverozapadnoj Hrvatskoj *in northwest Croatia*
na sjeveru *in the north*
u tom pravcu *in that direction*
prema sjeveru *towards the north*
Nije mi jasno. *It is not clear to me.*
po mom mišljenju *in my opinion*
autocesta *motorway, trunk road*
na krivom putu *on the wrong road*
Nemaš pravo. *You are not right.*
pravi put *right road*
Nisam baš siguran. *I am not quite sure.*
U pravu si. *You are right.*
s tobom *with you*
napraviti kratku pauzu *to make a short break*

True or false?

a Lijepo je biti na planinama kada pada snijeg.
b Sandra daje kartu Rudolfu.
c Jasna je u pravu kada kaže da su na pravom putu.

....

Insight

There are many places to visit in and around Zagreb. To the northwest is the old town of Varaždin, once the capital of Croatia. It is fast becoming an industrial town but the centre still retains its old-world charm. The castle and the town hall both date from the 16th century.

To the south is the Plitvice National Park. This is one of the most beautiful spots in inland Croatia with numerous lakes

(Contd)

connected by waterfalls surrounded by dense forests. Both places are within a couple of hours' drive from Zagreb. The coast is not really accessible on a one-day trip.

Insight

Large numbers of tourists visit Croatia by car. It is easy, if somewhat expensive, to hire a car from any one of a number of international hire companies that operate there. If you are driving and you need petrol (**benzin**) stop at a **benzinska stanica**. The road network is good on the whole and connects all major places of interest. Tourists that go straight to the coast are missing out on the historic towns, relaxing spa sites and countryside of inland Croatia. Visitors to such places can usually find accommodation in hotels, motels and private rooms at moderate rates.

Key phrases

◀) CD2, TR 2, 02:03

How to:

▶ say that you agree with someone	**Slažem se s vama.** (to someone with whom you use **vi**) **Slažem se s tobom.** (to someone with whom you use **ti**)
▶ say that someone is right or that someone is wrong	**U pravu si (ti).** **Nemate pravo. (vi).**
▶ say that you are sure of something	**Ja jesam siguran.** (male speaking, using the long form of **biti** for added emphasis) **Ja jesam sigurna.** (female speaking)

- ▶ say that you are not quite sure of something

  Nisam baš siguran.
  (male speaking)
  Nisam baš sigurna.
  (female speaking)
- ▶ say that it is not clear to you   **Nije mi jasno.**
- ▶ say that *in your opinion* ...   **po mom mišljenju**
- ▶ express satisfaction

  Zadovoljan sam.
  (male speaking)
  Zadovoljna sam.
  (female speaking)
- ▶ use expressions relating to the weather

  loše vrijeme
  dobro vrijeme
  sunce sija
  pada kiša
  pada snijeg
- ▶ use expressions relating to direction and position

  u sjeverozapadnoj Hrvatskoj
  na sjeveru
  prema sjeveru
  u tom pravcu
  na krivom putu
  na pravom putu

How it works

S vama with you (personal pronouns in the instrumental case)

You already know that after **s** (*with*) you use the instrumental case. So in the sentence **Slažem se s vama** you are using the instrumental case of **vi**. The pattern of cases for all the personal pronouns is as follows with some revision notes:

nom.	acc.	gen.	dat.	ins.
ja	me, mene	me, mene	mi, meni	mnom(e)
ti	te, tebe	te, tebe	ti, tebi	tobom

(Contd)

nom.	acc.	gen.	dat.	ins.
on	ga, njega	ga, njega	mu, njemu	njim(e)
ona	je, ju nju	je, nje	joj, njoj	njom(e)
mi	nas, nas	nas, nas	nam, nama	nama
vi	vas, vas	vas, vas	vam, vama	vama
oni	ih, njih	ih, njih	im, njima	njima

a The short form of the pronoun comes first.
b The forms for **ono** are the same as for **on**.
c The preferred short form of **ona** in the accusative is **je**.
d Sometimes an **e** is added to the end of the pronoun in the instrumental case.
e The extra letter is added when the pronoun is used without a preposition (e.g. **Idem s njim. Zadovoljan sam njome**).
f The short forms are unstressed.
g The forms which are spelt the same (e.g. **nas, nas**) are stressed when used as long forms.
h The cases for **one** and **ona** are the same as for **oni**.

Nije mi jasno and word order

This kind of expression is called an impersonal expression.
The phrase **nije jasno** *it is not clear* is formed by taking the neuter nominative form of the adjective **jasan** and using the **je** form from the verb **biti**. You have already come across some examples:

Lako je.	*It is easy.*
Teško je.	*It is difficult.*
Jasno je.	*It is clear.*

The **je** comes in second place because it is a short form and so cannot come at the beginning. The negative **nije** is not a short form:

Nije lako.	*It is not easy.*
Nije teško.	*It is not difficult.*
Nije jasno.	*It is not clear.*

You can add to these expressions the dative case of the personal pronouns to mean *to me* or *for me*, etc. Take care with the order of the short forms as je must come after the dative:

Lako mi je.	*It is easy for me. (I find it easy)*
Teško mu je.	*It is difficult for him. (he finds it difficult)*
Jasno im je.	*It is clear to them.*
Nije joj lako.	*It is not easy for her.*
Nije nam teško.	*It is not difficult for us.*

Study the word order in the following questions:

Je li ti jasno?	*Is it clear to you?*
Da li vam je jasno?	*Is it clear to you?*

Remember that je is an exception as far as short forms are concerned as it may occur at the beginning when introducing a question with the form **Je li ...?**

Points of the compass

The basic points of the compass are:

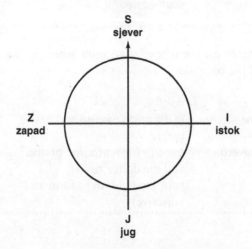

To say *in the north*, etc. you use the preposition **na** (and dat.):

na sjeveru	*in the north*
na istoku	*in the east*

To say *towards the south*, etc. you use the preposition **prema** (and dat.):

prema jugu	*towards the south*
prema zapadu	*towards the west*

The adjectives *northern*, etc. are:

sjeverni	*northern*
istočni	*eastern*
južni	*southern*
zapadni	*western*

They only have the definite forms that end in -i. And you can make compounds like *northwestern*:

sjeverozapadni	*northwestern*
jugoistočni	*southeastern*

Insight

Remember to use the following patterns when talking about points of the compass:

sjever	*north*
na sjeveru	*in the north* (use **na** and dative case)
prema sjeveru	*towards the north* (use **prema** and the dative case)
sjeverni	*northern* (add -**ni** to form an adjective)

Idioms

a There are a number of ways of saying *you are right/wrong* (**u pravu** followed by short from of **biti**):

U pravu ste.	*You are right.*
U pravu je.	*S/he is right.*
U pravu su.	*They are right.*

Negative of **biti** followed by **u pravu**:

Niste u pravu.	*You are wrong.*
Nismo u pravu.	*We are wrong.*

Imati followed by **pravo**:

Imaš pravo.	*You are right.*

Negative of **imati** followed by **pravo**:

Nemaju pravo.	*They are wrong.*

There are also adjectives:

kriv *wrong*   **prav** *right*

Mi smo na pravom putu.	*We are on the right road.*
Ovo je krivi telefonski broj.	*This is the wrong telephone number.*

b The intensifying **baš** that may be added after many words to mean *quite* or *really*:

Nisam baš siguran.	*I am not quite sure.*
Baš sam zadovoljan.	*I am quite satisfied.*
Baš smo žedni.	*We are really thirsty.*

c To form the expression *in my opinion*, etc.:

The expression **po mom mišljenju** is formed from the preposition **po** followed by the dative case of **moj** and of the word **mišljenje** *opinion*.

The words **moj** and **tvoj** are often shortened:

> **moj** + **em** = **mom**   **tvoj** + **em** = **tvom**

Study the following examples:
po njegovom mišljenju   *in his opinion*
po našem mišljenju   *in our opinion*

This expression is similar in meaning to:
čini mi se   *it seems to me*
mislim da ...   *I think that ...*

_____

Practice

1 Supply the correct cases of the personal pronoun indicated
in the brackets:
  a Zadovoljni smo (oni).
  b Konobar (ona) daje jelovnik.
  c Idu s (mi) u kino.
  d Zadovoljna je (ja).
  e Da li (oni) gledate?
  f Nisu zadovoljni (on).
  g Gledaš li (ja).
  h Idem u kazalište s (vi).
  i Ne gledaju (ja).
  j Je li zadovoljan (ti)?

◀》 **CD2, TR 2, 03:20**

2 Form a question for the following answers:
  a Teško mi je.
  b Nije joj lako.
  c Nije im jasno.
  d Jasno mi je.

3 Answer the following questions affirmatively and then negatively:

   a Da li vam je teško?

   b Je li im jasno?

   c Je li mu jasno?

   d Je li ti lako?

4 Fit the correct question words taken from the box to the following questions (you must use all the question words only once):

   a _____ se zovete?

   b _____ soba imaju u stanu?

   c _____ kompjutor imate?

   d _____ ide Rudolf sutra?

   e _____ ideš u grad?

   f _____ govori hrvatski?

   g _____ je Varaždin?

   h _____ Sandra želi kupiti?

> Koliko   Tko   Što   Kamo   Kakav   Kako   Gdje   Kada

5 Match the answers to the questions:

a Je li Jasna u pravu?	**i**	Ne, nismo.
b Da li ste u pravu?	**ii**	Ne, nisam u pravu.
c Tko ima pravo?	**iii**	Da, u pravu je.
d Jesmo li na pravom putu?	**iv**	Rudolf ima.

6 Change the following sentences to include the phrase **po mišljenju**. Look at the examples and take care to use the adjective of the name of the person or the correct form of moj, etc.:

Examples: Jasni se čini da pada kiša.

              Po Jasninom mišljenju, pada kiša.

Mislimo da idemo prema Zagrebu.
Po našem mišljenju, idemo prema Zagrebu.

a Rudolf misli da su Sandra i Mark u hotelu.
b Čini joj se da je Rudolf na poslu.
c Sutra idem, čini mi se, u kazalište.
d Sandra i Mark misle da otvoren bazen radi svaki dan.

Comprehension 1

Zagreb je glavni grad Hrvatske. Privredni je i kulturni centar s oko milijun stanovnika. U Zagrebu je park Maksimir sa zoološkim vrtom. Zoološki vrt otvoren je od devet sati do sumraka. U blizini parka Maksimir i Zoološkog vrta nalaze se sportski tereni: Stadion i kompleks "Dinamo" i Sportsko-rekreacijski centar.

Ako putujete prema sjeveru od Zagreba stižete do Slovenije. Ako putujete prema istoku stižete do Srbije. Ako putujete prema zapadu i prema jugozapadu stižete do Jadranskog mora. Ljeti tamo ima mnogo turista. Glavni gradovi na obali su Dubrovnik, Split, Zadar i Rijeka. Blizu obale su otoci – Hvar, Brač, Mljet, Korčula ... Obala je divna, otoci su lijepi i more je plavo.

True or false?

a U Zagrebu živi oko milijun stanovnika.
b Dubrovnik je jedan od glavnih gradova na obali.
c Mnogo turista dolazi na more.

QUICK VOCAB

privredni *economic*
kulturni *cultural*
milijun *million*
stanovnik *inhabitant*
zoološki vrt *zoo*
otvoren *open*
sumrak *dusk*
u blizini *in the vicinity*

stizati, stižem *to arrive*
Jadransko more *Adriatic Sea*
obala *coast*
blizu (preposition with gen.) *near*
otok *island*
plav *blue*

Comprehension 2

Read the passage and answer the questions that follow.

When they stop during their excursion at the café, Mark asks Jasna about the weather on the coast. Sandra joins in their conversation.

Mark	Jasna, kakvo je vrijeme na moru?
Jasna	Toplo. Ljeti sunce sija skoro svaki dan. Volite li more?
Mark	Da. Volim ga, i volim plivati u moru.
Jasna	Sandra, slažete li se s Markom?
Sandra	Da, slažem se s njim. Baš mi se sviđa ovdje u Zagrebu i u blizini Zagreba. Ali želimo također vidjeti obalu i Jadransko more.
Jasna	Jadransko more je jako lijepo. Rudolf i ja idemo na odmor u kolovozu. Idemo na more. Hoćete li poći s nama?
Sandra	Hvala na pozivu. To je dobra ideja. Idemo s vama.
Jasna	Sandra, da prijeđemo na ti. Idemo zajedno na more, sad smo prijatelji.
Sandra	U pravu si, Jasna.

toplo *warm*
skoro *almost*
plivati *to swim*
jako *very*
ići na odmor *to go on holiday*
poći *to go, set off*
Hvala na pozivu. *Thanks for the invitation.*

dobra ideja *a good idea*

Da prijeđemo na ti. *Let's start to use* **ti** *to one another.*

1 Kakvo je vrijeme na obali?
 a Loše.
 b Pada kiša.
 c Toplo je.

2 Što Sandra i Mark žele vidjeti?
 a More.
 b Planine.
 c Zagreb.

3 Kada idu Jasna i Rudolf na odmor?
 a Idu na more.
 b Idu u kolovozu.
 c Idu svaki mjesec.

_____

Test yourself

Here you can check some of the things you have learnt in this unit. Look at the questions that follow and choose the right answer:

1 What is the word for *mountain*?
 a planina
 b rijeka
 c polje

2 What does **kiša** mean?
 a snow
 b rain
 c river

3 How would Rudolf say *I am sure*?
 a Imam pravo.
 b Slažem se.
 c Siguran sam.

4 If you need petrol when driving, where would you stop?
  a glavni kolodvor
  b benzinska stanica
  c garaža

5 What does the word **cesta** mean?
  a road
  b seven
  c certain

6 Which phrase is closest to telling someone that you understand what you have been told?
  a lako mi je
  b po mom mišljenju
  c jasno mi je

7 In which circumstances would you say to someone
U **pravu ste**?
  a when you think the other person is in the wrong
  b when you think the other person has said something right
  c when you think the other person wants a cup of coffee

8 Someone has asked Jasna to complete a difficult task. What does she say?
  a lako je
  b teško je
  c zadovoljna sam

9 What is **Jadransko more**?
  a Mediterranean Sea
  b a Croatian island
  c Adriatic Sea

10 Which of the following would most likely indicate that you agree with someone's suggestion?
  a To je dobra ideja.
  b To je loša iseja.
  c To je stara ideja.

11

Povratne karte
Return tickets

In this unit you will learn how to
- *Express that things happened in the past (using the past tense form of the verb)*
- *Talk more about travelling*
- *Ask what happened*
- *Ask how long ago something happened*

Dialogue

Prijatelji su govorili o odmoru. Htjeli su ići na otok Hvar. Jasna je išla u putničku agenciju s Markom i Sandrom. Htjeli su kupiti avionske karte za Split. U Splitu će kupiti karte za brod.

CD2, TR 3

Jasna	Dobar dan. Molim vas, koliko koštaju avionske karte za Split?
Agent	Da li hoćete povratne karte ili u jednom smjeru?
Jasna	Povratne. Idemo sljedeći tjedan u petak, a vraćamo se dva tjedna kasnije.
Agent	Jedna povratna karta košta osamsto kuna. Petkom ima dva aviona. Prvi ide prije podne u deset i petnaest sa zagrebačkog aerodroma. Drugi ide poslije podne u petnaest i trideset.

Jasna	Koliko dugo traje put avionom od Zagreba do Splita?
Agent	Četrdeset minuta.
Jasna	Mislim da moramo rezervirati karte za prvi avion.
Sandra	Imaš pravo, jer poslije dolaska u Split moramo stići na brod za otok. Molim vas, gospodine, želimo četiri povratne karte za prvi avion u petak sljedećeg tjedna. Vraćamo se natrag dva tjedna kasnije, u petak.
Agent	Dobro ...

The vocabulary layout changes here: we shall give imperfective and perfective forms of the infinitives of new verbs where appropriate (not every verb has two forms). We shall also give the **ja** forms when the present tense is not formed directly from the infinitive. Don't forget that in any pair of verbs, the imperfective always comes first.

QUICK VOCAB

putnička agencija *travel agency*
avionska karta *air ticket*
U Splitu će kupiti ... *In Split, they will buy ...*
za (preposition with acc.) *for*
brod *boat*
povratna karta *return ticket*
karta u jednom smjeru *one-way ticket*
sljedeći tjedan *next week*
vraćati se, vratiti se *to return*
kasnije *later*
osamsto *800*
avion (avionom) *aeroplane* (by air – instrumental)
aerodrom *airport*
Koliko dugo traje put ...? *How long does the journey last ...?*
od ... do ... (followed by gen.) *from ... to ...*
jer *since, for*
stizati, stići (stižem, stignem: stizao, stigao/stigli) *to arrive*
natrag *back*

Čovjek je gledao u kompjutorski ekran i rezervirao njihove karte.
Jasna je platila i izašli su iz agencije. Te večeri, išla je k Rudolfu.

Rudolf	Što se desilo danas u agenciji? Je li sve bilo u redu?
Jasna	Sve je bilo u redu. Nisam imala problema. Kupili smo karte.
Rudolf	Onda, idemo u petak. Sjajno. Bili smo na Hvaru prije tri godine. Sjećaš li se?
Jasna	Da, sjećam se. Ali smo tada išli u hotel. Možemo li iznajmiti privatne sobe u Hvaru?
Rudolf	Možemo. Moramo odlučiti s Markom i Sandrom gdje želimo boraviti. Jedan kolega na poslu rekao mi je da je iznajmio privatnu sobu u Hvaru kod ljubazne gazdarice. Moram ga sutra pitati za njenu adresu.

kompjutorski ekran *computer screen*
plaćati, platiti *to pay*
te večeri *that evening*
dešavati se, desiti se *to happen*
Sve je bilo u redu. *Everything was OK.*
problem *problem*
onda *then*
sjajno *wonderful, smashing*
prije tri godine *three years ago*
privatna soba *private room*
iznajmljivati, iznajmiti (iznajmljujem, iznajmim) *to rent*
odlučivati, odlučiti (odlučujem, odlučim) *to decide*
boraviti *to stay*
kolega *colleague, person at work* (like **tata** this is a masculine word with feminine endings; see Unit 7)
reći (past tense rekao, rekli) *to tell*
ljubazan *kind*
gazdarica *landlady*
adresa *address*

(Verbs which end in **-ovati** and **-ivati** regularly form the present tense by changing to **-ujem**, **uješ**, etc: **putovati-putujem**; **iznajmljivati-iznajmljujem**.)

True or false?

a Jasna je kupila avionske karte u putničkoj agenciji.
b Put avionom od Zagreba do Splita traje trideset minuta.
c Rudolf i Jasna su bili na Hvaru prije tri godine.

Insight

In the last few years Croatian has changed some words and adopted new ones. There is a tendency to avoid foreign forms of words when it is possible to make up a new one from Croatian roots, especially in official usage. Consequently, you will find the word **računalo** instead of **kompjutor** for *computer*. Also, for air travel you will find other words being used: **zrakoplov** *aeroplane*, **zračna luka** *airport*, **zrakoplovna tvrtka** *aeroplane company*.

Insight

The town of Hvar is on the island of Hvar: when talking about the island, you say **Idem na Hvar** or **Ja sam na Hvaru** using the preposition **na**. The preposition **na** is the one normally used when talking about islands in general. However, when talking about the *town* of Hvar, you say **Idem u Hvar** or **Ja sam u Hvaru** using the preposition **u**. Generally speaking, the preposition **u** is used when talking about towns with one or two exceptions.

Insight

There are basically two types of accommodation (**smještaj**) available to tourists on the coast. There are hotels used by all the large tour companies and private rooms. Many people who live on the coast or on one of the Adriatic islands have converted their houses to take in paying guests during the summer. This is a relatively inexpensive form of accommodation. You can book such rooms at a travel agency on arrival at your destination. They are regularly checked to ensure that standards are maintained and you can book either a room (**soba**) or a small holiday flat (**apartman**).

Key phrases

🔊 **CD2, TR 3, 02:21**

How to:

▶ use words for travelling on holiday	odmor avion brod aerodrom
▶ use words for tickets and reservations	avionska karta za Split povratna karta karta u jednom smjeru kupiti karte za brod rezervirati kartu
▶ use words for the journey	Koliko dugo traje put? Idemo u Split. Vraćamo se iz Splita.
▶ use words for staying	boraviti hotel privatna soba gazdarica
▶ ask what happened and how long ago	Što se desilo? Je li sve bilo u redu?

How it works

Past tense

Prijatelji su govorili o ...	*The friends spoke about ...*
Htjeli su ići ...	*They wanted to go ...*
Jasna je išla ...	*Jasna went ...*
Čovjek je gledao ...	*The man looked at ...*
Sve je bilo u redu.	*Everything was OK.*
Nisam imala problema.	*I did not have any problems.*
Kupili smo karte.	*We bought the tickets.*

64

The past tense is formed using two parts: one taken from the infinitive of the verb indicating something in the past and the other from **biti** *to be*.

a One part is formed using a part of the infinitive. There are three types of infinitive:

▶ Infinitives that end in a vowel before **-ti**; remove the **-ti** at the end:

govoriti	**govori-**
gledati	**gleda-**

Treat this part like an adjective that agrees with the subject of the verb:

masc. singular add **-o**	masc. plural add **-li**
gledao, govorio	**gledali, govorili**
fem. singular add **-la**	fem. plural add **-le**
gledala, govorila	**gledale, govorile**
neut. singular add **-lo**	neut. plural add **-la**
gledalo, govorilo	**gledala, govorila**

There is a small subgroup of verbs ending in **-jeti** in the infinitive that have an exception in the masculine singular (**vidjeti, željeti, živjeti, htjeti**):

masc. singular	*masc. plural*
vidio	**vidjeli**
želio	**željeli**
živio	**živjeli**
htio	**htjeli**

▶ Infinitives that end in **-sti**; remove the **-sti** then follow the same pattern as just seen:

jesti-	**je-**

masc. singular	masc. plural
jeo	**jeli**
fem. singular	fem. plural
jela	**jele**

neut. singular	neut. plural
jelo	**jela**

▶ Infinitives that end in -ći; learn the past tense forms
separately:

moći	moga-
ići	iša-
reći	reka-

masc. singular	masc. plural
mogao, išao, rekao	**mogli, išli, rekli**
fem. singular	fem. plural
mogla, išla, rekla	**mogle, išle, rekle**
neut. singular	neut. plural
moglo, išlo, reklo	**mogla, išla, rekla**

The -a- that appears just before the adjective ending in the
masculine singular disappears in the other forms in this category.

b Along with this part of the past tense taken from the infinitive,
use the relevant form of **biti**:

Morali su kupiti avionske karte.	*They had to buy air tickets.*
Čovjek je gledao u kompjutorski ekran.	*The man looked at the computer screen.*
Sve je bilo u redu.	*Everything was OK.*
Kupili smo karte.	*We bought the tickets.*

The part of **biti** you use depends on the subject of the verb. So,
if the subject is **ja** you use **sam**, if it is **ti** you use **si**, etc. If Jasna
wanted to say *I spoke …* she would use the form **ja sam govorila**
(or **govorila sam** without **ja**), whereas Rudolf would say **ja sam
govorio**.

Word order with the past tense

The rules for the order of enclitics (short forms) apply when
forming the past tense in Croatian and care has to be taken.

The short forms of **biti** cannot occur as the first word of the sentence or phrase. So you say:

On je gledao u komjutorski ekran. *or* **Gledao je u kompjutorski ekran.**

Ja sam govorila o odmoru. (fem.) *or* **Govorila sam o odmoru.**

Mi smo bili na Hvaru. *or* **Bili smo na Hvaru.**

The word order, when using the short forms of the personal pronouns, follows a set pattern that you first met in Unit 9, e.g. **Rekao mi je** (*he told me*, using **mi** the dat. case of **ja**). The pattern is:

- **i** short form of **biti** (except **je**)
- **ii** dat. case
- **iii** gen. case
- **iv** acc. case
- **v** **se** (reflexive verbs only)
- **vi** **je** (short form from **biti**)

Look at the following examples:

Dala sam joj knjigu.	*I gave a book to her.*
Dala sam joj je.	*I gave it to her.*
Dali smo mu sok.	*We gave a fruit juice to him.*
Dali smo mu ga.	*We gave it to him.*
Dao mi je knjigu.	*He gave a book to me.*
Dao mi ju je.	*He gave it to me.*

(**ju** is used as the accusative case when the **je** form from **biti** is present)

Rekli su nam.	*They told us.*
Vratili smo se.	*We returned.*
Vratio se.	*He returned.*

(reflexive verbs usually omit **je** in the **on/ona/ono** forms of the past tense)

Negative past tense

To form the negative of the past tense in Croatian replace the short forms of **biti** with their negative equivalents. Note the effect this has on word order as the negative forms are not enclitics (short forms):

Rekao mi je.	*He told me.*
Nije mi rekao.	*He did not tell me.*
Dali smo mu ga.	*We gave it to him.*
Nismo mu ga dali.	*We did not give it to him.*
Vratio se.	*He returned.*
Nije se vratio.	*He did not return.*
Rekli su nam.	*They told us.*
Nisu nam rekli.	*They did not tell us.*
Dala sam joj je.	*I gave it to her.*
Nisam joj je dala.	*I did not give it to her.*

Asking a question in the past tense

You make questions in the past tense by following the patterns for asking questions with **biti**. There are two ways of forming a question.

a Using the short form:

Da li ste bili na Hvaru?	*Have you been on Hvar?*
Da li smo rekli Rudolfu?	*Did we tell Rudolf?*

b Using the long form:

Jeste li bili na Hvaru?	*Have you been on Hvar?*
Jesmo li rekli Rudolfu?	*Did we tell Rudolf? (or Have we told Rudolf?)*

The normal rules for the order of short forms still apply:

Da li ste mu dali knjigu?	*Did you give a book to him?*
Jesu li vam rekli?	*Did they tell you?*

With **je** as an exception:

Je li vam dao kavu.	*Did he give you a coffee?*

Aspect with the past tense

The English language has a variety of forms in the past tense:

> I did return.
> I have returned.
> I was returning.
> I had returned, etc.

Croatian has only the one form, based on the infinitive and **biti**. However, it can express all the varieties of English because of aspects. As you have already seen, Croatian has two aspects, an imperfective and a perfective. You have seen the differences between them in the infinitive and the imperative (command forms). They have similar differences in the past tense: the imperfective describes an incomplete or continuous action and the perfective describes a completed or momentary action. The first verb in the following list is the imperfective of the pair:

davati, dati	*to give*
vraćati se, vratiti se	*to return*
pisati, napisati	*to write*
piti, popiti	*to drink*
čitati, pročitati	*to read*
uzimati, uzeti	*to take*

Jučer je čitao knjigu, a njegov brat je gledao televiziju.	*Yesterday he was reading and his brother watched television.*

(i.e. both actions occur at the same time and without indicating when they were concluded)

Pila je mlijeko svaki dan, ali je danas popila sok.	*She drank (used to drink) milk every day, but today she drank fruit juice.*

(i.e. drinking milk was a daily occurrence, not limited to one completed occasion, but today she drank (up) a juice)

Jučer je pročitao knjigu.   *He read the book yesterday.*

(i.e. the action was completed)

Kad se vratio kući, napisao je   *When he returned home he wrote*
bratu pismo.   *a letter to his brother.*

(i.e. both actions were completed one after the other)

Some verbs only have one form that is both imperfective and perfective. These are verbs taken from foreign languages (e.g. **rezervirati, telefonirati**) and a small group of others (e.g. **ručati, vidjeti**).

Using *vi* in the past tense

Vi can be used to refer either to one person or to many people. When it is used to refer to one person, you must always use the masculine plural form:

Jasna, da li ste bili na Hvaru?   *Jasna, have you been on Hvar?*
Rudolfe, jeste li rekli Jasni?   *Rudolf, have you told Jasna?*

The same rule applies to using adjectives with **vi**:

Jasna, jeste li sigurni?   *Jasna, are you sure?*

....

Insight

Do not forget that the part of the past tense formed from the infinitive has to agree with the subject and that the appropriate form of **biti** will follow this if there is no named subject. Look at these examples:

Jasna je jela.   *Jasna was eating.*
Jela je.   *She was eating.*

Mi smo putovali vlakom.	We travelled by train.
Putovali smo vlakom.	We travelled by train.
Rudolf i Mark su kupili karte.	Rudolf and Mark bought the tickets.
Kupili su karte.	They bought the tickets.

Nisam imala problema

The -a ending on **problem** tells you that this word is being used in the genitive case, i.e. *I didn't have any problems*. The genitive case in Croatian can be used to indicate what in English would be expressed by *some* or *any*, as opposed to a single object. Compare the following sentences:

To nije moj problem.	That is not my problem.
Nisam imala problema.	I didn't have any problems.
Gdje je kruh?	Where is the bread?
Imate li kruha?	Have you got any bread?

Practice

1 Answer the following questions based on the **Dialogue** in this unit:
  a Kamo je Jasna išla s Markom i Sandrom?
  b Što su tamo htjeli kupiti?
  c Da li su kupili povratne karte ili u jednom smjeru?
  d U koliko sati ide prvi avion iz Zagreba?
  e Koliko košta karta?
  f Što moraju kupiti u Splitu?
  g Kada se vraćaju?
  h Kada je Jasna išla k Rudolfu?
  i Kada su Jasna i Rudolf bili na Hvaru?
  j Tko je uzeo privatnu sobu u Hvaru?

2 Formulate questions for the following answers:
   a Pio sam mlijeko svaki dan.
   b Napisao sam pismo.
   c Rudolf mi je dao knjigu.
   d Da, bio sam na Hvaru.
   e Ne, nisam bila u Dubrovniku.
   f Rezervirali su karte u putničkoj agenciji.
   g Otišli su na odmor u subotu.
   h Bili smo u Dubrovniku prije pet godina.
   i Povratna karta za Split košta osamsto kuna.
   j Ne, Rudolf nije radio u toj zgradi.

3 Choose the correct emboldened aspect in the sentences:
   a **Pisao/Napisao** sam mami svaki dan.
   b Da li vam je konobar **davao/dao** kavu?
   c Kad smo se vratili u Zagreb **uzimali/uzeli** smo taksi.
   d Pijem mlijeko svaki dan, ali sam danas **pio/popio** čašu vode.

4 Make the following sentences negative (take care with the word order):
   a Išli smo na Hvar prije tri godine.
   b Konobar mi je dao salatu.
   c Konobar mi ju je dao.
   d Kupili su avionske karte u putničkoj agenciji.
   e Kupili su ih u putničkoj agenciji.
   f Vratila sam se jučer iz Dubrovnika.
   g Čitao je novine.
   h Čitao ih je.

◀ CD2, TR 3, 03:34

5 Complete the missing parts of the dialogue:
   Dobar dan.
   Hello. I want to buy a plane ticket to Dubrovnik.
   Da li hoćete povratnu kartu ili u jednom smjeru?
   A one-way ticket, please. How much does it cost?
   Karta u jednom smjeru za Dubrovnik košta petsto kuna.

At what time is there a plane on Mondays from Zagreb?
Ima tri aviona. Prvi ide prije podne u deset sati. Drugi ide
poslije podne u petnaest sati i petnaest minuta. Treći ide
navečer u dvadeset sati.
I want a ticket for Monday in the evening.
Mogu vam, ako želite, rezervirati hotel.
I have a private room in Dubrovnik.
Dobro. Izvolite kartu.
Thank you. Goodbye.
Molim. Do viđenja.

Izvolite kartu. *Here is your ticket.*

6 Make up sentences using the pictures, as in the example:
   a Koliko dugo traje put avionom od Zagreba do Splita?
   Četrdeset minuta.

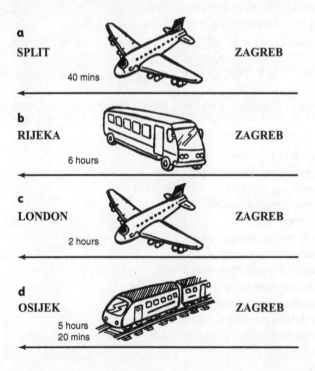

a
SPLIT   ZAGREB
40 mins

b
RIJEKA   ZAGREB
6 hours

c
LONDON   ZAGREB
2 hours

d
OSIJEK   ZAGREB
5 hours
20 mins

Comprehension 1

Zvonko je jučer išao na Glavni kolodvor. Tamo je htio kupiti voznu kartu.

Zvonko	Molim vas, želim rezervirati kartu za Osijek.
Čovjek	Da li hoćete kartu prvog ili drugog razreda?
Zvonko	Prvog. Idem prekosutra.
Čovjek	Prekosutra je nedjelja. Prvi vlak ide u osam i trideset ujutro.
Zvonko	Kada ide drugi?
Čovjek	Drugi ide u jedanaest sati. A onda vlakovi idu skoro svaki sat.
Zvonko	Dajte mi, molim vas, jednu kartu za vlak u jedanaest sati.
Čovjek	Da li hoćete povratnu kartu ili u jednom smjeru?
Zvonko	Ne znam kada se vraćam.
Čovjek	Nije važno, gospodine. Karta vam važi mjesec dana.
Zvonko	Moram se vratiti do srijede. Mogu li rezervirati mjesto u Osijeku kad saznam točan datum povratka?
Čovjek	Možete, gospodine. Idite na kolodvor u Osijeku dan prije povratka.
Zvonko	Dajte mi, molim vas, jednu povratnu kartu za Osijek.

vozna karta *train ticket*
karta prvog razreda *first-class ticket*
karta drugog razreda *second-class ticket*
vlak *train* (**vlakovi** – plural)
skoro *almost*
Karta vam važi mjesec dana. *Your ticket is valid for a month.*
do srijede *by Wednesday*
rezervirati mjesto *to reserve a seat*
saznati, saznam *to get to know, find out*
kad saznam *when I know* (find out)
točan datum povratka *the exact date of return*
dan prije povratka *the day before you come back* (lit. *the day before return*)

174

True or false?

a Prvi vlak za Osijek ide u 10.00 ujutro.
b Zvonko ne zna kad se vraća iz Osijeka.
c Zvonko mora ići na kolodvor u Osijeku dva dana prije povratka.

Comprehension 2

Read the passage and answer the questions that follow:

Rudolf je otišao na posao. Razgovarao je sa svojim kolegom o sobama u Hvaru. Rudolf je htio saznati sve o tim sobama. Pitao ga je koliko koštaju privatne sobe i kakve su. Njegov kolega mu je rekao da sobe nisu skupe. Dao mu je adresu jedne žene koja izdaje apartman. Apartman je na prvom katu s velikom kuhinjom, kupaonicom i dvije spavaće sobe. Ima pogled na more i na jednu staru crkvu. U blizini kuće nalazi se dobar riblji restoran. Blizu Hvara se nalaze mali otoci. Iz Hvara na te otoke svaki dan voze čamci. Tamo se možete sunčati i kupati. U Hvaru je sve lijepo.

koja izdaje *who lets out, rents*
izdavati, izdajem *to let, rent out*
crkva *church*
čamac *boat*
sunčati se *to sunbathe*
kupati se *to bathe*

QUICK VOCAB

1 Što gazdarica izdaje?
  a Privatnu sobu.
  b Hotel.
  c Apartman.

2 Kakav restoran je blizu njene kuće?
  a Ribliji restoran.
  b Kavana.
  c Restoran s roštiljem.

3 Što možete raditi na malim otocima?
   a Igrati nogomet.
   b Sjediti na obali.
   c Sunčati se.

Test yourself

Here you can check some of the things you have learnt in this unit.
Look at the questions that follow and choose the right answer:

1 Which phrase would you use to ask for a *return ticket*?
   a karta u jednom smjeru
   b povratna karta

2 Which form of the past tense would you use to complete the
sentence **Moj prijatelj je ... vlakom?**
   a putovao
   b putovala
   c putovali

3 Which form would a woman use to say that she has bought
her ticket for the boat **Ja sam ... kartu za brod?**
   a kupio
   b kupila
   c kupili

4 You and your Croatian colleague arrive at a meeting by taxi.
How would you respond if asked **Kako ste stigli?**
   a Stigli su taksijem.
   b Stigao si taksijem.
   c Stigli smo taksijem.

5 Which word would you choose to fill the gap when asking
your Croatian colleague if he or she has ever been to England:
Da li ste već... u Engleskoj?

a bili
b bila
c bio

6 Rudolf and Jasna are telling Mark and Sandra that they have bought the tickets for their journey. What would they say?
   a Kupili su karte.
   b Kupile smo karte.
   c Kupili smo karte.

7 If a man wanted to say that he has finished his coffee, what would he say?
   a Pio sam kavu.
   b Popio sam kavu.

8 Jasna is telling Rudolf that she was returning home when she met Sandra by accident in the street and they went for a coffee. How would she begin saying *I was returning home when ...* ?
   a Vraćala se kući kada ...
   b Vratila sam se kući kada ...
   c Vraćala sam se kući kada ...

9 How would you fill the gap to say that Mark has his own ticket: **Mark ima ... kartu?**
   a njegovu
   b njenu
   c svoju

10 You ask your friend if he has bought the tickets for the journey you are planning. He replies simply: **Nisam imao problema.** What might this mean?
   a He has not got a clue what you are talking about.
   b He has bought the tickets and so no need to worry.
   c He has not bought any tickets as they are sold out.

12

Imam telefonski broj
I have the telephone number

In this unit you will learn how to
- *Talk about future events*
- *Ask questions about the future*
- *Talk on the telephone*
- *Report on events*
- *Make indirect questions*
- *Express my/your in other ways*

Dialogue

Prijatelji su rezervirali apartman kod gospođe Bilčić. Stigli su u Split avionom. Otišli su direktno u luku, gdje su kupili karte za brod. Sada stoje na pristaništu u Hvaru sa prtljagom.

CD2, TR 4

Sandra	Što ćemo raditi večeras? Nadam se da nećemo biti suviše umorni.
Jasna	Tko će biti umoran? Ići ćemo u grad i naručit ćemo lijepu večeru u nekom restoranu. Rudolf, znaš li put do gospođe Bilčić?
Rudolf	Ne mogu naći njenu adresu. Mislio sam da mi je tu negdje u džepu. Bio sam siguran da ništa nisam zaboravio. Imam njen telefonski broj. Javit ću joj se. Idem na poštu. Čekajte me ovdje.

luka *harbour*
stajati, stojim *to be standing*
pristanište *quay*
prtljaga *luggage*
nadati se, nadam se *to hope*
suviše *too much*
umoran *tired*
neki *some, a certain*
misliti, mislim *to think*
... da mi je tu negdje u džepu *... that it's here somewhere in my pocket*
ništa *nothing*
zaboravljati, zaboraviti *to forget*
Javit ću joj se. *I'll call her.*
javljati se, javiti se *to contact, be in touch*
čekati, čekam *to wait*

Na pošti Rudolf razgovara s gospođom Bilčić preko telefona.

Bilčić	Halo.
Rudolf	Halo. Molim vas, možete li mi reći da li je gospođa Bilčić kod kuće?
Bilčić	Na telefonu je. Tko govori?
Rudolf	Ovdje Rudolf Šimunić, iz Zagreba. Rezervirao sam apartman kod vas. Rekao sam da ćemo stići danas.
Bilčić	Oprostite, gospodine. Ne sjećam se. Jeste li mi pisali?
Rudolf	Nisam. Telefonirao sam.
Bilčić	Da, sada se sjećam. Ja sam vas pitala da li možete stići prekosutra.
Rudolf	Da, a nismo mogli ...
Bilčić	Sve je u redu. Apartman je spreman. Gdje ste?
Rudolf	Stigli smo u Hvar. Međutim, izgubio sam vašu adresu.
Bilčić	Nema problema. Adresa mi je Dalmatinska ulica broj 5. Da li ste je zapisali?
Rudolf	Jesam. Hvala vam lijepo. Doći ćemo odmah.
Bilčić	Molim lijepo. Do viđenja.
Rudolf	Do viđenja.

halo (on the telephone) *hello*
na telefonu je *speaking* (lit. *I'm on the telephone*)
telefonirati *to telephone*
Pitala sam da li možete ... *I asked if you could ...*
spreman *ready, prepared*
međutim *however*
gubiti, izgubiti *to lose*
nema problema *no problem*
Adresa mi je ... *My address is ...*
zapisivati, zapisati (zapisujem, zapišem) *to note down*
odmah *immediately*

True or false?

a Rudolf traži adresu gospođe Bilčić.
b Rudolf je rezervirao apartman preko telefona.
c Gospođa Bilčić je rekla da apartman nije spreman.

Insight

When making a telephone call, whoever picks up the phone
at the other end may just say **halo** *hello*, a greeting largely
reserved for use on the phone. Otherwise, the first word
might be simply **Molim?** An alternative way for Rudolf
to begin would have been **Ovdje Rudolf Šimunić. Molim
vas, dajte mi gospođu Bilčić.** When you have asked for the
person you wish to speak to, the response may be **Tko ga/je
traži?** *Who wants him/her?*, or **na telefonu je** *he/she is on the
telephone.*

When calling another town or country you'll need the **pozivni
broj** *code number* and when calling an office or a firm you
may need to ask **Molim vas, dajte mi interni broj ...** (*Please
give me extension number ...*).

Key phrases

◆) CD 2, TR 4, 02:10

How to:

▶ make telephone calls and to respond on the phone	halo
	Molim vas, dajte mi ...
	Tko ga/je traži?
	Na telefonu je.
	preko telefona
▶ use ways of expressing *my*, etc.	adresa mi je
▶ say *somewhere*, *nothing*	negdje mi je u džepu
	ništa nisam zaboravio
▶ report events and questions	Rekao sam da ćemo stići ...
	Pitala sam da li možete stići ...
	Pitala sam možete li stići ...

How it works

Future tense

When expressing the future you use the short form of **htjeti** (the same as the long form without the initial **ho-**). You have already met some of these forms in the Dialogues of Units 4 and 11:

ja	ću	mi	ćemo
ti	ćeš	vi	ćete
on/a/o	će	oni/e/a	će

This is used together with the infinitive of another verb:

Ja ću ići.	*I shall go.*
Rudolf će telefonirati.	*Rudolf will telephone.*

As this is a short form it may not come at the beginning of a sentence. If you omit the personal pronoun, the short form comes after the infinitive. If the infinitive ends in **-ti**, omit the **-i** at the end and pronounce it as one word with a silent **-t:**

naručit ćemo   *we shall order*

Infinitives that end in **-ći** are not shortened:

ići ćemo   *we shall go*

The short form of **htjeti,** like the short form of **biti,** takes second place and goes in front of other short forms:

Javit ću joj se.   *I shall contact (telephone) her.*
Odmah ću joj se javiti. *I shall contact her immediately.*

When asking a question use either the long form or the short form following the patterns you already know with **da li ...** or **... li ...,** unless there is a question word when you use the short form:

Hoćemo li ići?   *Shall we go?*
Da li ćemo ići?   *Shall we go?*
Što ćemo raditi večeras? *What shall we do this evening?*
Tko će biti umoran?   *Who will be tired?*

The negative is simply formed by using the negative of **htjeti** in front of the infinitive of the other verb:

Nećemo biti kod kuće.   *We shall not be at home.*
Nećemo ići na izlet.   *We shall not go on the excursion.*

As with the past tense, aspects are important in the future tense to distinguish between actions intended to be either continuous or incomplete (imperfective) and completed or momentary (perfective):

Pit ću mlijeko.   *I'll drink milk.* (not just once)
Pisat ćemo ti.   *We'll write to you.*

Naručit ćemo večeru. *We'll order dinner.* (completed)
Odmah ćemo doći. *We'll come immediately.*

Insight

Verbal aspects are important when using past and future tenses. You use the perfective aspect of the verb to express that you have completed or intend to complete the action in question and the imperfective aspect to express the fact that the action was done many times, was in the process of being done but not completed in the past or will be done frequently or not completed in the future.

Perfective aspect
Kupio sam sendvič i pojeo sam ga. *I bought a sandwich and ate it.*

Two actions took place one after the other, the first one completed before the second, which was also completed.

Napisat ću pismo mami sutra. *I shall write a letter to mum.*

This is a single action to be completed in the future.

Imperfective aspect
Kupovao sam sendvič *I was buying my sandwich*
 kada sam video Jasnu u *when I saw Jasna in the*
 samoposluzi. *supermarket.*

In other words, I was in the process of buying my sandwich when I was interrupted because I saw Jasna (action not completed).

Pisat ću mami svako dan. *I shall write to mum every day.*

This is an action that I intend to perform many times in the future.

Indirect speech

The following is an example of indirect (or reported) speech. Compare it with the same in direct speech:

Indirect

Rekao sam da ćemo stići danas.	*I said that we would arrive today.*

Direct

'Stići ćemo danas,' rekao sam.	*'We shall arrive today,' I said.*

In English, when you say *I said that ...* or *I am telling you that ...*, we have a set of rules that determines the tense that follows. In Croatian, the situation is simpler. You use the tense of the verb that was used or would have been used in the original statement. So:

Indirect

Rekao je da će doći.	*He said that he would come.*

Direct

'Doći ću,' rekao je.	*'I'll come,' he said.*

The same pattern is followed in all similar sentences in Croatian, for example:

Mislim da ...	*I think that ...*
Siguran sam da ...	*I am sure that ...*
Nadam se da ...	*I hope that ...*

Recreate what was originally said or thought and use the tense from that recreated sentence.

Indirect questions

Here is an example of an indirect question, compare it with the direct question:

Indirect

Možete li mi reći da li je gđa Bilčić kod kuće?	*Can you tell me if Mrs Bilčić is at home?*

Direct

Da li je (Je li) gđa Bilčić kod kuće?	*Is Mrs Bilčić at home?*

In English, you use the word *if* in indirect questions. In Croatian, you begin the second part of the sentence with the question form da li (or li on its own after the verb as in an ordinary question) and use the tense of the verb from the original question:

Indirect

Pitala sam možete li stići   prekosutra. *I asked if you could arrive the day after tomorrow.*

Direct

Možete li stići prekosutra? *Could you arrive the day after tomorrow?*

Negdje, ništa

Look below to see how these words are formed in Croatian.

gdje *where*	**tko** *who*
negdje *somewhere*	**netko** *someone*
nigdje *nowhere*	**nitko** *nobody*
igdje *anywhere*	**itko** *anyone*
što *what*	**kada** *when*
nešto *something*	**nekad** *once, formerly*
ništa *nothing*	**nikad** *never*
išta *anything*	**ikad** *anytime*

There are other forms for *anywhere*, etc. formed with either **bilo** or **god** in this pattern: **bilo gdje** *anywhere*, **gdje god** *anywhere*, **što god** *anything*, **bilo tko** *anyone*, etc.

Uzeo je nešto.	*He took something.*
Netko je došao.	*Someone came.*

If the verb or any other part of the sentence is negative, you *must* use the negative word from the list just given. This is sometimes heard in colloquial speech in English (e.g. *He didn't tell me nothing* rather than *He did not tell me anything* or *He told me nothing*):

Ništa nisam zaboravio.	*I have forgotten nothing.*
Nije bio nigdje.	*He has not been anywhere.*
Nikad nije uzeo ništa.	*He has not taken anything ever.*

Use of personal names and cases

People's names follow the normal rules for case endings where possible. Men's names follow the masculine and women's names the feminine pattern of endings. Foreign names also change if they fit the usual pattern, i.e. men's names ending in a consonant and women's names in -a. Surnames also change according to the normal patterns, but surnames that end in a consonant do not change when they are used for a woman. Study the following examples:

Ići ću s Rudolfom.	*I shall go with Rudolf.*
Dala je novac Marku.	*She gave the money to Mark.*
Gledaju Zvonka.	*They are looking at Zvonko.*
Vidio sam Sandru.	*I saw Sandra.*
Gledaju Rudolfa Šimunića.	*They are looking at Rudolf Šimunić.*
Gledaju Jasnu Kušan.	*They are looking at Jasna Kušan.*
Javio se gospođi Bilčić.	*He called Mrs Bilčić.*

Tko će biti umoran?

After the word **tko** verbs and adjectives are always singular and take masculine endings:

Tko će biti umoran?	*Who will be tired?*
Tko je došao?	*Who has come?*

The same rule applies to **netko**:

Netko je došao.	*Someone has come.*

More about possession

The dative case of **ja**, etc. may be used in order to show possession:

Adresa mi je ...	*My address is ... (lit. the address to me is ...)*

This is normally to express something close such as personal possessions or members of the family:

Sestra joj je u Londonu.   *Her sister is in London.*
Roditelji su mi u Zagrebu.   *My parents are in Zagreb.*

Moj, etc. and cases

The possessive adjectives **moj**, **tvoj**, **svoj** are unusual as they generally omit the -je- which you would expect in the middle of the word. Here is the full pattern of endings, along with the optional vowels which are sometimes added to all adjectives:

	Masc. sing.	Fem. sing.	Neut. sing.	Masc. plural	Fem. plural	Neut. plural
nom.	moj	moja	moje	moji	moje	moja
acc.	nom/gen	moju	moje	moje	moje	moja
gen.	mog(a) mojeg(a)	moje	mog(a) mojeg(a)	mojih	mojih	mojih
dat.	mom(e) mojem(u)	mojoj	mom(e) mojem(u)	mojim(a)	mojim(a)	mojim(a)
ins.	mojim	mojom	mojim	mojim(a)	mojim(a)	mojim(a)

The accusative of masculine adjectives is either the same as the nominative (for inanimate objects) or the same as the genitive (for people and animals).

All adjectives have the optional extra letters at the end, e.g. **dobrog(a)**, **starom(e)** and **starom(u)**. They are added when the adjective is used without a noun:

Jeste li vidjeli mladog čovjeka?   *Did you see the young person?*
Ne, vidio sam staroga.   *No, I saw the old one.*

Practice

1 Put the following into the future tense:
   a Išli smo u dobar restoran.
   b Javio joj se.
   c Našli smo stolicu u blagovaonici.
   d Tko je stigao?
   e Što ste radili na odmoru?
   f Da li si mu dao ključ?
   g Nisu došli k nama.
   h Nisam bio na Hvaru.

2 Put the following into indirect speech, beginning with **Rekao/
   Rekla je da ...** as in the example. Imagine that you have asked
   the receptionist in your hotel for information. You have to
   report the answer to your friend who is waiting by the door.
   Remember to take care with the order of short forms which
   have to come immediately after **da** ...:

   Example: Sigurno će vaše pismo stići sutra.
            Rekao/Rekla je da će naše pismo sigurno stići sutra.

   a Možete kupiti novine tamo kod lifta.
   b Zaboravio sam vaše avionske karte.
   c Dobit ćete ih sutra.
   d Dat ću vam vaš novac sutra.
   e Prodajemo razglednice, koverte i marke u hotelu.
   f Ovo nije vaše pismo.
   g Danas će biti lijepo vrijeme.
   h Nismo izgubili ključ od vaše sobe.
   i Netko vas je tražio u hotelu.
   j Ne znam odakle je bio.

3 Make the following into indirect questions, beginning with
   Pitao/Pitala sam da li ... You have asked the question and
   now you have to tell someone what you asked, as in the
   example (vi is here used to refer to one person politely):

Example: Hoćete li doći sutra na večeru?
Pitao/Pitala sam da li će doći sutra na večeru.

a Da li ste zaboravili gdje stanujemo?
b Da li će danas biti lijepo vrijeme?
c Je li gospođa Bilčić kod kuće?
d Znaš li gdje mi je ključ?
e Da li će Rudolf doći u London?
f Da li ste bili u Engleskoj?
g Da li si bila u Engleskoj?
h Mogu li dobiti čašu vode?
i Možete li doći sutra?
j Idemo li k tvom bratu sutra?

4 Pick the most appropriate form of **negdje, ništa,** etc. from the box to fit these sentences. Use each word once only:
a _____ je došao.
b Mislio sam da _____ nisam zaboravio.
c Naša prtljaga mora biti _____ u našoj sobi.
d _____ nisam uzeo tvoju knjigu.
e Našao je _____ u svom džepu.
f Nije bio _____ u Engleskoj.

: negdje   netko   nigdje   ništa   nikad   nešto :

5 Match the question on the left to the correct answer on the right:
a Gdje je bio vaš novac?   **i** Nikad nisam bila.
b Jesi li bila u Engleskoj?   **ii** Vaš telefonski broj.
c Tko je došao?   **iii** Jasna.
d Što ste našli u džepu?   **iv** U mom džepu.

◀) **CD2, TR 4, 03:03**

6 Fill in the missing part of the telephone conversation:
Molim?
Good day. Is Mr Šimunić at work?
Da, na poslu je. On je u svom uredu.

Put me through to his extension, please.
Halo. Rudolf Šimunić ovdje.
Hello. 'Your name' here.
Da, sjećam vas se.
*I have forgotten your address. Could you tell me where
  you work?*
Moja zgrada je u Ilici, broj dvanaest.
May I come by you today?
Naravno. Dođite u dva sata. Čekat ću vas.
Thank you. Goodbye.
Molim. Do viđenja.

QV · **Ilica** is one of Zagreb's main streets

Comprehension 1

Barry Smith je Englez. On je na odmoru u Hvaru. Ušao je u poštu
i prišao šalteru.

◈ CD2, TR 4, 04:29

Barry	Dobar dan. Želim nazvati Englesku.
Službenik	Kabina tri je slobodna. Uđite i okrenite broj.
Barry	Molim vas, recite mi koji je pozivni broj za Englesku. Zaboravio sam ga.
Službenik	Pozivni broj je nula nula četiri četiri.
Barry	Hvala.
Službenik	Molim.

Barry se javio mami da joj kaže da je stigao na otok i da je sve u
redu. Izašao je iz kabine. Opet je prišao šalteru i platio račun.

QUICK VOCAB

ušao je (ući) *he went in*
prišao je *he went up to*
(**prići** – the verb is used without **je** as it is contained in the first part of
  the sentence **ušao je**)
šalter *counter*
nazvati *to call*

službenik *clerk*
slobodan *free*
okrenuti broj (okrenem) *to dial the number*
koji je pozivni broj ... *which is the code number*
nula *zero*
izašao je (izaći) *he went out*
platiti *to pay*
račun *bill*

True or false?

a Barry Smith je ušao u poštu.
b Htio je nazvati sestru.
c Platio je račun.

Comprehension 2

Read the passage and answer the questions that follow:

Barry Smith je učio hrvatski u Engleskoj. Kad je bio u Hvaru,
našao je vrlo dobar riblji restoran. Nije znao sve riječi iz jelovnika.
Konobarica je bila djevojka iz Zagreba, i govorila je engleski.

Barry	Molim vas, što znači ova riječ 'dagnje' na engleskom?
Konobarica	Na engleskom to znači 'mussels', gospodine.
Barry	A kako se kaže 'zubatac' na engleskom?
Konobarica	Ne znam. 'Zubatac' je jedna vrsta morske ribe. Da li znate, gospodine, kako se kaže na hrvatskom 'squid'?
Barry	Naravno. To su 'lignje'.

🎧 CD2, TR 4, 05:17

vrlo *very*
konobarica *waitress*
djevojka *girl, young lady* (unmarried woman)
Što znači ova riječ? *What does this word mean?*
na engleskom *in English*

Kako se kaže ...? *How is ... said?/How do you say ...?*
vrsta *kind, sort*
morska riba *salt water* (lit. *sea*) *fish*
na hrvatskom *in Croatian*

1 Što Barry uči u Engleskoj?
   a Francuski.
   b Hrvatski.
   c Engleski.

2 Kako se kaže 'dagnje' na engleskom?
   a Squid.
   b Mussels.
   c Sea fish.

3 Što je 'zubatac'?
   a To je vrsta ribe.
   b To su lignje.
   c To je salata.

Test yourself

Here you can check some of the things you have learnt in this unit. Look at the questions that follow and choose the right answer:

1 Choose the appropriate word to fill the gap when you are telling your Croatian friend that you intend to rent an apartment in Hvar: **Ja ... iznajmiti stan u Hvaru:**
   a ću
   b ćete
   c ćemo

2 Choose the appropriate word to fill the gap when you are telling your Croatian colleague that the two of you will share a taxi to go to your next business meeting: **Ići ... taksijem:**

    a ćete
    b ćemo
    c će

3 You are on holiday and you do not intend to eat in the hotel.
Complete the phrase: **Ja ... jesti u hotelu:**
    a neće
    b nećeš
    c neću

4 You are asking Rudolf and Jasna if they intend to go on
holiday this year. Complete the phrase: **... li ići na odmor:**
    a Hoćete
    b Hoćemo
    c Hoćeš

5 Which of the two options would you use to complete the
question **Da li ... vlakom?**
    a putovat ćeš
    b ćeš putovati

6 Match the sentence on the left with the reported sentence on
the right:

a Doći ću sutra u osam sati.	**i** Rekla je da su ručali u dobrom restoranu.
b Čekala sam vas ispred pošte.	**ii** Rekla je da će doći sutra u osam sati.
c Bit ćemo u gradu večeras.	**iii** Rekla je da nas je čekala ispred pošte.
d Ručali smo u dobrom restoranu.	**iv** Rekla je da će biti u gradu večeras.
e Vidjet ćemo vas u Zagrebu.	**v** Rekla je da će nas vidjeti u Zagrebu.

13

Na plaži
On the beach

In this unit you will learn how to
- *Express dates, numbers above 100 and further expressions of time*
- *Express feelings, intentions and moods*
- *Say* oneself

Dialogue

Svi ljudi na odmoru u Hvaru vole *Paklene otoke*. Danas se Sandra i Jasna sunčaju na plaži jednog od tih otoka. Provode dan u razgovoru.

Sandra	Jasna, koji je danas datum?
Jasna	Danas je dvadeset prvi kolovoz.
Sandra	Kad smo stigli u Hvar?
Jasna	Stigli smo desetog kolovoza.
Sandra	Ne ostaje nam mnogo vremena. Ponekad sanjam da ćemo ostati mjesecima na otoku.
Jasna	Znam što hoćeš reći. Zaista je ovdje divno. Kad sam bila dijete, imala sam namjeru živjeti na nekom otoku, negdje daleko od mojih roditelja.
Sandra	A što sad misliš?
Jasna	Više nemam tu namjeru. Sad sam pesimist.

svi ljudi *all people*
Pakleni otoci *Hell's Islands*
plaža *beach*
jedan od tih otoka *one of those islands*
provoditi, provesti (provodim, provedem: provodio, proveo)
 to spend (of time)
Koji je danas datum? *What is the date today?*
Danas je dvadeset prvi kolovoz. *Today is 21 August.*
desetog kolovoza *on 10 August*
Ne ostaje nam ... *There does not remain for us ...*
ostajati, ostati (ostajem, ostanem) *to remain, stay*
mnogo vremena *much time*
ponekad *sometimes*
sanjati *to dream*
mjesecima *for months*
htjeti reći *to want to say, to mean*
namjera *intention*
sam (adj. sama, samo) *alone*
 (note this word is pronounced with a long falling tone and sounds
 completely different from the short form of **biti**, **ja sam**)
Nemam više tu namjeru. *I no longer have that intention.*
rođen sam *I was born*
tisuću devetsto sedamdeset pete godine *in 1975*
pesimist *pessimist*
Ne smiješ biti ... *You mustn't be ...*
mlad *young*
Što ti je! *What's with you! What's up!*
dobro raspoložen *in a good mood*
pjevati *to sing*
biti veselo društvo *to be jolly company*
cijeli dan *for the whole day*

QUICK VOCAB

Jasna	Nemoj misliti da sam tužna. Sretna sam. Međutim, ne radujem se povratku u Zagreb.
Sandra	Zašto?
Jasna	Zato što ne znam koliko još dugo mogu podnositi Rudolfovo ponašanje. Ljutim se na njega. Njegova majka misli da sam ja kriva zato što nismo u braku. Ali, on se nije htio vjenčati. Pričali smo o toj mogućnosti u prošlosti. Ali kasnije više nije htio razgovarati o tome. Ovih dana me je pitao da li ja želim da se mi vjenčamo. Po mom mišljenju, još jednom moramo iskreno razgovarati o budućnosti. Bit će sve u redu čim počnemo govoriti o našim osjećajima.
Sandra	Slažem se. Moraš misliti na sebe, a ne na njega.
Jasna	Dobro mi je sada. Htjela sam ti ispričati što se dešava. Što ćemo raditi sad? Hoćeš li da se idemo kupati?
Sandra	Da, kupa mi se.

QUICK VOCAB

tužan *sad*
sretan *happy*
radovati se, radujem se (with dat.) *to look forward to*
Zašto? *Why?*
zato što *because*
Koliko još dugo ...? *For how much longer ...?*
podnositi *to tolerate*
ponašanje *behaviour*
ljutiti se na (with acc.) *to be angry with*
kriv *wrong, guilty, at fault*
vjenčati se *to get married*
pričati *to tell, talk*
prošlost (fem. noun) *the past*
Više nije htio da ... *He no longer wanted to ...*
ovih dana *these days, recently*
još jednom *once more*
iskreno *sincerely*
budućnost (fem. noun) *the future*
čim *as soon as*
počinjati, početi (počinjem, počnem) *to begin*

osjećaj *feeling, emotion*
misliti na sebe *to think of/about oneself*
Dobro mi je. *I'm OK, I feel fine.*
dešavati se, desiti se *to happen*
kupati se *to bathe*
Kupa mi se. *I feel like going for a swim.*

True or false?

a Jasna je imala namjeru živjeti daleko od kuće.
b Jasna nije lijepo pjevala.
c Rudolfova majka misli da je njen sin kriv zato što nije oženjen.

Insight

The island of Hvar is one of a group of larger islands including Brač and Korčula off the Adriatic coast between Split and Dubrovnik. Hvar is the furthest to reach from a port on the mainland, but the journey still takes only a couple of hours by ferry. The larger islands are surrounded by smaller ones and the so-called **Pakleni otoci** (*Hell's Islands*) are only a few hundred yards from the entrance to Hvar's small fishing port. They have the best beaches on Hvar and there are always boats waiting to take you over.

Key phrases

◀) CD2, TR 5, 02:24

How to:

▶ ask the date today and reply	Koji je danas datum?
	Danas je dvadeset prvi
	kolovoz.
▶ ask when something happened and reply	Kad ...
	Desetog kolovoza ...

▶ state the year when someone was born	Rođena (fem.) Rođen (masc.) sam tisuću devetsto sedamdeset pete godine.
▶ use further expressions of time	mjesecima mnogo vremena cijeli dan čim u prošlosti u budućnosti ovih dana
▶ use expressions which show intentions	Znam što hoćeš reći. Imam namjeru… Ne smiješ… Kupa mi se.
▶ use expressions related to mood	Što ti je! tužna sam/tužan sam sretna sam/sretan sam ljutim se na njega/nju radujem se povratku dobro sam raspoložen/a biti veselo društvo on je kriv/ona je kriva osjećaj
▶ say *oneself*	moraš misliti na sebe

How it works

◀) CD2, TR 03:52

Numbers – above 100

sto	100	sto devedeset jedan	191
dvjesta	200	dvjesta tri	203
trista	300	trista sedamdeset	370
četiristo	400	četiristo osamnaest	418
petsto	500	petsto šezdeset devet	569

šeststo	600	šeststo trideset dva	632
sedamsto	700	sedamsto dvadeset četiri	724
osamsto	800	osamsto osamdeset osam	888
devetsto	900	devetsto četrdeset pet	945
tisuća	1 000	tisuća sto jedan	1 101
milijun	1 000 000		

tri milijuna petsto pet tisuća šeststo pedeset tri   *3 505 653*

You might hear some Croatian speakers say **dvjesto** and **tristo**.

The word for *thousand* is often used in its accusative form **tisuću**.

◀) **CD2, TR 5, 05:13**

Dates

To express dates you use ordinal numbers (see Unit 6), remembering that only the last part of such a number becomes an adjective. To say *today is …* use the nominative case, and to say *on a date* use the genitive case:

Koji je datum danas?	*What is the date today?*
Danas je treći siječanj.	*Today is 3 January.*
Danas je osamnaesti travanj.	*Today is 18 April.*
Danas je dvadeset osmi prosinac.	*Today is 28 December.*
Kad smo stigli?	*When did we arrive?*
Stigli smo …	*We arrived …*
trinaestog veljače.	*on 13 February.*
dvadeset prvog srpnja.	*on 21 July.*
tridesetog travnja.	*on 30 October.*

To express a year use the formula *one thousand nine hundred …* and to say *in* a year use the ordinal numeral and the word for *year* **godina**, in the genitive case:

Kada ste rođeni?	*When were you born?*
Tisuću devetsto sedamdeset druge godine.	*In 1972.*
Tisuću devetsto pedeset sedme godine.	*In 1957.*
Tisuću devetsto osamdeset prve godine.	*In 1981.*

Expressions of time

Mjesecima *for months* is expressed by using the instrumental plural case of the word **mjesec**. Similar expressions can be formed for other periods of time:

Čekali smo te satima.	*We waited for you for hours.*
Tražili su ga danima.	*They searched for him for days.*
tjednima	*for weeks*
godinama	*for years*

Other expressions of time can be formed by using *still, yet, more*:

Nemam više tu namjeru.	*I no longer intend to* (lit. *have the intention*).
Više nije htio da ...	*He no longer wanted to ...*
Dok sam još bio dijete ...	*While I was still a child ...*
Još nije došao.	*He has not come yet.*
Još jednom.	*Once more.*
više – with negative	*no longer*
još (uvijek)	*still*
još – with negative	*yet*

Adverbs

Adverbs are words that often end in *-ly* in English: *sincerely, beautifully*, etc. They are formed in one of two ways in Croatian.

a use the nominative neuter form of the adjective:

Masc.	Fem.	Neut.
lijep	lijepa	lijepo
iskren	iskrena	iskreno
tužan	tužna	tužno
sretan	sretna	sretno

b use the nominative masculine form of adjectives which end in **-ski**:

Masc.	Fem.	Neut.
prijateljski	prijateljska	prijateljsko

They are frequently used to add meanings to verbs (whereas adjectives add meanings to nouns):

Lijepo si pjevala.	*You sang beautifully.*
Razgovarali smo iskreno.	*We talked sincerely.*
Tužno su me gledali.	*They looked at me sadly.*
Govorila je sa mnom prijateljski.	*She spoke with me in a friendly fashion.*

Hoćeš li da se idemo kupati?

You know that the verbs **željeti** and **htjeti** are used in a similar way to the English *I want to* … A difference occurs when talking about what we want others to do. Compare the following:

Hoćeš li da se idemo kupati?	*Do you want us to go for a swim?*
Ovih dana me je pitao želim li ja da se mi vjenčamo.	*Recently he's been asking if I want us to get married.*

(emphasis added by use of pronouns **ja** and **mi** in Croatian)

In English. we still use a construction with the infinitive, but, in Croatian, we say the equivalent of *I want that you do something*.

Kupa mi se

You don't have to say that *you want* all the time, you can add more of an inner feeling by saying *you feel like*. The equivalent expression in Croatian is formed by making the verb reflexive and using the dative case for the person concerned:

Kupa mi se.	*I feel like bathing.*

(**kupa** – on form of verb: **mi** – dat. of **ja**: **se** – reflexive enclitic)

Jede mi se.	*I feel like eating.*
Ide mi se u kino.	*I feel like going to the cinema.*
Pije mi se čaj.	*I feel like (a drink of) tea.*

Insight

You have now met different ways of saying that you *want* or *like* something:

Želim kavu.	*I want a coffee.*
Hoću piti kavu.	*I want a coffee.*
Pije mi se kava.	*I feel like some coffee.*

All three sentences mean that you want coffee, with the provision that the last is not so strong:

| Volim plivati. | *I like (or I love ...) swimming.* |
| Sviđa mi se plivanje. | *I like (or I am fond of ...) swimming.* |

Both sentences mean that you like swimming, except that in the second sentence it is not quite so strongly expressed.

To say *oneself*

In English, there are a number of words like *myself*, *yourself* and *oneself*, etc. In Croatian, there is just one word that has all these meanings. It changes according to case in the following pattern:

nom. acc. gen.	**sebe**
dat.	**sebi**
ins.	**sobom**

The meaning of the word depends on the context of the sentence:

Misli na sebe.	*Think about yourself.*
Pogledaj sebe.	*Look at yourself.*
Zadovoljan je sobom.	*He is pleased with himself.*
Kupio je sebi novine.	*He bought a newspaper for himself.*

Aspects with *početi*

After the verb **počinjati, početi** (and others that mean *to begin* or ones which mean *to finish*) you must use an imperfective infinitive:

On počinje čitati.   *He is beginning to read.*
Počeo sam piti mlijeko.   *I began to drink my milk.*

Jedan od tih otoka

The phrase *one of …* is made up of **jedan** followed by **od** and the genitive case. Remember that **jedan** is an adjective and its ending will depend on what is being discussed:

jedan od tih otoka   *one of those islands*
otok (masc.), **jedan** (masc.)
jedna od tih kavana   *one of those cafés*
kavana (fem.), **jedna** (fem.)

u jednoj od tih kavana   *in one of those cafés*
(use the feminine dative as you are saying the equivalent of)
u jednoj kavani od tih   *in one café out of those*

Unusual noun categories (*vrijeme*)

Vrijeme is unusual in that it adds **-en-** before its neuter case endings:

	Singular	Plural
nom.	vrijeme	vremena
acc.	vrijeme	vremena
gen.	vremena	vremena
dat.	vremenu	vremenima
ins.	vremenom	vremenima

It also loses **-ij-** when it adds case endings.

A small group of nouns follows the same pattern as **vrijeme** and adds -en- before the case endings: e.g. **ime** (*name*), **breme** (*burden*). They are all neuter nouns which end in -me.

Unusual adjective categories

In this unit, some adjectives do not strictly follow the patterns you have learnt so far.

	Singular			Plural		
Svi	Masc.	Fem.	Neut.	Masc.	Fem.	Neut.
nom.	sav	sva	sve	svi	sve	sva
acc.	nom/gen	svu	sve	sve	sve	sva
gen.	sveg(a)	sve	sveg(a)		svih	
dat.	svem(u)	svoj	svem(u)		svim(a)	
ins.	svim	svom	svim		svim(a)	

The adjective is treated as if it has a soft ending, and -e is used in place of -o in masculine and neuter singular endings.

Remember that **svi** (masc. plural) also means *everyone* and **sve** (neut. singular) also means *everything*:

Svi su došli.   *Everyone came.*
Sve je bilo na stolu.   *Everything was on the table.*

Veselo Singular	Masc.	Fem.	Neut.
nom.	veseo	vesela	veselo

The masculine nominative ends in -o, while all other endings are added to **vesel-**.

A similar adjective to **veseo** is **topao** *warm*:

Topao Singular	Masc.	Fem.	Neut.
nom.	**topao**	**topla**	**toplo**

Practice

◄ CD2, TR 5, 06:30

1 Write out and say the following numbers in words: 567, 239, 807, 301, 1500, 3790.

◄ CD2, TR 5, 07:24

2 Write out and say the following dates. Take care with getting the right case to match the meaning of the sentence:

  a Danas je   (14 March).
  b Danas je   (1 June).
  c U četvrtak bit će   (8 August).
  d Vratit ćemo se   (on 3 September).
  e Englezi su stigli u Dubrovnik (on 25 June).
  f Idemo u Zagreb   (on 27 December).
  g Rođen sam   (in 1980).
  h Rođena je   (in 1962).
  i Rođen sam   (on 25 May) (in 1971).
  j Rođena je   (on 11 January) (in 1935).

3 Fill in the most appropriate words from the box to complete the time expressions in the following sentences. Use each word once only:

  a Radujem se povratku na Hvar u _____.
  b Živjeli su na Braču _____.
  c _____ nisu došli.
  d Ne ostaje nam mnogo _____.
  e To se dešavalo u _____.
  f Sunčaju se na plaži po _____ dan.
  g _____ dođe Rudolf, recite mu da sam se javio.

4 Complete the sentences with the correct form of **htjeti**:

   a _____ li vi da idemo u Varaždin vlakom?

   b Pitao me je, _____ li ja da dođe na večeru!

   c Rudolf mi je rekao da Mark _____ ostati cijeli dan na plaži.

   d Sandra je _____ da joj Jasna priča o svemu.

5 In the sentences that follow make an adverb from the adjective given in brackets. All the adjectives are given in the nominative masculine form:

   a (Tužan) je išao prema trgu.

   b Bilo smo u kavani i (veseo) smo pjevali.

   c Mogu ti (iskren) reći da nikad nisam bio tamo.

   d Mi smo razgovarali vrlo (prijateljski) cijeli dan.

6 Match the question on the left to the correct answer on the right:

   a Mogu li ti reći nešto?   **i** Htio sam te vidjeti.

   b Ideš li na odmor?   **ii** Dobro sam raspoložena, hvala.

   c Zašto si došao?   **iii** Ne moraš, ako ne želiš.

   d Kako si danas?   **iv** Imala sam namjeru, a sada nisam sigurna.

7 Replace the verbs **htjeti** and **željeti** with a phrase meaning *I feel like* in the following sentences:

   a Hoću piti čaj.

   b Hoćemo ići u grad danas.

   c Ona se želi kupati.

   d Hoću ići na plažu danas.

◀) **CD2, TR 5, 09:39**

   8 Complete the missing parts of the dialogue:

      Što vam je?

      I am sad.

      Zašto?

Because I do not feel like going home.
Možete se vratiti sljedeće godine.
I intend to return.
Onda, nemojte se ljutiti na mene.
*I am not angry with you. I am looking forward to my
   return.*
Vidim da ste sada sretni.

9 Provide the correct form of **sebe** in these sentences:
  a Jasna je pogledala _____.
  b Jesu li zadovoljni _____?
  c On misli samo na _____.
  d Kupili smo _____ avionske karte za Dubrovnik.

_____

Comprehension 1

Sandra i Mark nisu imali mnogo vremena dan prije polaska na
Hvar. Sandra je spakovala majice, šorceve, kupaće kostime, čarape,
donje rublje, sandale i cipele za njih. Mark je uzeo ljetne hlače,
laganu crvenu jaknu i košulje. Ima jednu zelenu košulju s kratkim
rukavima. Nije uzeo svoje sivo odijelo. Sandra je uzela svoju žutu
jaknu, suknju i crnu haljinu. Bili su sigurni da nisu ništa zaboravili.
Ali nisu znali de će biti tako toplo. Morali su kupiti šešire i mlijeko
za sunčanje u prodavaonici u Hvaru.

dan prije polaska *the day before departure*
pakovati, spakovati (pakujem, spakujem) *to pack*
majica *T-shirt*
šorc *shorts*
kupaći kostim *swimming costume*
čarapa *sock*
donje rublje *underwear*
sandale (fem. plural noun) *sandals*
cipele (fem. plural noun) *shoes*
ljetne hlače (fem. plural noun) *summer trousers*
lagan *light*
crven *red*

QUICK VOCAB

jakna *jacket*
košulja *shirt*
zelen *green*
s kratkim rukavima *with short sleeves*
sivo odijelo *grey suit*
žut *yellow*
suknja *skirt*
haljina *dress*
tako *so*
šešir *hat*
mlijeko za sunčanje (or **ulje za sunčanje**) *suntan lotion*

True or false?

a Sandra je spakovala cipele za njih.
b Mark ima jednu crvenu košulju s kratkim rukavima.
c Kupili su mlijeko za sunčanje u Zagrebu.

Comprehension 2

Here are some descriptions of resorts and hotels. Read the descriptions and answer the questions that follow.

Pag je turistički grad. Smješten je u tihom zaljevu, u blagoj mediteranskoj klimi s mnogo sunčanih dana, kristalnim morem s malim i velikim plažama.

Hotel Bellevue (B kategorija) kapacitet: 320 kreveta. Svaka soba ima tuš, WC. Svaki balkon ima pogled na more. Hotel ima vlastitu plažu, rekreacioni centar i frizerski salon.

Turističko naselje Medena smješteno je u Segetu, malom ribarskom mjestu (4km od Trogira, 30km od Splita i 7km od aerodroma). Naselje ima restoran, grill-bar s terasom, terasu za ples, salu za konferenciju, frizerske salone, supermarket, bazen s toplom morskom vodom, terene za sport i dječje igralište.

Hotel Kompas: Cjenovnik po osobi/danu

	noćenje/doručak	polupansion	puni pansion
jednokrevetna soba	921 Kn	1012 Kn	1102 Kn
dvokrevetna soba	795 Kn	858 Kn	921 Kn
trokrevetna soba	740 Kn	800 Kn	841 Kn

QUICK VOCAB

turistički *tourist* (adj.)
Smješten je ... *It is situated ...*
u tihom zaljevu *in a quiet bay*
u blagoj mediteranskoj klimi *in a gentle Mediterranean climate*
sunčan dan *sunny day*
krevet *bed*
svaki *each, every*
tuš *shower*
WC *toilet* (pron. ve-tse)
balkon *balcony*
vlastit *own*
frizerski salon *hairdressing salon*
ribarski *fishing* (adj.)
terasa *terrace*
ples *dance, dancing*
sala za konferenciju *conference hall*
morska voda *salt water*
dječje igralište *children's playground*
cjenovnik po osobi/danu *price list per person/day*
noćenje/doručak *overnight/breakfast*
polupansion *half board*
puni pansion *full board*
jednokrevetna soba *one-bedded room*
dvokrevetna soba *two-bedded room*
trokrevetna soba *three-bedded room*

1 Kakav grad je Pag?
   a Ribarski.
   b Industrijski.
   c Turistički.

2 Gdje je smješteno turističko naselje 'Medena'?

   a U malom mjestu.

   b U gradu.

   c Na plaži.

3 Koliko košta po osobi/danu dvokrevetna soba, polupansion, u Hotelu 'Kompas'?

   a 1012 Kn

   b 858 Kn

   c 795 Kn

Test yourself

Here you can check some of the things you have learnt in this unit. Look at the questions that follow and choose the right answer:

1 If Jasna says that she is **dobro raspoložena** does this mean that she is:

   a happy

   b sad

   c bored

2 If you wanted to be in good company what would you look for?

   a tužno društvo

   b teško društvo

   c veselo društvo

3 You see a friend of yours who looks upset. Which question would be the least appropriate?

   a Kako si?

   b Što ti je?

   c Koliko imaš godina?

4 Which of the following phrases means *in 1999*?
   a tisuću devetsto devedeset deveta godina
   b tisuću devetsto devedeset devete godine
   c tisuću devetsto devedeset devetu godinu

5 If your birthday is **petnaestog veljače**, when is it?
   a on 15 January
   b on 15 February
   c on 15 March

6 If your birthday is **desetog prosinca**, when is it?
   a on 10 October
   b on 10 November
   c on 10 December

7 Complete the phrase to say that you are no longer a student:
Nisam ... student:
   a više
   b još uvijek
   c dok

8 Complete the sentence to say that your son is still going to
school: **Moj sin ... ide u školu:**
   a više
   b još uvijek
   c dok

9 Which form of the word is correct for you to say that you and
your friend ate well: **... smo jeli?**
   a Dobar
   b Dobri
   c Dobro

10 Which of the two infinitives would you use to complete the
sentence *I began to write the letter* (**Počeo sam ... pismo**)?
   a pisati
   b napisati

14

Ako pada kiša ...
If it rains ...

In this unit you will learn how to
- *Say if using different levels of possibility and the conditional*
- *Further understand aspects*
- *Use expressions for the weather and verbs of movement*
- *Say that you can see/hear somebody doing something*

Dialogue

🔊 **CD2, TR 6**

Jasna je ustala rano. Odlučila je da ide u grad. Ostavila je poruku za Rudolfa.

Rudolf

Izašla sam po kruh za doručak. Kad ustaneš, stavi ručnike na balkon da se osuše. Da smo ih sinoć stavili na balkon, bili bi već suhi. Ako vidiš Sandru ili Marka, reci im da sam otišla u grad po kruh. Imam prijedlog za danas. Ako bude toplo, možemo ići na plažu. Ako bi padala kiša, mogli bismo ići u samostan.

Tvoja Jasna

ustajati, ustati (ustajem, ustanem) *to get up*
rano *early*
odlučiti *to decide*
ostavljati, ostaviti *to leave*
poruka *message*
izlaziti izaći (izlazim, izađem: izlazio, izašao) *to go out*
po kruh *for bread*
stavi (stavljati, staviti) *put* (command form)
ručnik *towel*
sušiti se, osušiti se *to dry*
Da smo … *If we had …*
bili bi *they would be*
suh *dry*
reci im *tell them* (imperative of **reći**)
odlaziti, otići (odlazim, odem: odlazio, otišao) *to go away*
prijedlog *suggestion*
Ako bude toplo... *If it is warm…*
Ako bi padala kiša... *If it were to rain…*
mogli bismo ići *we could go*
samostan *monastery*

Kad je Rudolf pročitao poruku, čuo je kako Jasna ulazi u apartman. Ušla je u njihovu sobu.

Jasna	Zdravo, Rudolfe. Gdje su Sandra i Mark? Nema ih u sobi.
Rudolf	Ne znam. Ja sam se upravo probudio.
Jasna	Previše spavaš.
	(Gleda kroz prozor.)
	Evo ih. Vidim kako dolaze s obale. Možda su išli rivom u grad.
Rudolf	Misliš li da će danas padati kiša? Vjetar ne puše, nebo je vedro i nema oblaka.
Jasna	Sve je moguće. Vjerojatno neće padati. Ako bude toplo, nema problema. Kada bi bilo hladno, ne bismo išli na plažu. Moramo imati i drugi plan.
Rudolf	U pravu si. Jesi li jutros vidjela gospođu Bilčić?
Jasna	Koga?
Rudolf	Našu gazdaricu. Hoću platiti račun.
	(Contd)

Jasna	Zašto?
Rudolf	Zato što se vraćamo prekosutra. Da postoji mogućnost, ostali bismo još. Ali ne postoji, jer imam sastanak početkom sljedećeg tjedna u Zagrebu.

Čuo je kako Jasna ulazi. *He heard Jasna coming in.*
ulaziti, ući (ulazim, uđem: ulazio, ušao) *to enter, come in*
Nema ih u sobi. *They're not in their room.*
upravo *just now*
buditi se, probuditi se *to wake up*
previše *too much* (also *too ...*)
spavati *to sleep*
gledati kroz prozor (gledati, pogledati) *to look through the window*
s obale *from the coast*
možda *perhaps*
riva (rivom) *promenade, esplanade* (along the promenade – instrumental)
Vjetar ne puše. *The wind is not blowing.*
Nebo je vedro. *The sky is clear.*
oblak *cloud*
mogući *possible*
vjerojatno *probably, likely*
Kada bi bilo hladno ... *If it were cold ...*
drugi plan *another plan*
koga *whom*
račun *bill, account*
postojati, postojim *to exist*
mogućnost (fem. noun) *possibility*
ostali bismo *we would stay*
sastanak *meeting*
početak *beginning*

True or false?

a Jasna je ustala kasno.
b Sinoć nisu stavili ručnike na balkon.
c Moraju se vratiti u Zagreb jer Rudolf ima sastanak.

Insight

Jasna need not worry about the weather on Hvar. All the islands of the Adriatic have excellent weather, but Hvar is particularly known for having no rain all summer. It is said that hotels are even prepared to refund money for each day of rain. So, it is unlikely that she would need her **kišobran** *umbrella* or her **kaput** *coat*.

Key phrases

◀) **CD2, TR 6, 02:05**

How to:

▶ describe levels of possibility	**možda**
	vjerojatno
	moguće
▶ use types of sentences using *if*	**Ako vidiš Sandru …**
	Ako bude toplo …
	Ako bi padala kiša …
	Kada bi bilo hladno …
	Da smo ih stavili …
▶ use expressions about the weather	**toplo je**
	hladno je
	vjetar puše
	nebo je vedro
	nema oblaka
▶ say you can *see/hear* someone doing something	**Čuo je kako Jasna ulazi u sobu.**
	Vidim kako dolaze s obale.
▶ use verbs of motion	**Izašla je iz sobe.**
	Otišla je u grad.
	Ušla je u sobu.

How it works

To say *if*

You need to know what is called the conditional part of the verb. This is formed by taking the past tense from the infinitive (**čitao**, **išli**, etc.) and combining it with the following short forms:

ja	bih	mi	bismo
ti	bi	vi	biste
on/a/o	bi	oni/e/a	bi

The conditional means *would* in English. It is often found in more formal and polite language, as a waiter might ask you in a restaurant **Što biste željeli, gospodine/gospođo?** (*What would you like, sir/madam?*) or as you first saw in Unit 2 in the phrase **ja bih kavu** *I would like coffee.*

These short forms, like others, tend not to come in first place in a sentence.

Like other short forms that are verbs, they come before short forms from personal pronouns.

In conversation, all forms of the verb are sometimes reduced to **bi**: **ja bi**, **vi bi**, etc.

The negative is formed by adding **ne** before the short form, which then allows it to come in first place:

Volio bih ...	*I would like ...*
Ne bih volio ...	*I would not like ...*

Questions are formed in one of two ways.

a Da li biste htjeli ...?	*Would you like ...?*

   (using the **da li** formula)

b Biste li htjeli ...?   *Would you like ...?*

(using the li formula, but this time the short form comes first).

There are three levels of possibility expressed in Croatian *if* sentences:

▶ **Ako je toplo, idemo na**   *If it is warm, we go to the beach.*
  plažu.

i.e. if A (it is warm) occurs, B (we go to the beach) occurs. Tenses
are the same as in English. Note that when talking about one
specific occasion in the future say **Ako bude toplo ...** This is
explained in more detail later.

▶ **Ako bi padala kiša, mogli**   *If it were to rain, we could go*
  bismo ići u samostan.   *to the monastery.*

i.e. I don't believe A will occur, but it might. Conditional in both
parts of the sentence. In such sentences **kada** may also be used to
mean *if*.

▶ **Da postoji mogućnost,**   *If the possibility existed, we*
  ostali bismo.   *would stay.*
  Da smo ih sinoć stavili na   *If we had put them on the balcony*
  balkon, bili bi suhi.   *last night, they would be dry.*

i.e. A is not possible or was not done, so the condition is not met
for B, which will not or did not occur. The verb with **da** is in the
appropriate tense, and the second verb is in the conditional.

Other tenses in Croatian

You have learnt all the most used parts of the verb in Croatian.
There are four other tenses: pluperfect, aorist, imperfect, future
exact. The first three are used rarely.

The pluperfect is formed by adding the past tense of **biti** to another
verb in the past tense (e.g. **Bio sam napisao pismo bratu.** *I had
written a letter to my brother*).

The aorist and imperfect are also past tenses (e.g. **rekoh** *I said* –
aorist; **Kako to bješe?** *How was that?* – imperfect).

The future exact is sometimes used with *if* clauses. It is formed
in two parts by joining another part of the verb **biti** (given in the
following pattern):

ja	budem	mi	budemo
ti	budeš	vi	budete
on/a/o	bude	oni/e/a	budu

This form uses the past tense from the infinitive in the following
way:

Ako bude padala kiša, ići	*If it rains we shall go to the*
ćemo u kino.	*cinema.*

It is used to indicate a precise point in the future, hence the formula
Ako bude toplo ... i.e. if A will occur then B will happen. Both
parts of the sentence are in future tenses, but it is not possible to
use the future formed from the short form of **htjeti** with **ako**.

Verbal aspect

You have now met a number of aspectual pairs. If we take the
imperfective (the first in any pair) as the basic verb, then we can
see three main trends in forming the perfective:

a The perfective verb is a shortened version of the imperfective:

ustajati	ustati	*to get up*
počinjati	početi	*to begin*
ostavljati	ostaviti	*to leave*

b The perfective verb is formed by adding a prefix to the
imperfective:

piti	popiti	*to drink*
čitati	pročitati	*to read*
pisati	napisati	*to write*

c The perfective verb belongs to a different type, often being an **i** verb:

sjećati se	**sjetiti se**	*to remember*
vraćati se	**vratiti se**	*to return*

Verbs of movement

The verb *to go* is **ići**. From this verb, you can form a number of other verbs by adding prefixes that specify the direction of the movement. From **ići**, you form the perfective form of the compound verb and an imperfective is formed by adding the same prefix to **-laziti**:

izlaziti	izaći	(followed by preposition **iz** + gen.)
to go out		
ulaziti	ući	(followed by preposition **u** + acc.)
to go in, enter		
odlaziti	otići	(prepositions vary)
to go away, leave		

Also:

dolaziti	**doći**	*to come, arrive*
izlaziti	**izići**	(same as **izaći**)
polaziti	**poći**	*to set off*
prelaziti	**prijeći**	*to cross*
prolaziti	**proći**	*to pass by*
silaziti	**sići**	*to go down, get off*
zalaziti	**zaći**	*to go behind*

They all follow the same verbal patterns. The **-laziti** forms are regular. The other forms end in **-đem**, etc. (except **otići**):

izaći	izađem
ući	uđem
otići	odem
prijeći	prijeđem

In the past tense, they all follow the same pattern: **on je izašao, ona je ušla, oni su otišli** (like **išao** but note **prijeći** becomes **prešao**).

Examples:

Izašao je iz sobe. *He came out of the room.*
Dolaze kući. *They are coming home.*
Prešli su most. *They crossed the bridge.*
Sunce je zašlo. *The sun set.*

Insight

Verbs of movement may be followed by a preposition depending on context and meaning:

Vlak je pošao u Zagreb. *The train departed for Zagreb.*
Jasna je prošla pored *Jasna passed by the theatre.*
kazališta.
Došli su do kolodvora. *They have got as far as the station.*
Otišli smo na ručak. *We went out for lunch.*

Sometimes a preposition may be used but it is not obligatory:

Prelaze rijeku. *They are crossing the river.*
Prelaze preko rijeke. *They are going across the river.*

It is warm

When specifying that *I am warm*, you add the relevant person in the dative case to the expression **toplo je** (which is the adverbial form – Unit 13). This is the same principle as we had with the phrases **lako mi je** and **Je li vam jasno?**

Toplo mi je. *I am warm.*
Je li vam hladno? *Are you cold?*
Vruće im je. *They are hot.*

Tko/koga

The words **tko** and **što** have case endings that resemble adjective endings:

nom.	**tko**	**što**
acc.	**kog(a)**	**što**
gen.	**kog(a)**	**čeg(a)**
dat.	**kom(u/e)**	**čem(u)**
ins.	**kim(e)**	**čim(e)**

The required case and ending are determined by the same rules as for all nouns and adjectives:

Koga si vidjela?	*Whom did you see?*
Kome je dao novac?	*To whom did he give the money?*
S kim su došli u grad?	*Who did they come to town with?*
	(or With whom ...?)
Iz čega izlazimo?	*What are we getting out of?*
Čime ste zadovoljni?	*What are you satisfied with?*

Netko/nešto and **nitko/ništa** change according to these patterns too. **Netko** and **nitko** lose the t in other cases, e.g. **nekog(a)/nikog(a)**.

When you use a preposition with **nitko** and **ništa** the word is split. Look at the following examples:

Jasna je sama.	*Jasna is alone.*
Nije došla ni s kim.	*She came with nobody.*
Nisam dobio pismo ni od koga.	*I did not receive a letter from anybody.*

Idiomatic phrases

▶ *to fetch*

Idem po kruh	*I am going for the bread.*
	(or I am going to fetch the bread.)

The normal way of saying *to fetch* is to say **ići po** followed by the accusative case.

▶ *To go along ...*

Idu rivom u grad.	*They are going along the promenade to town.*

The place along which one moves is put into the instrumental case:
Išli su ulicom ... *They went down the street* ...

▶ *They are not in* ...
  Nema ih u sobi.   *They are not in their room.*

You know **nema** followed by the genitive case means *there is not* or
there are not. It is also commonly used to mean *they are out*
(i.e. *not at home*):

Nema ga.   *He is not in/not at home/not here.*

▶ *At the beginning of* ...

This is often expressed by the word **početkom** (instrumental case of
početak beginning) followed by the genitive case:

Početkom mjeseca.   *At the beginning of the month.*

The phrase **na početku** is also used.

The expression **krajem** and **na kraju** is used to mean *at the end*:

Krajem idućeg tjedna.   *At the end of next month.*

▶ *To see/hear someone doing something*
  Čuo je kako Jasna   *He heard Jasna coming into*
    ulazi u apartman.   *the apartment.*
  Vidim kako dolaze   *I can see them coming from*
    s obale.   *the beach.*

In Croatian, you express this by literally saying *he heard how Jasna
comes into the apartment, I can see how they come*. The verb of
perception is followed by **kako** and the other verb is in the present
tense:

Gledali su kako ti ljudi   *They watched those people talking*
  razgovaraju ispred hotela.   *in front of the hotel.*

Practice

1 Supply the word for *if* (**ako, ako/kad, da**) in each of the
following sentences:

    a _____ smo bili u Hvaru, bilo bi nam previše vruće.

    b _____ dođeš k meni, vidjet ćeš ga.

    c _____ si došao k meni, vidio bi ga.

    d _____ pada kiša, išli bismo u kino.

    e _____ bi padala kiša, išli bismo u kino.

    f _____ imate moj novac, ostavite ga na stolu za mene.

    g _____ je vidiš, reci joj da ću sutra biti kod kuće.

    h _____ je znao kamo je otišla, rekao bi mi.

    i _____ je vrijeme lijepo, išli bismo rivom.

    j _____ biste htjeli ići u kazalište, dao bih vam moju kartu.

2 You are on holiday with a friend. Leave him/her a note and
say the following:

    I woke up early this morning.

    I decided to go to the beach before breakfast.

    If I return at 9 o'clock we can go to breakfast together.

    If I do not return at nine, do not wait for me.

    Go to breakfast. I shall buy something at the beach.

    I shall see you at 10 o'clock in our room.

3 Complete the following sentences with the most appropriate
verb of motion from the box. Each verb is given in its correct
form.

    a Autobusi su _____ most.

    b Kamo_____?

    c Jasna je _____ iz sobe.

    d Jću _____, čim budem mogla.

    e Sunce _____ na Zapadu.

    f Mi _____ kuću gdje sam rođen.

> zalazi   izašla   prolazimo   idete   doći   prešli

4 Complete these sentences with the most appropriate prepositions. Pay attention not only to the sense of the sentence but also to the case ending of the noun that comes after the preposition:

 a Neki ljudi vole gledati _____ prozor.
 b Satima smo stajali _____ trgu.
 c Rudolf, idite _____ kruh.
 d Ja sam _____ Engleske.
 e Sutra idemo _____ Korčulu.
 f Gosti su sjedjeli _____ stolom.
 g Dolazimo _____ obale.
 h Rudolf je _____ kuće.

5 Replace the words in brackets with their correct case forms:

 a (tko) pišete pismo?
 b (što) je Rudolf zadovoljan?
 c (nitko) nisam vidio.
 d (što) se sjećaš?
 e Nisam se sjećao (ništa).
 f Na (tko) se ljutiš?
 g (tko) je hladno?
 h Jesi li dao moj novac (netko)?

6 Match the question on the left to the correct answer on the right:

 a Da li vam je hladno?   **i** Ne znam, nema je kod kuće.
 b Hoće li padati kiša danas? **ii** Početkom rujna.
 c Gdje je Jasna?   **iii** Nije, hvala.
 d Kad idete kući?   **iv** Možda.

Comprehension 1

These are weather forecasts covering different regions of Croatia:

VRIJEME

Danas: toplo

Središnja Hrvatska
Ujutro slab mraz i kratkotrajna magla. Danju sunčano sa slabim vjetrom. Jutarnja temperatura od –3 do 2, a dnevna od 11 do 15C.

Slavonija i Baranja
Ujutro mraz i magla. Danju sunčano i toplo. Jutarnja temperatura od –2 do 5, a dnevna od 12 do 16C.

Gorski kotar i Lika
Ujutro magla, a danju sunčano. Vjetar slab. Jutarnja temperatura od –3 do 2, a dnevna od 10 do 15C.

Istra i Hrvatsko primorje
Ujutro u obalnom području sumaglica, a danju vedro ili malo oblačno. Vjetar slab. Jutarnja temperatura od 3 do 7, a dnevna od 11 do 16C.

Dalmacija
Sunčano. Vjetar slab. Jutarnja temperatura od 3 do 10, a dnevna od 12 to 16C.

slab *weak, light*
mraz *frost*
kratkotrajan *short-lived*
magla *fog*
jutarnji *morning* (adj.)

obalan *coastal*
područje *region*
sumaglica *mist*
oblačno *cloudy*

True or false?

a U Središnjoj Hrvatskoj vrijeme je danju sunčano.
b Nema sumaglice u Istri.
c Slab vjetar puše u Dalmaciji.

CROATIA

- ○ Sunce
- ◐ Promjenljivo
- ● Oblačno
- ◉ Pljuskovi
- ◍ Magla
- ↗ Moguća kiša
- ☂ Kiša

ZAGREB
RIJEKA
SL.BROD
OSIJEK
PULA
ZADAR
ŠIBENIK
SPLIT
DUBROVNIK

Comprehension 2

◀) CD2, TR 6, 03:10

Read or listen to the passage and answer the questions that follow:

Margaret Turner je turistkinja iz Engleske. One je na odmoru u hotelu na Korčuli. Jednog dana, poslije doručka, nije mogla naći svoju tašku. Pitala je konobara da li je vidio njenu tašku. Rekao je da nije. Izašla je iz restorana i prišla recepciji.

Margaret	Molim vas, gdje je policijska postaja?
Recepcija	Zašto, gospođo? Što vam se desilo?
Margaret	Netko mi je ukrao tašku.
Recepcija	Što ste imali u taški?
Margaret	Imala sam novčanik, putovnicu i putničke čekove.
Recepcija	A koje je boje vaša taška?
Margaret	Crvena.
Recepcija	Netko ju je predao recepciji. Evo je. Ne trebate policajca. Mislim da ćete naći sve svoje stvari u njoj.

turist (masc.) **turistkinja** (fem.) *tourist*
taška (**u taški** – **k** does not change to **c** here) *handbag*
policijska postaja *police station*
krasti, ukrasti (kradem, ukradem; krao, ukrao: followed by dat.
  meaning *from me*) *to steal*
novčanik *wallet, purse*
putovnica *passport*
putnički čekovi *traveller's cheques*
A koje je boje ...? *And what colour is ...?*
policajac *policeman*

1 Što je gospođa Turner izgubila?
   a Izgubila je tašku.
   b Izgubila je doručak.
   c Izgubila je ključ od sobe.

2 Koga je gospođa Turner pitala?
   a Pitala je policajca.
   b Pitala je konobara.
   c Pitala je konobaricu.

3 Gjde je našla svoju tašku?
   a U restoranu.
   b U policijskoj postaji.
   c Na recepciji.

Test yourself

Here you can check some of the things you have learnt in this unit.
Look at the questions that follow and choose the right answer:

1 Choose the correct word to complete the sentence: ... **smo**
   kupili karte, mogli bismo ići u kazalište večeras:
   a Ako
   b Da
   c Što

2 Choose the correct word to complete the sentence: ... **bude lijepo vrijeme, ići ćemo na odmor:**
   a Ako
   b Da
   c Što

3 Choose the correct word to complete the sentence: ... **je bilo lijepo vrijeme, išli bismo na odmor:**
   a Ako
   b Da
   c Što

4 Rudolf says that he would like to stay longer but has to go to Zagreb. Complete his sentence: **Ostao ... još, ali moram ići u Zagreb:**
   a bi
   b bismo
   c bih

5 Rudolf wants to say that he and Jasna would not go to England for a holiday this year. Complete his sentence: ... **išli u Englesku na odmor ove godine:**
   a Ne bih
   b Ne bismo
   c Ne biste

6 Choose the correct verb to complete this sentence: ... **svaki dan u sedam sati:**
   a Ustajem
   b Ustanem

7 Choose the correct verb to complete this sentence: ... **sam pismo mami i poslao sam ga:**
   a Pisao
   b Napisao

8 Jasna could not see anybody. Complete her sentence: **Nisam vidjela...**:

   a ko

   b koga

   c nikoga

9 Jasna asks from whom Rudolf has received a letter. Complete her question: **Od ... si dobio pismo?**

   a ko

   b koga

   c nikoga

10 Jasna went to fetch the wine. How would you complete the following: **Jasna je otišla po ...?**

   a vino

   b vinu

   c venom

15

Kako se osjećate?
How do you feel?

In this unit you will learn how to
- *Refer to health and parts of the body and call a doctor*
- *Express degrees of forbidding*
- *Form comparative and superlative adjectives such as* good, better, best

Dialogue

Jednog jutra Sandra i Mark su se probudili u svojoj hotelskoj sobi u Zagrebu. Vrijeme je postajalo hladnije i kiša je sve više padala. Mark se nije osjećao dobro.

♦ CD2, TR 7

Sandra	Kako se osjećaš? Ne izgledaš dobro.
Mark	To je istina. Uopće se ne osjećam dobro. Boli me glava. Nisam dobro spavao.
Sandra	Zašto?
Mark	Zato što nisam mogao spavati od kašlja.
Sandra	Ništa nisam čula.
Mark	Otišao sam u kupaonicu. Nisam se vratio dok nisam prestao kašljati. Nisam te htio probuditi.
Sandra	Ne brini se. To nije ništa opasno. Samo si prehlađen. To će proći.
Mark	Lako je tebi govoriti. Ne smijem biti u krevetu. Znaš da uskoro s Rudolfom putujem u Osijek.

hotelska soba *hotel room*
postajati, postati (postajem, postanem) *to become*
sve više *all the more*
osjećati se, osjetiti se (dobro) *to feel* (well)
izgledati (dobro) *to look* (well)
istina *truth*
uopće ne ... *not at all ...*
boli me glava (boljeti) *I have a headache.* (lit. *the head hurts me*)
kašalj *cough, coughing*
čuti (čujem) *to hear*
dok ne ... *until ...*
prestati (prestanem) *to stop*
kašljati (kašljem) *to cough*
brinuti se (brinem se) *to worry*
opasan *dangerous*
biti prehlađen *to have a cold*
To će proći. *It will pass.*
Ne smijem. *I must not.*
uskoro *soon*
kola za hitnu pomoć *ambulance*
Ne moraš ... *You do not have to ...*
bolnica *hospital*
ambulanta *clinic*
liječnik *doctor*
što prije *as soon as possible*

Kasnije netko kuca na vrata. Sandra ih otvara.

Liječnik	Dobar dan. Jeste li vi gospođa Bryant?
Sandra	Jesam. Izvolite, uđite. Moj muž je bolestan.
Liječnik	Dobar dan, gospodine. Kako se osjećate?

(Contd)

Mark	Osjećam se vrlo loše, doktore. Mnogo kašljem, slab sam, a i grlo me počinje boljeti.
Liječnik	Da vidim. Imate temperaturu. Molim vas, otvorite usta. Imate i infekciju. Ukratko, prehlađeni ste, gospodine. Nije ništa opasno. Vi mlađi ljudi brže ozdravljate nego stariji ljudi. Uskoro ćete se osjećati bolje.
Mark	Najteže mi je ležati u krevetu. Moram se sutra vratiti na posao.
Liječnik	*(Sandri)* Gospođo, neka vaš muž ostane u krevetu najmanje tri dana. Dat ću vam najjači lijek protiv te infekcije. Posao će ga čekati.

QUICK VOCAB

kasnije *later*
kucati na vrata *to knock at the door*
bolestan *ill*
loš *bad*
slab *weak*
grlo *throat*
da vidim ... *let me see ...*
imati temperaturu *to have a temperature*
usta (neut. plural) *mouth*
infekcija *infection*
ukratko *in short, briefly*
mlađi *younger*
brže *quicker, more quickly*
ozdravljati, ozdraviti *to recover, get better*
nego *than*
stariji *older*
bolje *better*
najteže mi je *most difficult for me is*
neka ... ostane *let* (him) *... stay*
najmanje *least, at least*
najjači *strongest*
lijek *medicine*
protiv (with gen.) *against*

True or false?

a Mark se nije osjećao dobro.
b Sandra je rekla da Mark mora ići u bolnicu.
c Liječnik je dao lijek protiv infekcije.

Insight

In the event of illness, any large hotel will be able to provide quick and easy access to a doctor. You may need to visit a doctor's surgery (**ordinacija**), a clinic (**klinika**) or a hospital (**bolnica**). When talking *about* doctors, the word **liječnik** is used, but when talking *to* them the word **doktor** is commonly used. You may need to find a dentist (**zubar**) too. Although, you will hopefully not need any of this information.

When visiting a doctor you may need to point out where the problem is. It may concern your hair (**kosa**), face (**lice**), eye (**oko**), ear (**uho**), nose (**nos**), lip (**usna**), chin (**brada**), neck (**vrat**), shoulder (**rame**), arm or hand (**ruka**), finger (**prst**), stomach (**stomak**), back (**leđa**) (neut. plural word like **vrata**), leg or foot (**noga**) or knee (**koljeno**).

Key phrases

◀) CD2, TR 7, 02:23

How to:

▶ ask how people feel, say how you feel	Kako se osjećate? Osjećam se dobro. Ne osjećam se dobro.
▶ remark on how people look	Ne izgledate dobro. Dobro izgledate.
▶ comment on someone's health	Boli me glava. Grlo me počinje boljeti. Kašljati.

		Moj muž je bolestan.
		Ti si prehlađen.
▶	understand comments from	Imate temperaturu.
	a doctor	Imate infekciju.
		Dat ću vam lijek protiv ...
		Uskoro ćete ozdraviti.
		Uskoro ćete se bolje osjećati.
▶	express degrees of restriction	ne možeš
		ne moraš
		ne smiješ
▶	use phrases connected with	što prije
	comparative forms	sve više

How it works

Comparative forms

There is one basic way to form the comparative of an adjective, i.e. the difference between *old* (**star**) and *older* (**stariji**). There are also three subcategories that are a variation on this basic form and some adjectives that do not follow this pattern at all. Most comparative adjectives end in soft consonants and take the appropriate adjective endings.

Basic form
To form the comparative of an adjective add -iji to the adjective:

star	*old*	**star + iji**	**stariji**	*older*
slab	*weak*	**slab + iji**	**slabiji**	*weaker*
sretan	*happy*	**sretan + iji**	**sretniji**	*happier*
tužan	*sad*	**tužan + iji**	**tužniji**	*sadder*

Subcategories
  i With these adjectives, you add -ji to the adjective. However, in the process of doing this the final consonant at the end of the adjective changes (d–đ, g–ž, h–š, k–č, s–š, t–ć, z–ž):

mlad	young	mlad + ji	mlađi	younger
blag	gentle	blag + ji	blaži	gentler
tih	quiet	tih + ji	tiši	quieter
jak	strong	jak + ji	jači	stronger
ljut	angry	ljut + ji	ljući	angrier

(ljut and ljući also mean *spicy hot* referring to food.)

ii With adjectives that end in -ak, -ek or -ok remove these letters and then proceed in a way similar to that in i:

težak	difficult	tež + ji	teži	more difficult
dalek	far	dal + ji	dalji	further
visok	tall	vis + ji	viši	taller

iii Some adjectives that end with -b, -p, -m, -v add -lji:

skup	expensive	skuplji	more expensive
kriv	wrong	krivlji	more wrong

Irregular comparatives

dobar	good	bolji	better
loš	bad	gori	worse
mali	small	manji	smaller
lak	easy	lakši	easier
lijep	beautiful	ljepši	more beautiful
velik	large	veći	larger

Superlative form

To form the superlative (i.e. *best, tallest*, etc.), add **naj-** to the beginning of the comparative adjective:

najstariji	oldest
najmlađi	youngest
najteži	most difficult (also heaviest)
najskuplji	most expensive
najbolji	best

More and less

The words for *more* and *less* of something are followed by the genitive case:

više *more*   **manje** *less*

Rudolf je kupio mnogo knjiga, ali je Mark kupio više.	*Rudolf bought many books, but Mark bought more.*

These words can also be used to mean *more* or *less* with *ordinary* adjectives. In fact, **više** has to be used to form the comparative of adjectives that end in **-ski**:

više prijateljski *more friendly*   **manje prijateljski** *less friendly*

Comparative of adverbs

The comparative and superlative form of adverbs is, as for ordinary adjectives, the neuter singular form:

Jasna lijepo pjeva, ali Sandra pjeva još ljepše.	*Jasna sings beautifully, but Sandra sings even more beautifully.*

Similarly:

Meni je teško, ali znam da je tebi teže.	*It is difficult for me, but I know that it is more difficult for you.*

To say *than*

There are two ways of saying *than*.

a Use **nego** with the same case endings before and after:

Njemu je teže nego tebi.	*It is more difficult for him than for you.*
Moja sestra je starija nego ja.	*My sister is older than me.*
Hladnije je u Londonu nego u Zagrebu.	*It is colder in London than in Zagreb.*

b Use the preposition **od** followed by the genitive case:

Moja sestra je starija od mene.	*My sister is older than me.*
Ta knjiga je skuplja od ove.	*That book is more expensive than this one.*

To say *as … as possible*

The phrase **što prije** means *as soon as possible*. Other similar phrases are formed by putting **što** in front of the comparative form of the adjective or adverb:

što teže	*as difficult as possible*
što lakše	*as easily as possible*

Other command forms

You have learnt how to tell someone to do something. There are other forms relating to other people.

To say *let him come* or *let them come*, use **neka** with the appropriate part of the verb:

Neka liječnik dođe što prije.	*Let the doctor come as soon as possible.*

To say *let me see* or *let us see*, use **da** with the appropriate part of the verb:

Da vidim vašeg muža.	*Let me see your husband.*

To say *… hurts*

The word **boljeti** is used in a way that is slightly different from the English expression:

Boli me grlo.	*My throat hurts* (aches).
Bole me leđa.	*My back hurts* (aches).

You are literally saying that *the throat hurts me*. The word **leđa** is one of those words like **kola**, i.e. it is a neuter plural word, so it has to be used with the plural form of the verb **bole**.

To say *until*

The word **dok** means *while*. When it is used with a negative verb it means *until*:

... dok nisam prestao kašljati   *... until I stopped coughing*

Subcategories of adjectives

There is another small group of adjectives like **bolestan** (*sick, ill*) that end in **-tan** and lose both the **-t-** and the **-a-** when they change case ending:

Mark je bolestan.	*Mark is ill.*
Sandra je bolesna.	*Sandra is ill.*

Subcategories of nouns

A number of words that refer to parts of the body do not follow the standard patterns:

a   uho/oko

The plural forms are feminine and follow a similar pattern:

nom.	**uši** *ears*	**oči** *eyes*
acc.	**uši**	**oči**
gen.	**ušiju**	**očiju**
dat.	**ušima**	**očima**
ins.	**ušima**	**očima**

b   ruka (fem.)/**noga** (fem.)/**prst** (masc.)

These words follow the normal patterns except in the genitive plural.

These forms are:

ruka	ruku
noga	nogu
prst	prstiju

The word **ruka** means both *hand* and *arm*.
The word **noga** means both *foot* and *leg*.
The word **prst** means both *finger* (**prst na ruci**) and *toe* (**prst na nozi**).

c rame

This word follows the same pattern as **vrijeme**:

nom.	**rame**
acc.	**rame**
gen.	**ramena**

It adds -en before the case endings.

Bole me ramena.   *My shoulders hurt (ache).*

d usta/leđa

These words are always in the plural and follow the pattern for neuter nouns:

Njegova usta su crvena.   *His mouth is red.*
Gledam njena leđa.   *I am watching her back.*

Insight

The English verb *to ask* can mean either *to ask a question (for information)* or *to request (someone to do something)*.
In Croatian, these meanings are expressed by two different verbs: **pitati** and **moliti**:

Pitala je da li imaju liječnika.   *She asked if they had a doctor.*
Zamolila je da liječnik dođe   *She asked that the doctor*
što prije.   *come as soon as possible.*

Practice

1 Fill in the missing parts of the dialogue:
Bolesnik je kod liječnika. Vi ste bolesnik.

♦ CD2, TR 7, 03:21

Liječnik	Kako se osjećate, gospodine?
Bolesnik	*I do not feel well.*
Liječnik	Da li vas nešto boli?
Bolesnik	*I have a headache./My head hurts.*
Liječnik	Kad vas je počela boljeti glava?
Bolesnik	*It began to ache/hurt yesterday.*
Liječnik	Moram priznati da ne izgledate dobro, gospodine. Da li vas još nešto boli?
Bolesnik	*I had a stomachache last week, but that has passed.*
Liječnik	Dat ću vam lijek. Ostanite kod kuće dok ne ozdravite.

2 Name the parts of the body indicated in the illustration:

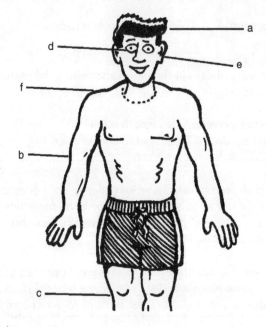

3 Change the adjectives in the sentences that follow into the required comparative forms with the correct case endings. They are given in brackets in the masculine nominative form:

   a Sandra je (star) od Jasne.
   b On je visok, ali je njegov brat (visok).
   c Jučer je rekao (mlad) sestri da danas neće doći na večeru.
   d Tko je (dobar), Mark ili Rudolf?
   e Moj kaput je (skup) od vašeg.
   f Bili smo zadovoljni (blag) klimom na Hvaru.
   g Da li si vidio (veseo) čovjeka?
   h Sjetila se njihove (velik) kuće u Varaždinu.

4 Give the superlative forms of the adjectives in brackets in Exercise 3.

5 Change the adverbs in brackets in the sentences that follow into the correct comparative form:

   a Jasna (lijepo) pjeva nego Sandra.
   b (Toplo) je na Hvaru nego u Zagrebu.
   c Zimi je (hladno) u Rusiji nego u Engleskoj.
   d Meni je (lako) ići na odmor nego tebi.

6 Match the question on the left to the correct answer on the right:

   a Moram li ja ići na   **i** Još nije.
      kolodvor s tobom?

   b Je li Rudolf pročitao   **ii** Ne mogu dok ne završim
      tu knjigu?   ovaj posao.

   c Kako je danas   **iii** Ne moraš.
      izgledala Jasna?

   d Ideš li u kino večeras?   **iv** Loše je izgledala.

Comprehension 1

Informacije o hotelu

▶ Molimo da svoj odlazak prijavite recepciji do 12 sati i da napustite sobu do 14 sati, jer zadržavanje sobe poslije 14 sati uvjetuje plaćanje za još jedan dan.

▶ Ako odlazite iz hotela molimo Vas da sobu zaključate i ključ predate na recepciji.

▶ Za Vaš auto stoje Vam na raspolaganju naše parkiralište i garaža uz minimalnu naplatu.

▶ Prema Vašoj želji peremo, glačamo i kemijski čistimo Vaše rublje u najkraće vrijeme.

▶ Prema Vašoj želji uslužujemo jela i pića u sobi uz naplatu servisa od 20%.

QUICK VOCAB

moliti *to ask, beg*
prijaviti *to announce*
napustiti *to leave*
zadržavanje *keeping*
uvjetovati *to cause, bring about*
plaćanje *payment*
Vas/Vaš (these words usually spelt with a capital letter when meaning one person)
zaključati *to lock*
predati *to hand over*
na raspolaganju *at* (your) *disposal*
parkiralište *car park*
garaža *garage*
uz minimalnu naplatu *for a minimal fee*
prema Vašoj želji *in accordance with your wishes*
prati (perem) *to wash*
glačati *to iron*
kemijski čistiti *to dry-clean*
rublje *laundry*
najkraće *shortest*
usluživati *to serve*
piće *drink*

True or false?

a Morate prijaviti svoj odlazak recepciji do 14 sati.
b Parkiralište i garaža za auto ne koštaju mnogo.
c Ne možete dobiti jela i pića u hotelskoj sobi.

Comprehension 2

Read the following passage and answer the questions that follow.

Kod liječnika

Rudolf se nije osjećao dobro. Imao je poslovni sastanak u gradu, ali je prije njega otišao k liječniku.

Liječnik	Dobar dan, gospodine Šimuniću. Kako ste?
Rudolf	Kad sam se jutros probudio, nisam se dobro osjećao. Ne znam što mi je. Sve me boli. Osjećam se sve gore kako dan prolazi.
Liječnik	Da li ste popili aspirin?
Rudolf	Nisam. Nisam znao što da radim. Rekao bih da sam inače zdrav čovjek.
Liječnik	U pravu ste, gospodine, jeste zdrav čovjek. Ali se možete razboljeti kao i svi drugi ljudi. Da pogledam vaše oči … i sada da pogledam u usta … Da, ja bih rekao da ste uhvatili neku infekciju. Dat ću vam antibiotik. Morate se odmarati. Uskoro će proći.

poslovni sastanak *business meeting*
popiti aspirin *to take an aspirin*
Nisam znao što da radim. *I didn't know what to do.*
inače *otherwise*
razboljeti se *to fall ill*
kao i *like, as well as*
uhvatiti infekciju *to catch an infection*
antiobiotik *antibiotic*
odmarati se *to rest*

1 Kada je Rudolf išao k liječniku?
  a Prije poslovnog sastanka.
  b Poslije poslovnog sastanka.
  c Odmah poslije posla.

2 Što Rudolfa boli?
  a Bole ga oči.
  b Boli ga glava.
  c Sve ga boli.

3 Što će liječnik dati Rudolfu?
  a Dat će mu aspirin.
  b Dat će mu antibiotik.
  c Dat će mu infekciju.

Test yourself

Here you can check some of the things you have learnt in this unit. Look at the questions that follow and choose the right answer:

1 What is the Croatian word for *eyes*?
  a prsti
  b uši
  c oći

2 What is the Croatian word for *arm*?
  a rame
  b ruka
  c noga

3 What does **usta** mean?
  a ear
  b lip
  c mouth

4 Complete the sentence to say that your back hurts: ... me leđa:

   a Boli

   b Bole

5 How would Rudolf say that he has a cold: ... sam?

   a Prehlađen

   b Prehlađena

   c Prehladeno

6 How would Jasna say that she does not feel well:
Ne osjećam se ... ?

   a dobar

   b dobra

   c dobro

7 How would you tell someone that they look better today: ...
izgledate danas?

   a Dobro

   b Bolje

   c Bolji

8 Complete the sentence to say that Jasna is tall but her sister is
taller: Jasna je visoka, ali je njena sestra ...:

   a visoka

   b više

   c viša

9 How would you say that Rudolf is the youngest in his family?

   a najstariji

   b najmlađi

   c najbolji

10 How would you advise someone that they have to study as
much as possible: Moraš ... studirati?

   a što prije

   b što više

   c što ljepše

16

Poslovni ugovor
Business contract

In this unit you will learn how to
- *Use words and expressions for a business meeting*
- *Form complex sentences joined in the middle by* which

Dialogue

Mark i Rudolf su putovali u Osijek na poslovne pregovore s gospodinom Markovićem. On je generalni direktor jedne osiječke firme. U vlaku, čitajući najnovije podatke o Markovićevoj firmi, Mark je slušao i sve što mu je Rudolf pričao o njoj. Pročitavši te podatke, Mark je počeo ispitivati Rudolfa detaljnije. Konačno su stigli u Osijek i odmah krenuli na sastanak. Ušli su u Markovićev ured.

Marković	Dobar dan, gospodo, dobro došli. želite li kavu?
Rudolf	Ja bih? A ti, Mark?
Mark	I ja bih isto, molim vas.

Čekaju kavu govoreći o svakodnevnim stvarima. Kava stiže, a poslovni pregovori počinju.

pregovor (usually used in plural) *negotiation*
generalni direktor *general manager*

246

osiječki (adj.) *Osijek, of Osijek*
čitajući *reading*
podatak (usually used in plural) *information*
pročitavši *having read*
ispitivati, ispitati (ispitujem, ispitam) *to question*
detaljnije *in more detail*
konačno *at last*
kretati, krenuti (krećem, krenem) *to set off*
gospoda *gentlemen*
govoreći *speaking, talking*
svakodnevni *everyday*

Marković	Ovdje, u našoj firmi, smatramo da možemo prodati vaše proizvode na našem tržištu.
Mark	Zašto?
Marković	Zato što sve zavisi od marketinga i znanja trendova koji se mijenjaju iz dana u dan. Imamo transportni odjel s kamionima, imamo svoje prodavaonice, imamo i svoj reklamni odjel.
Mark	Vidim da imate razvijenu infrastrukturu. Tražite li pravo na uvoz, ili proizvođenje pod licencijom?
Marković	Tražimo isključivo pravo na uvoz. To je naš kratkoročni plan za sljedeću godinu dana. Poslije toga, razmotrit ćemo situaciju, i ako budemo imali uspjeha, otvorit ćemo pregovore ponovo.
Mark	Jeste li razmišljali kako ćete platiti za robu?
Marković	Platit ćemo transferom preko banke.
Mark	Poslat ću faks u London o našem razgovoru.
Marković	Mogu vam reći da su svi naši uvjeti napisani u ovom pismu. Možete ga poslati u London.

smatrati *to consider*
tržište *market*
proizvod *product*
Zavisi od ... (followed by gen.) *It depends on ...*
marketing *marketing*

znanje *knowledge*
trend *trend*
koji *which*
mijenjati se, promijeniti se *to change*
proizvođenje pod licencijom *production under licence*
isključiv *exclusive*
kratkoročni plan *short-term plan*
za sljedeću godinu dana *for the next year*
razmatrati, razmotriti *to examine, discuss*
uspjeh *success*
otvarati, otvoriti *to open*
iz dana u dan *from day to day*
transportni odjel *transport department*
kamion *lorry*
reklamni odjel *advertising department*
razvijen *developed*
infrastruktura *infrastructure*
pravo na uvoz *right to import*
ponovo *again*
razmišljati, razmisliti *to think about, consider*
roba (sing. noun) *goods*
transfer preko banke *bank transfer*
slati, poslati (šaljem, pošaljem) *to send*
faks *fax*
uvjet *condition*
napisan *written*

True or false?

a Gospodin Marković hoće prodati proizvode Markove firme.
b Gospodin Marković nema kamiona.
c Gospodin Marković će platiti za robu transferom preko banke.

Insight

One of the first things you will be offered when visiting, either socially or on business, is coffee. The basic type of coffee is **turska kava** *Turkish coffee*. Coffee made in this way is strong and served in small cups. It is also becoming increasingly popular to drink espresso coffee and instant coffee.

Insight

For many years after the Second World War the state of Yugoslavia had a communist government and an economy in which there was little room for private enterprise. Following Croatian independence industry has largely been privatized and modern forms of information technology and commercial practice have been rapidly introduced.

Insight

Podatak means *a piece of information*. It is usually found in the plural **podaci**. If you want to find the information counter in a hotel or public building look for the sign **Informacije**.

Key phrases

◀) **CD2, TR 8, 02:05**

How to:

▶ use words and expressions
  connected with business and
  commerce

poslovni pregovori
proizvod
tržište
marketing
proizvođenje pod licencijom
kratkoročni plan
roba
transfer preko banke
faks

How it works

How to say *which*

The word **koji** has two uses. It is used to join together two parts of a sentence and to ask questions.

a Joining together:

Sve zavisi od marketinga i od znanja trendova. Oni se mijenjaju iz dana u dan.	*Everything depends on marketing and on knowledge of trends. They change from day to day.*

We can join these two sentences together:

Sve zavisi od marketinga i od znanja trendova koji se mijenjaju iz dana u dan.	*Everything depends on marketing and on knowledge of trends which change from day to day.*

The word **koji** is the equivalent of English *which* or *who*. It is an adjective and its ending depends on to what it refers from the first part of the sentence and how it is used in the second part of the sentence. In the example, **koji** refers to **trendovi** *trends* and therefore it has to have a plural masculine ending. It is then used as the subject of the second part of the sentence and so has to be in the nominative case. It follows the same pattern of case endings as **moj**, so it has both **kojem/kojeg** and **kome/koga** forms. The long forms are used when referring to objects, short forms when referring to people.

Briefly, **koji** takes either singular or plural and masculine, feminine or neuter endings depending on to what it refers; while its case depends on how it is used. Look at the following example:

To je čovjek koga sam jučer vidio.	*That is the man whom I saw yesterday.*

In this example, **koga** refers to **čovjek** and so is masculine singular.
It is used as the object of the verb **vidio** and so it is accusative
(i.e. it is the thing that is seen and not the person who sees):

To je pismo u kojem su napisani uvjeti.	*That is the letter in which the conditions are written.*
To je čovjek kome sam dao novac.	*That is the person to whom I gave the money.*

(**Kojem** is used as the word refers to an object and **kome** is used
because the word refers to a person.)

The word for *which* after **to** *that* and **sve** *everything* is **što**:

Mark je slušao sve što je Rudolf govorio.	*Mark listened to everything which Rudolf was saying.*

b Making questions:

In questions, **koji** means *which*:

Koju knjigu želite?	*Which book do you want?*
Koji je vaš stan?	*Which is your flat?*
Koja žena je uzela ključ?	*Which woman took the key?*
Kojoj ženi ste dali ključ?	*To which woman did you give the key?*

It means *which one* from a larger number of possible options.

Reading, having read, written, etc.

These patterns of a verb are not often found in the spoken
language. They are examples of a formal or bookish style.
However, you may come across them in newspapers or documents.
They are easily formed.

a Čitajući *reading*:

This is formed by adding **-ći** to the **oni** form of the verb.

It is the equivalent of the part of the verb that ends in -ing in English. It often means *while doing*, *by doing* or *in doing* as in the following examples:

Slušajući radio, pisao je pismo.	*While listening to the radio he was writing a letter.*
Čitajući podatke, slušao je i sve što mu je Rudolf pričao.	*Reading the information he also listened to everything which Rudolf told him.*

It is used when referring to two actions performed by the same subject that occur at the same time. It is formed only from imperfective verbs.

b **Pročitavši** *having read*:

This is formed by replacing -o at the end of the masculine past tense with -vši:

Pročitavši novine, počeo sam spremati večeru.	*Having read the newspaper I began to prepare dinner.*
Došavši u hotel, Sandra je uzela ključ od sobe.	*Having arrived at the hotel Sandra took the key to the room.*

It is used when referring to two actions, the first being completed before the second takes place, performed by the same subject. It is formed only from perfective verbs.

c Napisan *written*:

This is the equivalent in English of saying *something is done*. They are adjectives and agree with the noun to which they refer like any other adjective:

Uvjeti su napisani u pismu.	*The conditions are written in the letter.*
Pismo je napisano.	*The letter is written.*
Pismo je bilo napisano.	*The letter was written.*

It is formed from the infinitive:

i Infinitives which end in -**ati** replace -**ti** with -**n**:
napisati   napisan
čitati   čitan

ii Most infinitives that end in -**iti** and -**eti** (-**jeti**) replace -**iti** and -**eti** (-**jeti**) with -**jen**, and as the ending begins with **j** this may cause a preceding consonant to change as with comparative adjectives that take the -**ji** ending (see Unit 15):
vidjeti   viđen

iii Infinitives that end in -**nuti** replace -**ti** with -**t**:
okrenuti   okrenut

Subcategories of nouns

The plural forms of these three nouns do not follow the usual pattern:

gospodin	**gospoda**	*gentlemen*
brat	**braća**	*brothers*
dijete	**djeca**	*children*

Although they refer to more than one gentleman, brother and child these words are feminine singular nouns and they follow the regular pattern for feminine singular nouns that end in -**a** (hence, **gospodo** is the vocative form of **gospoda**). Adjectives that describe them also follow the regular pattern of feminine singular endings, while verbs are plural. Study the following examples:

Djeca su visoka.	*The children are tall.*
Imaju visoku djecu.	*They have tall children.*
Gospoda su govorila engleski.	*The gentlemen were speaking English.*

In the last example, the verbal element from **biti** is plural, while the ending on **govorila** is feminine singular.

More about time

In the phrase **za sljedeću godinu dana** the word **dana** has no
meaning. It is often found after the words **tjedan** *week*, **mjesec**
month and **godina** *year* without adding anything extra to the sense
of the word.

More about cases

You have now reached a stage in Croatian when you can
understand and produce for yourself sentences and phrases that
are grammatically quite complicated. You have learnt all the
basic forms of the verbs, case endings for adjectives (including
comparative and superlative) and nouns. You have also learnt the
basic meanings of those cases that often do away with the need
for little words in English, such as *to*, *of*, *by*, etc. There is another
example of the use of the instrumental case in this Unit. Look at
these examples:

Gospodin Marković će platiti robu transferom preko banke.	*Mr Marković will pay for the goods by a transfer through the bank.*
Mark će poslati pismo gospodina Markovića faksom.	*Mark will send Mister Marković's letter by fax.*

In both sentences, the instrumental case is used to mean *by*. The
case refers to the *instrument* by which an action is performed.

Insight

A native speaker of Croatian may understand what you want
to say even if you use the incorrect case ending because the
context of your conversation makes only one meaning likely.
However, cases are one of the important foundations of the
language and getting them wrong can lead to mistakes and
misunderstanding. They are not always easy for an English
speaker, but perseverance will enable you to master them and
will help smooth communication with people. Indeed, using
cases properly will certainly impress your new Croatian friends.

Practice

1 Mark has to inform his office in London about his conversation with Mr Marković. Follow the guidelines that follow in order to write a brief letter about the event as if you were Mark. Do not try to use complicated language, split the ideas up into separate sentences. Your intention is to convey the basic points of information:

▶ *Say that you spoke with Mr Marković today.*

▶ *Say that he wants the exclusive right of import of our products from London.*

▶ *Say that you spoke about the conditions of the business contract with him.*

▶ *You are sending those conditions by fax.*

▶ *Say that you think the conditions are good. Mr Marković said that he would pay for the goods by bank transfer.*

2 Put the correct form of **koji** into the sentences that follow:

a To je ugovor (koji) sam jučer pročitao.

b Govorio sam s gospodinom Markovićem, (koji) je generalni direktor te firme.

c Moja sestra, (koji) živi u Engleskoj, radi u bolnici.

d Ovo je najbolja knjiga (koji) imam.

e Da li je to čovjek (koji) ste dali ključ od moje sobe?

f To je škola u (koji) radim.

3 Put the correct form of **koji** into the sentences that follow:

a (Koji) faks šaljete u London?

b Od (koji) konobara ste dobili čašu vode?

c U (koji) sobi je gospodin Bryant?

d (Koji) žena je ušla u poštu?

e O (koji) ugovoru govorite?

f (Koji) sportom se bavite?

4 Make the bold parts of the following sentences plural:

a **Dijete je bilo** kod kuće.

b **Čovjek je ušao** u hotel.

   c Vidjeli smo **gospodina** u uredu.
   d **Gost je sjedio** u našoj dnevnoj sobi.
   e Dobili su čašu vode.
   f Dobila je pismo od **mlađeg brata**.
   g **Kiosk** je ispred kolodvora.
   h Nema **lijepog parka** u tom gradu.
   i Nema **ga** kod kuće.
   j Vidjeli su **njenog muža** u kavani.

5 Match the question on the left to the correct answer on the right:

a Kamo šaljete faks?	**i** Vlakom.
b Kakvog čovjeka ste vidjeli tamo?	**ii** Jesu.
c Jesu li djeca bila u školi danas?	**iii** U London.
d Kako ćete putovati u Zagreb?	**iv** Visokoga.

Comprehension 1

Rudolf je napisao kratko pismo u kojem je rezervirao dvije sobe u jednom osiječkom hotelu.

> Štovani gospodine,
> Želio bih rezervirati u Vašem hotelu dvije jednokrevetne sobe za osmi listopad. Ostali bismo tu jednu noć.
> Srdačno Vas pozdravlja
> Rudolf Šimunić.

The letter has a formal and polite tone, indicated by using the formula **Štovani gospodine** *Respected sir* and the conditional forms of the verb. The end formula **Srdačno Vas pozdravlja Rudolf Šimunić** (lit. *Cordially greets you Rudolf Šimunić*) is also polite. You will learn more about letter writing in Unit 18. If they were to stay for four days in Osijek, Rudolf would have reserved the rooms **od osmog do dvanaestog listopada**.

True or false?

a Rudolf je rezervirao jednu sobu u Osijeku.
b Rudolf je rezervirao jednokrevetne sobe u Osijeku.
c Rudolf i Mark su ostali jednu noć u Osijeku.

Comprehension 2

🔊 **CD2, TR 8, 02:32**

Read or listen to the passage and answer the following questions:

Odmah poslije sastanka Mark je napisao kratku poruku koju je htio poslati faksom svom šefu u London. Kao svi veći hoteli u Zagrebu i Hrvatskoj, i njihov hotel ima faks.

Štovani gospodine,
Danas sam razgovarao sa gospodinom Markovićem. Razgovor je bio vrlo koristan. Šaljem Vam njegovo pismo zajedno sa ovim pismom. Preporučujem da pažljivo proučite njegove uvjete za ugovor. Mislim da možemo s njim surađivati. Naš kolega iz Zagreba, gospodin Šimunić, smatra da u Osijeku nećemo dobiti bolju ponudu.
Srdačno Vas pozdravlja
Mark Bryant

šef *boss*   **proučiti** *to study*
koristan *useful*   **surađivati** *to cooperate*
pažljivo *carefully* **ponuda** *offer*

QV

1 Odakle Mark šalje svoj faks?
    a Iz ureda gospodina Markovića.
    b Iz njihovog osječkog hotela.
    c Sa glavne pošte.

2 Što preporučuje Mark svom šefu?

   a Da pažljivo prouči Markovićeve uvjete?

   b Da pažljivo pročita njegovu poruku.

   c Da dođe u Zagreb.

3 Što smatra Rudolf?

   a Da neće dobiti ništa više od gospodina Markovića.

   b Da neće dobiti bolju ponudu u Osijeku.

   c Da je bolje da i Markov šef dođe u Osijek.

Test yourself

Here you can check some of the things you have learnt in this unit. Look at the questions that follow and choose the right answer:

1 What is the Croatian word for *product*?

   a tržište

   b proizvod

   c uspjeh

2 What does the word **roba** mean?

   a goods

   b thief

   c robot

3 What might you do in a **kamion**?

   a fly across the desert

   b deliver goods by road

   c sail down the river

4 Put the correct form of **koji** into the sentence: **Mark je čitao knjigu ... je jučer kupio:**

   a koja

   b koji

   c koju

5 Put the correct form of **koji** into the sentence: **Jasna je čekala Sandru ... je već bila u gradu:**
   a koja
   b koga
   c koju

6 Put the correct form of **koji** into the sentence: **Mark je vidio gospodina s ... je razgovarao:**
   a koji
   b koja
   c kojim

7 Put the correct form of **koji** into the sentence: **Pregovori o ... je Mark pisao svojoj firmi bili su teški:**
   a kojima
   b koji
   c kojih

8 Jasna has bought some wine. How does Rudolf ask her which wine she has bought: **... vino si kupila?**
   a Koji
   b Koja
   c Koje

9 Sandra is telling Jasna about a book she has been reading. How does Jasna ask which book she is talking about: **O ... knjizi govoriš, Sandra?**
   a kojem
   b kojoj
   c koja

10 You want to say that the children are in the garden. Supply the missing verb **biti** in the past tense in this sentence: **Djeca ... u vrtu:**
   a su bila
   b je bila
   c su bili

17

U Osijeku
In Osijek

In this unit you will learn how to
- *Say more numbers*
- *Ask questions with* whose?
- *Use reflexive verbs*
- *Talk about changing money*
- *Make general enquiries at hotel reception (Units 17 and 18 also include general revision exercises)*

Dialogue

Poslije sastanka Rudolf i Mark su izašli na ulicu. Mark je morao promijeniti novac. Zaustavli su se ispred banke i ušli. Mark je čekao u redu. U banci je bilo četvoro ljudi.

Mark	Kako danas stoji kurs?
Službenik	Za koju valutu?
Mark	Za engleske funte.
Službenik	Danas je funta četrnaest kuna.
Mark	Želim promijeniti sto funti. Da li primate putničke čekove?
Službenik	Primamo, gospodine. Potpišite ovdje i ovdje i dajte mi, molim vas, putovnicu.

zaustavljati se, zaustaviti se *to stop*
banka *bank*
četvoro ljudi *four people*
Kako danas stoji kurs? *What is the exchange rate today?*
službenik *desk clerk, counter clerk*
valuta *currency*
funta *pound*
primati, primiti *to receive, to accept*
putnički ček *traveller's cheque*
potpisivati, potpisati (potpisujem, potpišem) *to sign*
putovnica *passport*

Poslije banke nastavili su put do hotela. Rudolf je prišao recepciji.
Na recepciji su radila dvojica.

Rudolf	Dobra večer. Rezervirao sam dvije jednokrevetne sobe.
Recepcija	Dobra večer. Na čije ime, gospodine?
Rudolf	Na ime Šimunić.
Recepcija	Samo trenutak, gospodine, da vas nađem u knjizi ... Da, tu ste. Rezervirali ste dvije sobe za jednu noć.
Rudolf	Točno.
Recepcija	Dat ću vam ključeve od soba, koje se nalaze na petom katu.
Rudolf	Naš vlak za Zagreb polazi rano ujutro. Želio bih sada platiti račun.
Recepcija	Naravno, gospodine. Kako želite platiti? U gotovom novcu ili na karticu?
Rudolf	Koje kartice primate?
Recepcija	Primamo American Express, Visa karticu i Mastercard.
Rudolf	Platit ću na karticu. A htio bih naručiti i telefonsko buđenje u šest sati i naručiti taksi za kolodvor.
Recepcija	U redu. U koliko sati trebate taksi?
Rudolf	Od koliko sati se služi doručak?
Recepcija	Od šest do devet sati u restoranu.
Rudolf	Onda, naručite, molim vas, taksi za petnaest do sedam.

nastavljati, nastaviti *to continue*
dvojica *two* (men)

Na čije ime? *In whose name?*
samo trenutak *just a moment*
nalaziti, naći (nalazim, nađem; nalazio, našao) *to find*
točno *exactly, right*
kat *floor, storey*
polaziti, poći (polazim, pođem; polazio, pošao) *to set off*
želio bih platiti račun. *I would like to pay the bill.*
gotov novac *cash*
na karticu *by credit card*
telefonsko buđenje *alarm call* (telephone)
naručivati, naručiti (naručujem, naručim) *to order*
služiti se, poslužiti se *to be served*

True or false?

a Mark želi promijeniti novac u hotelu.
b Primaju putničke čekove u banci.
c Rudolf će platiti račun na karticu.

Insight

Money can be changed in a bank, bureau de change (**mjenjačnica**) and in the larger hotels. Hotels often charge a higher fee for changing money than do the banks. Hotels and larger shops also accept major credit cards.

Key phrases

◀) CD2, TR 9, 02:03

How to:

▶ find somewhere to change money   u banci
   u mjenjačnici
▶ ask for the rate of exchange and in the currency   Kako danas stoji kurs?
   za engleske funte
▶ ask in whose name a booking is and to reply   Na čije ime?
   Na ime ...

▶ pay the bill	**Želio bih platiti.**
▶ be asked how you want to pay	**Kako želite platiti?**
▶ pay the bill ... cash	**u gotovom novcu?**
... credit card	**na karticu?**
▶ order an alarm call	**naručiti telefonsko buđenje**
▶ book a taxi	**naručiti taksi**
▶ ask when breakfast is served	**Od koliko sati se služi doručak?**

How it works

More about numbers

In addition to the ones you have already learnt, there are two further sets of numbers. The first one refers to groups of children or to groups in which there are both men and women. The second refers to groups of men.

a Children/mixed groups

These are as follows:

dvoje	2	**petoro**	5
troje	3	**šestoro**	6
četvoro	4	**sedmoro**	7

Higher numbers follow the same pattern, i.e. they add **-oro** to the number. However, they are not so frequently used when referring to groups of more than ten. They are usually used alone (**dvoje** means *two children* or more often *a man and a woman*), or in combinations with the genitive case:

Vidio sam dvoje djece.   *I saw two children.*
Petoro ljudi je došlo.   *Five people came.* (adults with children perhaps)

When you use these numbers as a subject the verb is singular with the neuter gender in the past tense.

b Groups of men

These are as follows:

dvojica	2	petorica	5
trojica	3	šestorica	6
četvorica	4	sedmorica	7

Higher numbers follow the same pattern, i.e. they add -orica to the number. However, they are rarely used when referring to groups of more than ten. They are usually used alone (**dvojica** can only mean *two men*) or in combinations with the genitive case:

Imam dvojicu braće.	*I have two brothers.*
Njih trojica su došla.	*The three of them came.*

These are feminine nouns and they follow the regular pattern of case endings for feminine nouns. When you use these numbers as a subject the verb is plural with the feminine singular ending in the past tense (like **djeca,** etc).

It is often possible to avoid using these numbers. You can say **dva djeteta** or **dva brata,** but the other forms with **dvoje** and **dvojica** are in common usage.

> **Insight**
>
> It is useful to remember that when someone tells you that they 'saw two people' and used the word **dvoje**, this would refer to a man and a woman. If they use the word **dvojica**, it means that they saw two men. There are no special forms to mean a group of women. Compare these statements:
>
> | | |
> |---|---|
> | **Vidio sam dvoje ljudi u parku.** | *I saw a couple in the park.* |
> | **Dvojica su ušla u kavanu.** | *Two men came into the café.* |
> | **Dve žene rade u uredu.** | *Two women are working in the office.* |
>
> The same rules apply to higher numbers.

Numbers as the subject

Subjects with **jedan**:

Jedan stol je u sobi.   *One table is in the room.*
Jedan stol je stajao u sobi.   *One table was standing in the room.*
Jedna stolica je stajala u sobi. *One chair was standing in the room.*

With **jedan**, you use a singular verb and the gender of the past
tense is determined logically. The same also goes for compound
numbers with **jedan**:

Trideset jedno dijete je stajalo   *Thirty-one children were standing*
  na ulici.   *on the street.*

(compound numbers are those above 20; numbers 11–20 are not
compound, they are one word, e.g. **jedanaest**)

Subjects with **dva/dvije**:

Dva službenika su radila   *Two desk clerks were working*
  u hotelu.   *in the hotel.*
Dvije žene su plivale u moru. *Two women were swimming in the sea.*

With **dva** and **dvije**, you use a plural verb and with the past tense,
use -a with **dva** (masc. and neut. nouns) and -e with **dvije** (fem.
nouns). The numbers **tri** and **četiri** follow the same pattern.
The same also goes for compound numbers:

Dvadeset četiri konobara su   *Twenty-four waiters worked in the*
  radila u hotelskom restoranu. *hotel restaurant.*

Subjects with **pet, šest**, etc.:

Pet kreveta je stajalo u sobi. *Five beds stood in the room.*
Dvanaest sati je prošlo.   *Twelve hours passed.*

With all other numbers, you use a singular verb and the gender of
the past tense is neuter. The same also goes for compound numbers:

Četrdeset osam sati je prošlo. *Forty-eight hours passed.*

To say *whose*

The word for *whose* is **čiji**. It is an adjective and follows the usual pattern for soft adjectives. It always adds endings to **čij-**:

Na čije ime?	*In whose name?*
Čija je to žena?	*Whose wife is that?*
U čijem stanu sjedimo?	*In whose flat are we sitting?*
Ispred čije kuće ste parkirali auto?	*In front of whose house did you park the car?*

More about reflexive verbs

Some verbs can be used either with or without the reflexive pronoun **se**. Compare the following sentences:

Zaustavili su se ispred banke.	*They stopped in front of the bank.*
Zaustavili su auto.	*They stopped the car.*
Školski dan se završava u četiri.	*The school day finishes at four.*
Rudolf je završio posao.	*Rudolf finished the job.*

The first sentence in each example uses **se**. The second sentence does not use **se** and it answers the question *what* (*What did they stop?* and *What did Rudolf finish?*). When you have an object in such sentences, you do not use **se**. Other examples are:

On se mijenja.	*He is changing.* (e.g. in personality)
Mark mijenja novac.	*Mark is changing money.*
Vratili smo se sa Hvara.	*We returned from Hvar.*
Vratili smo ključ recepciji.	*We returned the key to reception.*

Practice

1 Tko ste vi?

Ja sam Mark Bryant. Ja sam Englez. Radim u Zagrebu. Imam trideset sedam godina. Oženjen sam.

Make up similar sentences for:

	Name	Nationality	City	Age	Married
a	Jasna	Croatian	Zagreb	23	no
b	Vjeko	Croatian	Split	48	yes
c	Margaret	English	Leeds	31	yes
d	Eva	German	Berlin	34	no

◄» CD2, TR 9, 03:08

2 You are at the spot marked X. You ask a female passer-by:
Molim vas, gospođo kako mogu doći do ...
   a kazališta?
   b pošte?
   c crkve?
   d glavnog trga?

Give the directions in Croatian.

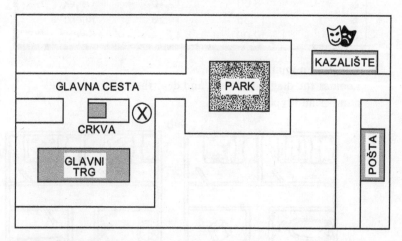

◄» CD2, TR 9, 04:23

3 You walk into a restaurant and sit down for dinner. Complete
the following dialogue between yourself and the waiter:
   Dobra večer.
   Good evening. Do you have the menu, please?

Da, izvolite, gospođo. Što biste željeli?
I would like soup, fish and salad.
Želite li nešto popiti, gospođo?
What would you recommend?
Imamo vrlo dobro bijelo vino.
Then, I would like the white wine, please.
A želite li nešto poslije?
May I have a coffee, please?
Naravno. Hvala.

4 You are looking at the railway timetable in Zagreb. At what
times do the following trains leave and at what times do they
arrive at their destinations?

U koliko sati polazi vlak?
Vlak polazi u _____ iz Zagreba, i stiže u _____ u Osijek.

Zagreb			
a	8.00	12.10	Osijek
b	11.35	14.20	Rijeka
c	12.00	17.55	Split

5 Kakav stan imate?
Look at the diagrams below and describe in Croatian the
number and types of room:

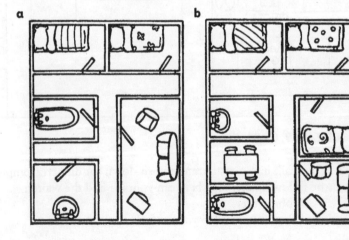

6 Fill in the date either in the nominative or the genitive as required:
  a Igram tenis s Markom u srijedu   (*24 March*)
  b Idem u Split početkom sljedećeg   (*1 June*)
     mjeseca
  c Danas je   (*3 August*)
  d Rudolf misli da će doći u London   (*18 November*)

Comprehension 1

Here is a recipe for the **zagrebački odrezak** that the friends ordered when they went to a restaurant in Unit 5.

> 6 velikih tankih telećih odrezaka
> sol i papar po ukusu
> 6 malih ploški kuhane šunke
> 6 malih ploški sira
> brašno
> jaje stučeno s malo mlijeka
> mrvice
> 3 velike žlice ulja
> 3 velike žlice maslaca

Stavite sol i papar na teleće odreske.
Stavite na polovicu odreska plošku šunke i na nju plošku sira.
Stavite jednu polovicu odreska na drugu.
Dobro pritisnite krajeve mesa.
Stavite odreske prvo u brašno, zatim u jaje i na kraju u mrvice.
Dobro zagrijte maslac i ulje i pržite odreske na umjerenoj vatri dok ne budu svijetlosmeđi s obje strane.
Odreske poslužite s miješanom salatom, kriškama limuna i pireom od krumpira.

tanak *thin*
teleći *veal* (adj.)
sol (fem.) *salt*

papar *pepper*
po ukusu *according to taste*
ploška kuhane šunke *slice of cooked ham*
ploška sira *slice of cheese*
brašno *flour*
jaje stučeno s malo mlijeka *egg beaten with a little milk*
mrvice *breadcrumbs*
ulje *oil*
maslac *butter*
polovica *half*
pritisnuti *to pinch* (together)
kraj *edge, end*
zatim *then, next*
na kraju *in the end, finally*
zagrijati *to heat, warm up*
pržiti *to fry*
na umjerenoj vatri *on a medium heat*
svijetlosmeđi *light brown*
s obje strane *on both sides*
miješana salata *mixed salad*
kriška limuna *wedge of lemon*
pire od krumpira *mashed potato*

Now check your comprehension of the recipe with the translation
that follows.

> *6 large thin veal cutlets*
> *salt and pepper according to taste*
> *6 small slices of cooked ham*
> *6 small slices of cheese*
> *flour*
> *egg beaten with a little milk*
> *breadcrumbs*
> *3 large spoons of oil*
> *3 large spoons of butter*

> *Put salt and pepper on the veal cutlets.*
> *Put a slice of ham on one half of the cutlet and a slice of*
> *cheese on top of that.*

Put one half of the cutlet over the other half.
Pinch the edges of the meat firmly together.
Put the cutlets first into flour, then into the egg, and at the end into the bread crumbs.
Heat the butter and oil and fry the cutlets on a medium heat until light brown on both sides.
Serve the cutlets with a mixed salad, wedges of lemon and mashed potato.

Comprehension 2

Read the following **mali oglasi** *small advertisements* and answer the questions that follow:

IZDAJEM trosoban komforan stan u centru Zagreba. Centralno grijanje, telefon. Plaćanje po dogovoru. Šifra 'Stan 1'.

IZDAJEM dvokrevetne sobe u vili na Braču. Blizu plaže i svih turističkih objekata. Posebni ulazi. Javite se na tel. 223 456 (Split).

IZDAJEM apartman u Dubrovniku. Dvije spavaće sobe, kupaonica i kuhinja. Balkon ima pogled na more. Tel. 155 677.

PRODAJEM poslovnu prostoriju u zgradi u centru Zagreba. Prodavaonica u prizemlju i ured na prvom katu. Šifra 'Posao'.

TRAŽIMO trosoban stan u centru Zagreba sa centralnim grijanjem i telefonom. Šifra 'Englezi'.

---

trosoban *three roomed*
komforan *comfortable*
grijanje *heating*
po dogovoru *by agreement*
šifra *box number*
vila *villa*
objekt *facility*

QUICK VOCAB

poseban ulaz *separate entry*
prostorija *space*
prizemlje *ground floor*

True or false?

a Stan u Zagrebu ima centralno grijanje.
b Nema posebnih ulaza u sobe na Braču.
c Netko u Zagrebu prodaje prodavaonicu u prizemlju.

Test yourself

Here you can check some of the things you have learnt in this unit.
Look at the questions that follow and choose the right answer:

1 What is a **putovnica**?
   a vehicle
   b passport
   c golf club

2 You are changing £50 into Croatian kunas. Which form of the
Croatian word for *pound* comes after **pedeset**?
   a funta
   b funte
   c funti

3 When would you use the word **sedmoro**?
   a when talking about a group of men and women
   b when talking about a group of women
   c when talking about a group of men

4 In which of the following circumstances would it be
appropriate to use the word **trojica**?
   a when talking about three children
   b when talking about three sisters
   c when talking about three brothers

5 How would you say that you want to pay a bill by credit card: **Platit ću ...?**
  a u kunama
  b na karticu
  c u gotovom novcu

6 Match the question on the left with the correct answer on the right:

  a Koliko imate braće?   **i** Moja.
  b Čija je ta kava?   **ii** Troje.
  c U koliko sati si završio ručak?   **iii** Vratio sam ga njoj.
  d Kome si vratio ključ?   **iv** Trojicu.
  e Koliko djece ima u vrtu?   **v** U tri.

18

Tri pisma
Three letters

In this unit you will learn more about
* *Writing letters and short messages for people both in a social and in a business context*

Štovani ...

Mark je dobio poslovno pismo od gospodina Markovića.

3. X. 2002.

Štovani gospodine Bryante,

Šaljem Vam kopiju pisma koje sam dobio iz Londona. Možemo sklopiti ugovor prema uvjetima koji su dogovoreni. Čestitam Vam na uspjehu u ovim našim pregovorima. Predložio bih Vam da još jednom dođete u Osijek na razgovor o mogućnosti uvoza i izvoza, a ja bih posjetio London poslije našeg sastanka.

Radujem se našoj budućoj suradnji.
Srdačno Vas pozdravlja

Marko Marković

QUICK VOCAB

kopija *copy*
sklopiti ugovor *sign a contract*
dogovoren *agreed*
čestitati (followed by dat.) *to congratulate* (someone)
predlagati, predložiti (predlažem, predložim) *to suggest*
izvoz *export*
posjećivati, posjetiti (posjećujem, posjetim) *to visit*
budući *future*
suradnja *cooperation*

Sandra je dobila kratko pismo od Jasne.

5. X. 2002.

Draga Sandra,

Morala sam ti odmah pisati. Ne možeš zamisliti što se sinoć
desilo! Rudolf me je zaprosio. Udat ću se za njega. Nije više
pitao da li bih ja htjela da se vjenčamo. Nestalo je to kolebanje.
Vodili smo ozbiljan razgovor o našim osjećajima i o praktičnim
stvarima. Previše sam uzbuđena da bih nastavila pisati. Javi se
što prije!

Voli te

Jasna

QUICK VOCAB

zamisliti *to imagine*
zaprositi *ask for a girl's hand in marriage*
nestajati, nestati (nestajem, nestanem) *to disappear*
kolebanje *hesitation*
voditi razgovor *to have a conversation*
praktičan *practical*
uzbuđen *excited*
nastavljati, nastaviti *to continue*

Sandra piše pismo mami i tati.

10. X. 2002.

Dragi mama i tata,

Ispričavam se što dugo nisam pisala. Otkad smo se vratili s
odmora život je postao burniji. Rudolf i Jasna će se vjenčati.
Još se ne zna kada će to biti, ali mislim da ćemo imati svadbu
tokom ove zime!

Druga stvar je još važnija. Mark je ovdje počeo otvarati tržište
za svoju londonsku firmu. Njegovi šefovi su, očito, jako
zadovoljni njime. Ponudili su mu da ostane u Zagrebu, i da
postane glavni predstavnik u cijelom ovom kraju Europe!
Naravno, mi smo dugo razgovarali o ponudi, i došli smo do
zaključka da bismo ovdje mogli lijepo živjeti. Odgovara nam
grad, našli smo prijatelje a nismo daleko od Londona (samo dva
sata avionom!). Mark je ovih dana imao mnogo posla u gradu,
dok sam ja tražila stan. Pravi stan!

Pored toga, pisala sam svojoj školi da dajem ostavku. Jasna
i moje prijateljice su me ohrabrile da ću naći posao kao
nastavnica engleskog jezika. Pravo da vam kažem, već sam
dobila posao u jednoj privatnoj školi za strane jezike.

Dolazimo u London za Božić. Pričat ćemo i tada o našem
boravku u Zagrebu i u drugim mjestima, ne samo u prošlosti
nego i u budućnosti.

Vole vas

Sandra i Mark

ispričavati se, ispričati se to apologize
otkad from when, since
buran stormy
Još se ne zna. It is still not known.
svadba wedding
tokom ove zime during this winter
važan important
očito evidently, obviously

nuditi, ponuditi *to offer*
doći do zaključka *to come to the conclusion*
odgovarati (with dat.) *to suit, correspond*
pravi *real*
ostavka *resignation*
ohrabrivati, ohrabriti (ohrabrujem, ohrabrim) *to encourage, cheer up*
nastavnica *teacher*
pravo da vam kažem *to tell you the truth*
privatna škola *private school*
strani jezik *foreign language*
Božić *Christmas*
tada *then*
ne samo ... nego i ... *not only ... but also ...*

True or false?

a Gospodin Marković je pozvao Marka u Osijek.
b Rudolf i Jasna će se vjenčati.
c Sandra je tražila stan za sebe i za Marka.

Key phrases

◀》 CD2, TR 10

Idiomatic and other phrases:

▶ sign a contract	sklopiti ugovor
▶ congratulations on your success	čestitam vam na uspjehu
▶ to have a conversation	voditi razgovor
▶ it is not yet known	još se ne zna
▶ to come to a conclusion	doći do zaključka
▶ to hand in one's resignation	dati ostavku
▶ to tell you the truth	pravo da vam kažem
▶ not only ... but also ...	ne samo ... nego i ...

How it works

Writing letters

There are a variety of formal and informal conventions used in writing letters.

a Formal

Beginning with:

Štovani gospodine ...	*Dear sir/Dear Mr ...*
Štovana gospođo ...	*Dear madam/Dear Mrs ...*

As you are addressing someone directly the vocative case is used. An alternative beginning is:

Štovani kolega
Štovana kolegice

The tone here is not quite so formal. The words **kolega** (masc. although ending in **-a**) and **kolegica** mean *colleague* but are more frequently used to refer to people with whom you work.

Such letters may end with:

Srdačno Vas pozdravlja ...	*Yours sincerely ...*

b Informal

Beginning with:

Dragi ...	*Dear ... (to a man)*
Draga ...	*Dear ... (to a woman)*

An alternative beginning is:

Zdravo ...!	*Hi ...! (to a man or woman)*

But, in both instances, you again use the vocative case for the name of the person to whom you are writing.

Such letters may end with:

Voli te ...   *Love ...* (when signed by one person)
Vole te ...   *Love ...* (when signed by more than one person)

An alternative ending is the less intimate:

Tvoj   *Yours* (signed by a man)
Tvoja   *Yours* (signed by a woman)

Another thing to bear in mind when writing letters is that there is a convention to spell **Vi/Vas**, etc. with a capital letter when addressing one person.

How to say *from*

When saying from a place use **iz** and when saying from a person use **od**. When you would normally use **na** with a noun to mean *being there* or *going there*, then you use **s/sa** to mean *from there*. Look at the following examples:

Izašli smo iz sobe.	*We have come out of the room.*
Dobio je pismo iz Zagreba.	*He received a letter from Zagreb.*
Dobio je pismo od svog šefa.	*He received a letter from his boss.*
Idemo na odmor.	*We are going on holiday.*
Bili smo na odmoru.	*We were on holiday.*
Vratili smo se s odmora.	*We have returned from holiday.*

How to say *then*

You have learnt two words for *then*:

onda *then next*

Stigli smo u Split, onda smo kupili karte za brod.	*We arrived in Split, then we bought tickets for the boat.*

tada *at that time*

Išli smo na Hvar na odmor.	*We went to Hvar on holiday.*
Tada sam bio još dijete.	*I was still a child then.*

Ispričavam se što

You usually use the word **da** to mean *that* in sentences such as the following:

Rekao mi je da ...	*He told me that ...*
Mislio sam da ...	*I thought that ...*

However, in certain expressions, the word **što** is used. These are in sentences in which you are about to give a reason for something. Look at the following examples:

Ispričavam se što ...	*I am sorry that ...* (meaning *I apologize for not having done something* after which you can expect an explanation)
Sretan sam što ...	*I am happy that ...* (meaning *I am happy due to the following reasons*)

Practice

1 You are in the tourist office in Zagreb. You want to know how much a particular journey costs and how long it takes. Make up the questions and answers as indicated in the example.

Example:

autobus, Rijeka, 250 kuna, 6 hours

Koliko košta autobusna karta za Rijeku?
Dvjesta pedeset kuna.

Koliko dugo traje put autobusom do Rijeke?
Šest sati.
  a avion, Dubrovnik, 900 kuna, 45 minutes
  b vlak, Osijek, 380 kuna, 5 hours 10 minutes
  c autobus, Split, 235 kuna, 5 hours 30 minutes

2 Look at the weather forecasts for the following towns and
answer the questions that follow:

Zagreb: Ujutro kratkotrajna magla, kasnije sunčano.
Pula: Vjetar slab. Dnevna temperatura od 22°C do 25°C.
Zadar: Ujutro oblačno. Dnevna temperatura od 20°C do 22°C.
Šibenik: Ujutro moguća kiša. Po podne slab vjetar.
Split: Jutarnja temperatura od 14°C do 18°C. Dnevna od 25°C
do 29°C.
Hvar: Cijeli dan sunčano i slab vjetar.
Dubrovnik: Ujutro sumaglica. Danju sunčano.

  a U kojem gradu je moguća kiša?
  b Koji grad ima dnevnu temperaturu od 20°C do 22°C.
  c U kojem gradu je sunčano cijeli dan?
  d Koji grad ima kratkotrajnu maglu?

3 Answer the following questions:
  a Kako se kaže na hrvatskom 'I have a headache'?
  b Kako se kaže na hrvatskom 'I am going to the doctor's'?
  c Što znači riječ 'razglednica' na engleskom?
  d Što znači 'zubna pasta' na engleskom?

4 You want to reserve a room at a hotel. Write a short letter
stating that you want a double room from 14 to 20 July.

◀》 **CD2, TR 10, 00:48**

5 You arrive at your hotel and you have some enquiries to make
at reception. Fill in your part of the dialogue:

Good evening.
Dobra večer, gospodine.

I would like an alarm call at 7.15 in the morning, please.
U redu, gospodine. Odlazite li sutra?
Yes, I have to go to London as soon as possible. I have a business meeting there. I want to book a taxi for the airport, please.
U koliko sati trebate taksi?
At 8.00, please. Where is breakfast served?
U restoranu, gospodine.
And I shall pay the bill now.
U redu, gospodine. Nadam se da ste zadovoljni našim hotelom?
Very pleased, thank you.

6 What do you say to people when:
   a meeting them for the first time?
   b greeting them in the morning?
   c saying goodbye?
   d saying good night?

Comprehension

Sandra je poslala pismo roditeljima. Tjedan dana kasnije javili su joj se njeni roditelji iz Londona. Imali su samo jednu poruku za Sandru i Marka 'Čestitamo vam!'

Key to the exercises

Unit 1
Dialogue True (T), False (F) **a** T **b** T **c** F

Practice **1 a** prijateljica **b** dobra večer **c** oprostite **2 a** Ja sam Jasna.
Ja sam Hrvatica. Govorim hrvatski. **b** Ja sam Rudolf. Ja sam Hrvat.
Govorim hrvatski. **c** Ja sam Sandra. Ja sam Engleskinja. Govorim
engleski. **3 a** Ja sam Hans. Ja sam Nijemac. Govorite li njemački?
Da, govorim njemački. **b** Ja sam Pierre. Ja sam Francuz. Govorite
li francuski? Da, govorim francuski. **c** Ja sam Ivan. Ja sam Rus.
Govorite li ruski? Da, govorim ruski. **4 a** Govorite li engleski?
b Govorite li francuski? **c** Govorite li hrvatski? **d** Govorite li srpski?
5 a dobro jutro **b** dobar dan **c** dobra večer **d** do viđenja **6** Dobra
večer. Kako ste?/Drago mi je. Ja sam .../Laku noć. **7 a** Da vas
upoznam. Ovo je Mark. Mark je moj muž. **b** Da vas upoznam.
Ovo je Sandra. Sandra je moja žena.

Comprehension **a** F **b** T **c** T.

Test yourself **1c, 2a, 3b, 4a, 5b, 6a, 7c, 8a, 9b, 10a**

Unit 2
Dialogue **a** F **b** F **c** T.

Practice **1 a** Volim. Ne volim. **b** Govorim. Ne govorim. **c** Jesam.
Nisam. **d** Volim. Ne volim. **e** Želim. Ne želim. **f** Želim ići. Ne želim
ići. **g** Volim ići. Ne volim ići. **h** Idem. Ne idem. **2 a** Voliš li kavu?
b Govoriš li engleski? **c** Jesi li ti Englez? **d** Voliš li London? **e** Želiš
li živjeti u Londonu? **f** Želiš li ići u grad? **g** Voliš li ići na posao?
h Ideš li na kavu? **3 a** ja sam/učim **b** ti želiš/ideš **c** mi razumijemo/
učimo **d** vi ste/učite. **4 a** grad **b** kavanu **c** školu **d** Zagreb **e** posao
f kavu **g** gradu **h** Londonu **i** školi **j** poslu **k** kavani **l** predgrađu.
5 a želimo/Londonu **b** želim/Zagrebu **c** ideš/kavu **d** živim/gradu

e živimo/predgrađu **f** volite/poslu. **6 a** ii **b** iv **c** i **d** iii. **7 a** dobra
b žedna **c** naše **d** vaš **e** moja/dobra **f** tvoja **g** gladan.

Comprehension **a** T **b** F **c** F.

Test yourself **1c, 2a, 3c, 4b, 5a, 6 a** iv, **b** i, **c** v, **d** ii, **e** iii

Unit 3
Dialogue **a** F **b** T **c** T.

Practice **1 a** Ja moram/mogu **b** ti govoriš/razumiješ **c** on dolazi/
radi **d** mi vidimo/idemo **e** vi ste/govorite **f** oni idu/rade. **2 a** parku
b kavane **c** trgu **d** drveta **e** grad **f** poštu. **3 a** Jasnu **b** spomenik
c kavu/sok **d** vino **e** školu **f** gospodina. **4 a** njen **b** njegovo **c** njena
d njihov **e** njihovo **f** njihov. **5 a** On je na lijevo ispred koldvora.
Nije daleko od pošte. **b** Gdje mogu kupiti marke i koverte? Gdje je
pošta? **c** Kamo Rudolf ide? Gdje radi? **d** Da, gleda Sandru. Sandra
je blizu zgrade. **6 a** ona **b** on **c** oni **d** ona **e** one **f** ono **g** oni **h** on.

Comprehension **a** T **b** F **c** T. **1** a **2** c **3** b.

Test yourself **1a, 2a, 3b, 4c, 5c, 6b, 7c, 8b, 9a, 10b**

Unit 4
Dialogue **a** F **b** F **c** F.

Practice **1 a** dvije kune **b** četiri kune **c** dvanaest kuna (osamnaest
kuna) **2 b** Sandra hoće razglednicu. Koliko košta razglednica?
Razglednica košta četiri kune. **c** Mark hoće pivo. Koliko košta
pivo? Pivo košta petnaest kuna. **d** Jasna hoće šampon. Koliko košta
šampon? Šampon košta dvadeset kuna. **e** Zvonko hoće marku.
Koliko košta marka? Marka košta dvije kune. **f** Velimir hoće
marku za Englesku. Koliko košta marka za Englesku? Marka za
Englesku košta dvanaest kuna. **3 a** marke/razglednice **b** parkove/
spomenici **c** hoteli **d** ljudi **e** zgrade **f** koverte. **4** Dobar dan. Imate
li razglednice?/Mogu li vidjeti velike razglednice?/Koliko košta
jedna velika razglednica?/Dajte mi tri, molim vas./Hvala.

Do viđenja. **5 a** Mark daje kavu Rudolfu. **b** Čovjek daje marku Jasni. **c** Mi dajemo sapun mami. **d** Žena daje pivo Velimiru. **e** Oni daju novac čovjeku. **f** Konobar daje vino Branki. **6 a** ii **b** iv **c** i **d** iii. **7 a** mogu **b** govorite **c** žive **d** jeste **e** idu **f** volim.

Comprehension **a** T **b** T **c** F. **1** b **2** c **3** c.

Test yourself **1c, 2a, 3b, 4c, 5b, 6c, 7a, 8a, 9b, 10c**

Unit 5
Dialogue **a** T **b** F **c** F.

Practice **1 a** mu **b** nam **c** vam **d** joj **e** im **f** mi **g** ti **h** joj **i** mi **j** nam. **2 a** Jasni **b** konobarima **c** čovjeka **d** zgradu **e** kavu **f** prijateljima **g** stolom/Jasnom **h** konobare **i** cigarete/novine **j** jezike. **3** Konobaru! Dobar dan. Da li imate jelovnik?/Hvala/Što mi preporučujete?/ Više volim meso. Ja bih meso i salatu, molim vas./Više volim crno, i mogu li dobiti čašu vode? **4 a** iii **b** i **c** ii **d** iv. **5 a** Imate li jelovnik? **b** Imate li ribu i salatu? **c** Dva piva, molim vas. **d** Mogu li dobiti čašu vode? **6** Dubrovnik. **7 a** Volite li pivo? **b** Volite li pivo? **c** Kamo idete sutra? **d** Želite li piti bijelo vino? **e** Volite li ići u grad? **f** Mogu li dobiti čašu vode? **8 a** kruha **b** parkova **c** salate **d** čovjeka **e** prijatelja **f** vina **g** ljudi **h** Engleza **i** kave **j** razglednica.

Comprehension **a** F **b** F **c** F. **1** c **2** c **3** b.

Test yourself **1a, 2b, 3c, 4c, 5a, 6 a** ii, **b** iv, **c** v, **d** iii, **e** i

Unit 6
Dialogue **a** T **b** F **c** F.

Practice **1 a** pij **b** popijte **c** dođi **d** uzmite. **2 a** sići **b** piti **c** doći **d** dati. **3 a** Marka/Sandre **b** centru **c** centar **d** centru **e** trga **f** trgu **g** hotela/ restorana **h** večeru **i** kolodvora **j** drveta/parku/stanice. **4 a** Jasni/ salatu **b** autobusom **c** Londona **d** Konobaru **e** Marku. **5 a** Idite ravno i skrenite u drugu ulicu desno. **b** Idite do glavne ceste, skrenite lijevo onda skrenite u prvu ulicu lijevo. **c** Idite do glavne ceste, skrenite

desno onda skrenite u prvu ulicu desno. **d** Idite ravno i trg je na
lijevo. **6** Hoću vas pozvati k meni danas./Žao mi je. Možete li doći
sutra?/U osam sati./Uzmite autobus četrnaest ili tramvaj šest preko
puta parka i siđite na sedmoj stanici. Moj stan je u bloku preko puta
kazališta./Moja adresa je ... Moj telefonski broj je ... **7 a** Idemo k
njemu. **b** Konobar joj je daje. **c** Gledamo ih na ulici. **d** Idite do njega.
e Moram ih kupiti. **f** Oni im moraju pisati. **g** Rudolf stanuje blizu
njega. **h** Oni je piju.

Comprehension **a** F **b** F **c** T. **1** b **2** b **3** a.

Test yourself **1b, 2a, 3a, 4c, 5c, 6b, 7c, 8b, 9b, 10a**

Unit 7
Dialogue **a** F **b** T **c** F.

Practice **1 a** star **b** vruć **c** svježa **d** odlično **e** žedna **f** skupa
g bijelo **h** velika. **2 a** lijepom **b** velike **c** skupe **d** treću **e** starog
f velike **g** glavni **h** dobru/gradskoj. **3 a** Pierre je Francuz. Živi u
Francuskoj. Radi u uredu. **b** Vjekoslav je Hrvat. Živi u Hrvatskoj.
Radi u restoranu. **c** Branka je Srpkinja. Živi u Srbiji. Radi u hotelu.
d Maša je Ruskinja. Živi u Rusiji. Radi u školi. **4 a** Brankinom
b Markove **c** Sandrinu **d** Markov, **e** Rudolfov **f** Velimirovu. **5** Jeste
li oženjeni, Rudolf?/Je li Jasna udata? **6 a** ii **b** iv **c** iii **d** i. **7** dvadeset
dva, četrdeset sedam, šezdeset četiri, dvadeset devet, sedamnaest,
jedanaest, četrdeset tri, trideset osam, sedamdeset sedam, pedeset
osam, devedeset, šezdeset jedan.

Comprehension **a** F **b** T **c** T. **1** a **2** a **3** a.

Test yourself **1c, 2a, 3c, 4b, 5a, 6c, 7b, 8a, 9c, 10b**

Unit 8
Dialogue **a** T **b** F **c** F

Practice **1 a** glavne **b** njegovom **c** crno **d** velikih **e** tvoju **f** udobnim.
2 a poslije **b** do **c** na **d** kroz **e** kod **f** iz. **3 a** U dnevnoj sobi imam

tri naslonjača, jedan stolić i televizor u uglu. **b** U kuhinji imam
frižider, zamrzivač i ormare. **c** Imam tamo radni stol i dvije police
s knjigama. **d** Imam veliki stol i šest stolica za goste. **4 a** iv **b** i
c ii **d** iii. **5 a** u osam i trideset (u pola devet) **b** petnaest do četiri
c sedam i deset **d** deset do sedam **e** od devet sati do pet i petnaest.
6 a prije podne **b** večeras **c** noću **d** sutra.

Comprehension **a** T **b** T **c** T. **1** b **2** c **3** b.

Test yourself **1a, 2c, 3b, 4b, 5a, 6b, 7a, 8b, 9a, 10c**

Unit 9
Dialogue **a** T **b** F **c** F.

Practice **1 a** Sviđaju im se ove knjige. **b** Sviđa mi se nogomet. **c** Da
li vam se sviđa plivanje? (Sviđa li vam se plivanje?) **d** Rudolfu se
sviđa košarka. **e** Sandri i Jasni se sviđa badminton. **2 a** Čovjek mu
ih daje. **b** Da li joj žena daje novac? **c** Vidim ga blizu spomenika.
d Ljudi je piju u kavani. **e** Mark je gleda. **f** Pišemo joj. **g** Dajem
im ih. **h** Sjeća ga se u Londonu. **3** Da li vam se sviđa plivanje?/
Bavite li se sportom?/I ja volim igrati rukomet. Gdje je rukometno
igralište?/Da li imaju zatvoren bazen?/U koliko sati radi?/Kada vi
idete u sportski centar? **4 a** svaki dan **b** svake subote **c** u srijedu
d zimi **e** od svibnja do rujna **f** petkom **g** u proljeće **h** u nedjelju
i u ožujku, **j** u subotu.

Comprehension **a** F **b** T **c** T. **1** b **2** b **3** a.

Test yourself **1b, 2c, 3b, 4c, 5b, 6 a** ii, **b** iii, **c** v, **d** iv, **e** i

Unit 10
Dialogue **a** F **b** T **c** T.

Practice **1 a** njima **b** joj **c** nama **d** mnome **e** ih **f** njime **g** me **h** vama
i me **j** tobom. **2 a** Da li vam je teško? **b** Je li joj lako? (Da li joj
je lako?) **c** Da li im je jasno? **d** Je li vam jasno? **3 a** Da, teško mi
je. Ne, nije mi teško. **b** Da, jasno im je. Ne, nije im jasno. **c** Da,

jasno mu je. Ne, nije mu jasno. **d** Da, lako mi je. Ne, nije mi lako.
4 a kako **b** koliko **c** kakav **d** kamo **e** kada **f** tko **g** gdje **h** što.
5 a iii **b** ii **c** iv **d** i **6 a** po Rudolfovom mišljenju **b** po njenom
mišljenju **c** po mom mišljenju **d** po njihovom mišljenju.

Comprehension **a** T **b** T **c** T. **1** c **2** a **3** b.

Test yourself **1a, 2b, 3c, 4b, 5a, 6c, 7b, 8b, 9c, 10a**

Unit 11
Dialogue **a** T **b** F **c** T.

Practice **1 a** u putničku agenciju **b** avionske karte **c** povratne karte
d u deset i petnaest **e** osamsto kuna **f** karte za brod **g** dva tjedna
kasnije **h** te večeri **i** prije tri godine **j** Rudolfov kolega na poslu.
2 a Što ste pili svaki dan? **b** Što ste napisali? **c** Tko vam je dao
knjigu? **d** Jeste li bili na Hvaru? **e** Jeste li bili u Dubrovniku? **f** Gdje
su rezervirali karte? **g** Kad su otišli na odmor? **h** Kad ste bili u
Dubrovniku? **i** Koliko košta povratna karta za Split? **j** Je li Rudolf
radio u toj zgradi? **3 a** pisao **b** dao **c** uzeli **d** popio. **4 a** Nismo išli na
Hvar prije tri godine. **b** Konobar mi nije dao salatu. **c** Konobar mi je
nije dao. **d** Nisu kupili avionske karte u putničkoj agenciji. **e** Nisu ih
kupili u putničkoj agenciji. **f** Nisam se jučer vratila iz Dubrovnika.
g Nije čitao novine. **h** Nije ih čitao. **5** Dobar dan. Želim kupiti
avionsku kartu za Dubrovnik./U jednom smjeru, molim. Koliko
košta karta?/U koliko sati ide iz Zagreba avion ponedjeljkom?/
Želim kartu u ponedjeljak navečer, molim./Imam privatnu sobu u
Dubrovniku./Hvala. Do viđenja. **6 a** Koliko dugo traje put avionom
od Zagreba do Splita? Četrdeset minuta. **b** Koliko dugo traje put
autobusom od Zagreba do Rijeke? Šest sati. **c** Koliko dugo traje put
avionom od Zagreba do Londona? Dva sata. **d** Koliko dugo traje
put vlakom od Zagreba do Osijeka? Pet sati i dvadeset minuta.

Comprehension **a** F **b** T **c** T. **1** c **2** a **3** c.

Test yourself **1b, 2a, 3b, 4c, 5a, 6c, 7b, 8c, 9c, 10b**

Unit 12

Dialogue **a** T **b** T **c** F.

Practice **1 a** Ići ćemo u dobar restoran. **b** Javit ću joj se. **c** Naći ćemo stolicu u blagavaonici. **d** Tko će stići? **e** Što ćete raditi na odmoru? **f** Da li ćeš mu dati ključ? **g** Neće doći k nama. **h** Neću biti na Hvaru. **2** Rekao/Rekla je **a** da možemo kupiti novine tamo kod lifta. **b** da je zaboravio naše avionske karte. **c** da ćemo ih sutra dobiti. **d** da će nam sutra dati novac. **e** da prodaju razglednice, koverte i marke u hotelu. **f** da to nije naše pismo. **g** da će danas biti lijepo vrijeme. **h** da nisu izgubili ključ od naše sobe. **i** da nas je netko tražio u hotelu. **j** da ne zna odakle je bio. **3** Pitao/Pitala sam **a** da li je zaboravio gdje stanujemo. **b** da li će danas biti lijepo vrijeme. **c** da li je gospođa Bilčić kod kuće. **d** da li zna gdje mi je ključ. **e** da li će Rudolf doći u London. **f** da li je bio/bila u Engleskoj. **g** da li je bila u Engleskoj. **h** da li mogu dobiti čašu vode. **i** da li mogu doći sutra. **j** da li idemo **4 a** netko **b** ništa **c** negdje **d** nikad **e** nešto **f** nigdje. **5 a** iv **b** i **c** iii **d** ii. **6** Dobar dan. Je li gospodin Šimunić na poslu?/Molim vas, dajte mi njegov interni broj./Halo. Ja sam .../Zaboravio sam vašu adresu. Možete li mi reći gdje radite?/Mogu li danas doći k vama?/Hvala. Do viđenja.

Comprehension **a** T **b** F **c** T. **1** b **2** b **3** a.

Test yourself **1a, 2b, 3c, 4a, 5b, 6 a** ii, **b** iii, **c** iv, **d** i, **e** v

Unit 13

Dialogue **a** T **b** F **c** F.

Practice **1** petsto šezdeset sedam, dvjesta trideset devet, osamsto sedam, trista jedan, tisuća petsto, tri tisuće sedamsto devedeset. **2 a** četrnaesti ožujak **b** prvi lipanj **c** osmi kolovoz **d** trećeg rujna **e** dvadeset petog lipnja **f** dvadeset sedmog prosinca **g** tisuću devetsto osamdesete godine **h** tisuću devetsto šezdeset druge godine **i** dvadeset petog svibnja/tisuću devetsto sedamdeset prve godine **j** jedanaestog siječnja/tisuću devetsto trideset pete godine. **3 a** budućnosti **b** godinama **c** još **d** vremena **e** prošlosti **f** cijeli **g** čim. **4 a** hoćete **b** hoću **c** hoće **d** htjela. **5 a** tužno **b** veselo **c** iskreno **d** prijateljski. **6 a** iii **b** iv **c** i **d** ii. **7 a** Pije mi se čaj.

b Danas nam se ide u grad. **c** Kupa joj se. **d** Danas mi se ide na plažu. **8** Tužan/Tužna sam./Zato što mi se ne vraća kući./Imam namjeru da se vratim./Ne ljutim se na vas. Radujem se povratku. **9 a** sebe **b** sobom **c** sebe **d** sebi.

Comprehension **a** T **b** F **c** F. **1** c **2** a **3** b.

Test yourself **1a, 2c, 3c, 4b, 5b, 6c, 7a, 8b, 9c, 10a**

Unit 14
Dialogue **a** F **b** T **c** T.

Practice **1 a** Da **b** Ako **c** Da **d** Da **e** Ako/Kad **f** Ako **g** Ako **h** Da **i** Da **j** Ako/Kad. **2** Probudio sam se rano jutros./Odlučio sam otići na plažu prije doručka./Ako se vratim u devet sati, možemo ići zajedno na doručak./Ako se ne vratim u devet, nemoj me čekati./Idi na doručak. Kupit ću nešto na plaži./Vidjet ću te u deset sati u našoj sobi. **3 a** prešli **b** idete **c** izašla **d** doći **e** zalazi **f** prolazimo. **4 a** kroz **b** na **c** po **d** iz **e** na **f** za **g** s **h** kod. **5 a** kome **b** čime **c** nikoga **d** čega **e** ničega **f** koga **g** kome **h** nekome. **6 a** iii **b** iv **c** i **d** ii.

Comprehension **a** T **b** F **c** T. **1** a **2** b **3** c.

Test yourself **1b, 2a, 3b, 4c, 5b, 6a, 7b, 8c, 9b, 10a**

Unit 15
Dialogue **a** T **b** F **c** T.

Practice **1** Ne osjećam se dobro./Boli me glava./Jučer me je počela boljeti./Bolio me je stomak prošlog tjedna, ali je to prošlo./**2 a** glava **b** ruka **c** noga **d** oko **e** uho **f** rame. **3 a** starija **b** viši **c** mlađoj **d** bolji **e** skuplji **f** blažom **g** veselijeg **h** veće. **4** najstarija/najviši/najmlađoj/najbolji/najskuplji/najblažom/najveselijeg/najveće. **5 a** ljepše **b** toplije **c** hladnije **d** lakše. **6 a** iii **b** i **c** iv **d** ii.

Comprehension **a** F **b** T **c** F. **1** a **2** c **3** b.

Test yourself **1c, 2b, 3c, 4b, 5a, 6c, 7b, 8c, 9b, 10a**

Unit 16

Dialogue **a** T **b** F **c** T.

Practice **1** Danas sam razgovarao s gosodinom Markovićem./
Želi isključivo pravo na uvoz naših proizvoda iz Londona./Pričao
sam s njim o uvjetima poslovnog ugovora./Šaljem te uvjete ovim
faksom./Mislim da su uvjeti dobri./Gospodin Marković je rekao
da će platiti za robu transferom preko banke./ **2 a** koji **b** koji
c koja **d** koju **e** kome **f** kojoj. **3 a** koji **b** kog **c** kojoj **d** koja **e** kojem
f kojim. **4 a** deca su bila **b** ljudi su ušli **c** gospodu **d** gosti su sjedjeli
e čaše **f** mlađe braće **g** kiosci su **h** lijepih parkova **i** ih **j** njihove
muževe. **5 a** iii **b** iv **c** ii **d** i.

Comprehension **a** F **b** T **c** T. **1** b **2** a **3** b.

Test yourself **1b, 2a, 3b, 4c, 5a, 6c, 7a, 8c, 9b, 10a**

Unit 17

Dialogue **a** F **b** T **c** T.

Practice **1 a** Ja sam Jasna. Ja sam Hrvatica. Radim u Zagrebu.
Imam dvadeset tri godine. Nisam udata. **b** Ja sam Vjeko. Ja sam
Hrvat. Radim u Splitu. Imam četrdeset osam godina. Oženjen sam.
c Ja sam Margaret. Ja sam Engleskinja. Radim u Leedsu. Imam
trideset jednu godinu. Udata sam. **d** Ja sam Eva. Ja sam Njemica.
Radim u Berlinu. Imam trideset četiri godine. Nisam udata.
2 a Idite do glavne ceste, skrenite lijevo, idite kroz park, kazalište
se nalazi na lijevo. **b** Idite do glavne ceste, skrenite desno, idite kroz
park, skrenite desno kod kazališta, idite ravno i pošta se nalazi na
lijevo. **c** Idite do glavne ceste, skrenite lijevo, idite ravno i skrenite u
prvu ulicu desno **d** Idite ravno, ne prema glavnoj cesti, glavni trg se
nalazi na desno. **3** Dobra večer. Imate li jelovnik, molim vas?/Ja bih
juhu, ribu i salatu./Što biste preporučili?/Onda, ja bih bijelo vino,
molim./Mogu li dobiti kavu, molim vas? **4 a** Vlak polazi u osam
sati iz Zagreba, i stiže u dvanaest i deset u Osijek. **b** Vlak polazi
u dvadeset pet do dvanaest iz Zagreba, i stiže u dva i dvadeset po
podne na Rijeku. **c** Vlak polazi u dvanaest sati iz Zagreba, i stiže u
pet do šest po podne u Split. **5 a** dvije spavaće sobe, dnevna soba,

kupaonica i kuhinja. **b** tri spavaće sobe, blagovaonica, dnevna soba, kuhinja i kupaonica. **6 a** dvadeset četvrtog ožujka **b** prvog lipnja **c** treći kolovoz **d** osamnaestog studenog.

Comprehension **a** T **b** F **c** T.

Test yourself **1b, 2c, 3a, 4c, 5b, 6 a** iv, **b** i, **c** v, **d** iii, **e** ii

Unit 18
Dialogue **a** T **b** T **c** T.

Practice **1 a** Koliko košta avionska karta za Dubrovnik? Devetsto kuna. Koliko dugo traje put avionom do Dubrovnika? Četrdeset pet minuta. **b** Koliko košta vozna karta za Osijek? Trista osamdeset kuna. Koliko dugo traje put vlakom do Osijeka? Pet sati i deset minuta. **c** Koliko košta autobusna karta za Split? Dvjesta trideset pet kuna. Koliko dugo traje put autobusom do Splita? Pet sati i trideset minuta. **2 a** U Šibeniku **b** Zadar **c** U Hvaru **d** Zagreb. **3 a** Boli me glava. **b** Idem k liječniku. **c** postcard **d** toothpaste. **4** Štovani gospodine, Želio bih rezervirati u Vašem hotelu jednu dvokrevetnu sobu od četrnaestog do dvadesetog srpnja. Srdačno Vas pozdravlja… **5** Dobra večer./Želio/Željela bih telefonsko buđenje u sedam i petnaest ujutro, molim./Da, moram ići u London što prije. Imam tamo poslovni sastanak. Želim naručiti taksi za aerodrom, molim./U osam sati, molim vas. Gdje se služi doručak?/A ja ću sad platiti račun./Vrlo zadovoljan/zadovoljna, hvala. **6 a** drago mi je **b** dobro jutro **c** do viđenja **d** laku noć.

Summary of language patterns

General

In this section, you will find tables of the basic endings to nouns, adjectives and verbs that you have learnt in this course.

Remember that Croatian has some important spelling rules. Some consonants change when they occur before the vowel **i** in nouns. **k** changes to **c**, **g** changes to **z**, **h** changes to **s**. For example:

kiosk	**kiosci**
knjiga	**u knjizi**
orah *walnut*	**orasi** *walnuts*

There are some exceptions, such as personal names (e.g. **Branka** to **Branki**) and other isolated examples (e.g. **taška** to **u taški**).

Another spelling rule concerns consonants that occur before **j**. This is particularly important when forming the comparative of the adjectives (see Unit 15 for details).

Croatian is spelt as it is pronounced. This has the following consequences:

a it tends to avoid double consonants except in the superlative form of adjectives
e.g. jak, jači, najjači

b when two consonants come into contact in a word because of losing the separating vowel the spelling of the word alters to match the pronunciation
e.g. težak (masc.) teško (neut.).
Judge your spelling according to pronunciation.

Masculine and neuter nouns and adjectives are affected by soft consonants. They are c, č, ć, dž, đ, j, lj, nj, š and ž. The most important effect is the change of o to e after one of these consonants. Note that some neuter nouns ending in e do not necessarily follow one of these consonants. You will find examples of these in this section.

Be aware that in some books, and other printed material, the letter đ appears as dj.

Nouns

Masculine

	singular	plural	singular	plural
nom.	grad	gradovi	prijatelj	prijatelji
voc.	grade	gradovi	prijatelju	prijatelji
acc.	grad	gradove	prijatelja	prijatelje
gen.	grada	gradova	prijatelja	prijatelja
dat.	gradu	gradovima	prijatelju	prijateljima
ins.	gradom	gradovima	prijateljem	prijateljima

In the singular of masculine nouns, the accusative of inanimate objects is the same as the nominative, while the accusative of animate beings (human and animal) is the same as the genitive.

Sometimes there is a penultimate a that disappears when case endings are added. The a reappears in the genitive plural:

Nijemac (nom.)   **Nijemca** (gen. singular)   **Nijemaca** (gen. plural).

Similarly, in nouns which end in two or more consonants these letters are usually separated in the genitive plural by a, like the word for a *student*:

student (nom.)   **studenta** (gen. singular)   **studenata** (gen. plural).

Most masculine nouns of one syllable add **-ov-** before case endings (like **gradovi**) or **-ev-** after a soft consonant (like **muževi**).

Most masculine nouns end in a consonant. Some, however, end in o which converts to l when case endings are added:

posao (nom.) **posla** (gen. singular).

Some masculine nouns end in **a**. They follow the pattern of the feminine nouns that end in **a** but all adjectives and verbs agree with them as if they were masculine: **Ovo je moj tata.**

Feminine

	singular	plural	singular	plural
nom.	žena	žene	stvar	stvari
voc.	ženo	žene	stvar	stvari
acc.	ženu	žene	stvar	stvari
gen.	žene	žena	stvari	stvari
dat.	ženi	ženama	stvari	stvarima
ins.	ženom	ženama	stvari	stvarima

Feminine nouns that end in a consonant have an alternative instrumental singular form with **-ju** (e.g. **stvar** to **stvarju**).

In nouns that end in two or more consonants before **a**, these letters are usually separated in the genitive plural by **a** (e.g. **marka** to **maraka**). Some also take the alternative ending **-i** (e.g. **torba** (*bag*) to **torbi**):

Neuter

	singular	plural	singular	plural
nom.	selo	sela	more	mora
voc.	selo	sela	more	mora
acc.	selo	sela	more	mora
gen.	sela	sela	mora	mora
dat.	selu	selima	moru	morima
ins.	selom	selima	morem	morima

In nouns that end with two or more consonants before o or e, these letters are usually separated by a in the genitive plural (e.g. pismo to pisama).

Some neuter nouns add -en- and others -et before adding the case endings:

vrijeme (nom.)   vremena (gen. singular)
dijete (nom.)   djeteta (gen. singular).

Adjectives

Masculine

	singular	singular (adjective ending in soft consonant)
nom.	star/stari	vruć/vrući
voc.	stari	vrući
acc.	(as nom. or gen.)	(as nom. or gen.)
gen.	starog(a)	vrućeg(a)
dat.	starom(e) (u)	vrućem(u)
ins.	starim	vrućim

Feminine

	singular	singular (adjective ending in soft consonant)
nom.	stara	vruća
voc.	stara	vruća
acc.	staru	vruću
gen.	stare	vruće
dat.	staroj	vrućoj
ins.	starom	vrućom

	singular	**singular** (adjective ending in soft consonant)
nom.	staro	vruće
voc.	staro	vruće
acc.	staro	vruće
gen.	starog(a)	vrućeg(a)
dat.	starom(e) (u)	vrućem(u)
ins.	starim	vrućim

Plural

	Masc.	**Fem.**	**Neut.**
nom.	stari	stare	stara
voc.	stari	stare	stara
acc.	stare	stare	stara
gen.	starih	starih	starih
dat.	starim(a)	starim(a)	starim(a)
ins.	starim(a)	starim(a)	starim(a)

The additional vowels are usually added when the adjective is used without a noun.

In some adjectives, the penultimate **a** disappears when you add case endings. This sometimes has consequences for spelling:

bolestan (masc.)	**bolesna** (fem.)
dobar (masc.)	**dobra** (fem.)
kakav (masc.)	**kakva** (fem.)
težak (masc.)	**teška** (fem.)

Here is the pattern of changes for **koji**, which is similar to **moj**, **tvoj** and **svoj** in having a shorter form without -je- in the middle:

	singular			**plural**		
	Masc.	**Fem.**	**Neut.**	**Masc.**	**Fem.**	**Neut.**
nom.	koji	koja	koje	koji	koje	koja
acc.	nom/gen	koju	koje	koje	koje	koja
gen.	kog(a)	koje	kog(a)	kojih	kojih	kojih
	kojeg(a)		kojeg(a)			
dat.	kom(e)	kojoj	kom(e)	kojim(a)	kojim(a)	kojim(a)
	kojem(u)		kojem(u)			
ins.	kojim	kojom	kojim	kojim(a)	kojim(a)	kojim(a)

Personal pronouns

nom.	ja	ti	on	ona	ono
acc.	mene	tebe	njega	nju	njega
	me	te	ga	ju, je	ga
gen.	mene	tebe	njega	nje	njega
	me	te	ga	je	ga
dat.	meni	tebi	njemu	njoj	njemu
	mi	ti	mu	joj	mu
ins.	mnom(e)	tobom	njim(e)	njom(e)	njim(e)

nom.	mi	vi	oni	one	ona
acc.	nas	vas	njih	njih	njih
	nas	vas	ih	ih	ih
gen.	nas	vas	njih	njih	njih
	nas	vas	ih	ih	ih
dat.	nama	vama	njima	njima	njima
	nam	vam	im	im	im
ins.	nama	vama	njima	njima	njima

Verbs

There are three basic categories of verb, distinguished by the vowel that occurs before the ending:

▶ **a category**

ja	čitam	mi	čitamo
ti	čitaš	vi	čitate
on/a/o	čita	oni/e/a	čitaju

▶ **e category**

ja	idem	mi	idemo
ti	ideš	vi	idete
on/a/o	ide	oni/e/a	idu

▶ **i category**

ja	radim	mi	radimo
ti	radiš	vi	radite
on/a/o	radi	oni/e/a	rade

There is not always an obvious link between the infinitive and the present tense. However, if you know the **ja** form of the present tense, you will be able to make all the other forms as almost all verbs follow one of these patterns. Important exceptions are **biti** and **moći** (see Unit 3) and **htjeti** (see Unit 4).

For how to make commands, see Unit 6.

For how to form the past tense, see Unit 11.

For how to form the future tense, see Unit 12.

For how to form the conditional and use *if* see Unit 14.

Glossary of grammatical terms

Adjective An adjective is a word used to qualify or describe a noun or pronoun, e.g. *Rudolf is tall.* **Rudolf je visok.** *She is young.* **Ona je mlada.**

Adverb Adverbs are used to qualify or modify an adjective or a verb, e.g. *She is very young.* **Ona je veoma mlada.** *Jasna sings well.* **Jasna dobro pjeva.**

Agreement Agreement is when words that are used together have the same grammatical number, gender or case.

Case Cases in Croatian are indicated by changes made to nouns, adjectives and pronouns. Croatian is presented in this book with six cases: nominative, vocative, accusative, genitive, dative, instrumental. Cases tell you the function of a noun in a sentence.

Comparative When making comparisons we need the comparative form of the adjective. In English, this is usually done by adding -er to the adjective or by putting *more* in front. *This shirt is cheaper than that one.* **Ova košulja je jeftinija nego ona.** *This coat is more expensive.* **Ovaj kaput je skuplji.**

Conditional This is a form of the verb to show that an event might have happened or might yet take place.

Enclitics Croatian has two forms of the verb *to be*: **biti** and *to want* **htjeti** in the present tense and two forms for personal pronouns in cases other than the nominative (see **Case** and **Pronoun**). The shorter form of these alternatives is called the enclitic with rules for when and how they are to be used.

Gender In English, the term gender refers to whether human beings or animals are male or female. In Croatian, as in many European languages, all nouns have a gender that is masculine, feminine or neuter. Sometimes the grammatical gender of a noun may tell you if the word refers to a male or female being but it is not primarily a biological reference. The word *table* **stol** is masculine, while *chair* **stolica** is feminine, while *sea* **more** is neuter. Adjectives that are used to describe these words must agree with the gender of the noun and change accordingly. There are rules that help you to determine the gender of nouns and to change adjectives to agree with them.

Imperative The imperative is the form of the verb used to give directions, instructions, orders or commands.

Infinitive The infinitive is the basic form of the verb often used when two verbs are seen together, e.g. *She likes to live in London*. **Ona voli živjeti u Londonu**. In English, the infinitive is formed from two words (*to live*), while, in Croatian, it is one word (**živjeti**) that ends either in **-ti** or in **-ći**.

Noun Nouns are words that name things and people, e.g. *room* **soba**, *person* **čovjek**.

Number Number is the term used to indicate whether words are singular or plural.

Object The object of a verb indicates what or who is on the receiving end of an action, unlike the subject, which tells you who is performing the action (see **Subject**). There are two types of object. The direct object indicates on what or whom the action is performed, e.g. *Rudolf likes coffee*. **Rudolf voli kavu**. *Coffee* is the direct object in this sentence as it is the object being liked and here is expressed in the accusative case. The indirect object in a sentence indicates what or who is the beneficiary of an action, e.g. *He bought a book for his sister.* **Kupio je sestri knjigu.** *Sister* is the indirect object in this sentence as she is the beneficiary of the action, the one for whom the book has been bought and here is expressed in the dative dase. Indirect objects in English are usually preceded by *to* or *for*.

Person Person is the term that refers to the separate parts of a verb. Verbs have six persons, three in singular (I, you, he/she/it) and three in plural (we, you, they) and verb endings change to indicate which person is the subject.

Plural See **Singular**

Possessive adjective A possessive adjective such as *my* and *mine* indicates who possesses what in a sentence. *This is my coffee. That coffee is yours.* **Ovo je moja kava. Ta kava je vaša.**

Preposition A preposition is a word that generally show relationships between people or things, e.g. *Jasna is in the room.* **Jasna je u sobi.**

Pronoun A pronoun is often used as a substitute for a noun that has usually been mentioned once already. *This is my husband. He is standing in the square.* **Ovo je moj muž. On stoji na trgu.** Such pronouns as *I* **ja**, *he* **on** are called personal pronouns and are often omitted in Croatian because the ending of the verb indicates the person (see **Person**), e.g. *This is my husband. He is standing in the square.* **Ovo je moj muž. Stoji na trgu.**

Reflexive verb These are constructions in which the word **se**, meaning *oneself*, accompanies the verb.

Singular The terms singular and plural are used to contrast between one and more than one, e.g. *book/books* **knjiga/knjige.**

Subject The subject names the person or thing who is performing the action of the verb of a sentence, e.g. *Rudolf likes coffee.* **Rudolf voli kavu.** Rudolf is the subject as he is the one who likes coffee and is expressed here in the nominative case.

Superlative The superlative part of the adjective is formed in English by adding *-est* to the adjective or by using *most. This shirt is the cheapest of all.* **Ova košulja je najjeftinija od svih.** *This coat is the most expensive.* **Ovaj kaput je najskuplji.**

Tense Tense indicates the time at which the action of the verb in a sentence takes place.

Verb Verbs usually indicate the action of a sentence, e.g. *He is playing football.* **On igra nogomet.** They may indicate sensations, e.g. *I feel fine.* **Osjećam se dobro.** They may also be used to show a state, e.g. *Today is a fine day.* **Danas je lijep dan.**

Verbal aspect The aspect of a verb tells you more about the quality of the action in a sentence. It tells you if the action was or will be completed, if the action took place or will take place on more than one occasion, if the action was or will be in process but not completed for some reason. Croatian has an imperfective aspect (for unfinished or regular actions, e.g. *to write* **pisati**) and a perfective aspect (for completed actions e.g. *to write* **napisati**). *He wrote to his brother every day.* **Pisao je bratu svaki dan.** *Yesterday he wrote a letter to his brother.* **Jučer je napisao pismo bratu.**

Taking it further

Visitors to Croatia

For the latest information regarding visits to Croatia, holidays and general information contact the Croatian National Tourist Office. It has branches in many countries.

Jonathan Bousfield, *The Rough Guide to Croatia* (Rough Guides, London, 2000) is full of easy-to-find and useful information for all types of travellers to Croatia.

Language

Damir Kalogjera (editor-in-chief), *Englesko–hrvatski i hrvatsko-engleski rječnik* (Naklada C, Zagreb, 1996) is a compact dictionary ideal for the beginner.

Željko Bujas, *Veliki hrvatsko–engleski rječnik and Veliki englesko-hrvatski rječnik* (Nakladni zavod Globus, Zagreb, 1999) is a more detailed dictionary in two volumes.

Your local university may offer courses in Croatian. Contact the Slavonic studies department or continuing education for evening classes and ask what is available.

Background information

For Croatia in the Balkan context, see Misha Glenny, *The Balkans 1804–1999: Nationalism, War and the Great Powers* (Granta Books, London, 1999).

For Croatia in the Yugoslav context, see Leslie Benson, Yugoslavia: *A Concise History* (Palgrave, Basingstoke/New York, 2001).

For Croatia in the breakup of Yugoslavia, see Laura Silber and Allan Little, *The Death of Yugoslavia* (Penguin and BBC Books, London, 1995).

For general Croatian history see Marcus Tanner, *Croatia: A Nation Forged in War* (Yale University Press, New Haven/ London, 1997).

Useful internet addresses

Croatian National Tourist Board	www.croatia.hr
Dalmatia	www.dalmacija.net
Istrian Tourist Association	www.istra.com
Matica hrvatska cultural organization	www.matica.hr
Zagreb city information	www.zagreb-touristinfo.hr

Croatian–English vocabulary

The following vocabulary consists of words used in the **dialogues** and **comprehension** passages of this course. Take note:

a the gender of nouns is indicated by **m** (masculine), **f** (feminine) or **n** (neuter) and by **pl** (plural) if it is a noun usually used in the plural

b adjectives are given in the masculine singular nominative ending without -i when possible, followed by the endings for feminine and neuter nominative singular indicating when the penultimate -a- disappears (e.g. **dobar, -bra, -bro**)

c verbs are given in pairs with the imperfective form first; where there is only one verb it either functions as both imperfective and perfective or is the form that you have learnt to use in the language patterns explained in this course

d the cases that follow prepositions are given.

a *and, but*
adresa *(f) address*
aerodrom *(m) airport*
agencija *(f) agency*
ako *if*
ali *but*
ambulanta *(f) clinic*
Amerika *(f) America*
antibiotik *(m) antibiotic*
apartman *(m) holiday apartment*
aperitiv *(m) aperitif*
aspirin *(m) aspirin*
atletski, -a, -o *athletic*
auto *(m) car*
autobus *(m) bus*
autobusni, -a, -o *bus*
autocesta *(f) motorway*

avion *(m) aeroplane*
avionski, -a, -o *aeroplane*

balkon *(m) balcony*
banka *(f) bank*
bar *(m) bar*
baš *quite*
baviti se *to take part in, to be occupied with*
bazen *(m) swimming pool*
benzin *(m) petrol*
benzinska stanica *(f) petrol station*
bez *without (with gen. case)*
bijel, -a, -o *white*
biti *to be*
blag, -a, -o *gentle*
blagajna *(f) checkout*
blagajnica *(f) checkout operator*

blagovaonica *(f) dining room*
blizina *(f) vicinity*
blizu *near (with gen. case)*
blok *(m) block of flats*
Bog *(m) God*
boja *(f) colour*
bolestan, -sna, -sno *ill*
bolnica *(f) hospital*
boljeti *to hurt, to ache*
bolji, -a, -e *better*
boraviti *to stay*
Božić *(m) Christmas*
brada *(f) chin*
brak *(m) marriage*
brašno *(n) flour*
brat *(m) brother*
brinuti se *to worry*
brod *(m) boat, ship*
broj *(m) number*
brz, -a, -o *quick, fast*
buditi se, probuditi se *to wake up*
budući, -a, -e *future*
budućnost *(f) future*
buran, -rna, -rno *stormy*

centar *(m) centre*
cesta *(f) road*
cigareta *(f) cigarette*
cijeli, -a, -o *whole*
cipele *(f pl) shoes*
cjenik *(m) price list*
crkva *(f) church*
crn, -a, -o *black*
crno vino *(n) red wine*
crven, -a, -o *red*
čaj *(m) tea*
čamac *(m) boat*
čarapa *(f) sock*
čaša *(f) glass*
ček *(m) cheque*
čekati *to wait*
čestitati *to congratulate*
četvrtak *(m) Thursday*

čiji, -a, -e *whose*
čim *as soon as*
činiti se *to seem*
čitati, pročitati *to read*
čovjek *(m) person, man*
čuti *to hear*

da *yes, that*
dalek, -a, -o *far, distant*
daleko od *far from (with gen. case)*
Dalmacija *(f) Dalmatia*
dan *(m) day*
Danska *Denmark*
davati, dati *to give*
desno *right*
dešavati se, desiti se *to happen*
detaljan, -ljna, -ljno *detailed*
dijete *(n) child*
direktno *directly*
divan, -vna, -vno *wonderful*
dječji, -a, -e *children's*
djevojka *(f) girl, young lady*
dnevni, -a, -o *day, daily*
do *up to, as far as (with gen. case)*
do viđenja *goodbye*
dobar, -bra, -bro *good, fine*
dobiti *to get, to receive*
dogovor *(m) agreement*
dogovoren, -a, -o *agreed*
dok *while*
doktor *(m) doctor*
dolaziti, doći *to come*
donje rublje *(n) underwear*
doručak *(m) breakfast*
dosta *enough, much (with gen. case)*
drago mi je *pleased to meet you*
drugi, -a, -o *other, another, second*
društvo *(n) company, society*
drvo *(n) tree*
dva, dvije *two*
džem *(m) jam*
džep *(m) pocket*

ekran *screen*
Engleska *England*
   engleski, -a, -o *English*
    Englez *(m) Englishman*
    Engleskinja *(f) Englishwoman*
evo *here is (with gen. case)*

faks *(m) fax*
fasada *(f) facade*
firma *(f) firm, company*
Francuska *France*
   francuski, -a, -o *French*
    Francuz *(m) Frenchman*
    Francuskinja *(f) Frenchwoman*
frizerski salon *(m) hairdressing salon*
frižider *(m) fridge*
funta *(f) pound*

garaža *(f) garage*
gazdarica *(f) landlady*
gdje *where*
generalni direktor *(m) general manager*
glačati *to iron*
gladan, -dna, -dno *hungry*
glavan, -vna, -vno *main*
gledati, pogledati *to look at*
godina *(f) year*
gori, -a, -e *worse*
gospodin *(m) Mr, gentleman*
gospođa *(f) Mrs, madame*
gospođica *(f) Miss, young lady*
gost *(m) guest*
gotov novac *(m) cash*
govoriti *to speak*
grad *(m) town*
gradski, -a, -o *urban*
grijanje *(n) heating*
grlo *(n) throat*
gubiti, izgubiti *to lose*

halo *hello (on telephone)*
haljina *(f) dress*

hlače *(f pl) trousers*
hladan, -dna, -dno *cold*
hokej *(m) hockey*
hotel *(m) hotel*
Hrvatska *Croatia*
   hrvatski, -a, -o *Croatian*
    Hrvat *(m) Croat (man)*
    Hrvatica *(f) Croat (woman)*
htjeti *to want*
hvala *thank you*

i *and*
ići *to go*
igralište *(n) pitch, court, playing area*
igranje *(n) game, playing*
igrati *to play*
ili *or*
imati *to have*
ime *(n) name*
inače *otherwise*
industrijski, -a, -o *industrial*
infekcija *(f) infection*
informacije *(f pl) information*
infrastruktura *(f) infrastructure*
interni broj *(m) extension (telephone)*
Irska *Ireland*
isključiv, -a, -o *exclusive*
iskreno *sincerely*
ispitivati, ispitati *to question*
ispod *under (with gen. case)*
ispred *in front of (with gen. case)*
ispričavati se, ispričati se *to apologize*
isti, -a, -o *same*
istina *(f) truth*
istok *(m) east*
Istra *(f) Istria*
Italija *(f) Italy*
iz *from (with gen. case)*
izdavati *to let out, to rent*
izgledati (dobro) *to look (well)*
izlaz *(m) exit*
izlaziti, izaći *to go out*

iznajmljivati, iznajmiti *to rent*
izvan *outside (with gen. case)*
izvolite *here you are*
izvoz *(m) export*

ja *I*
jaje *(n) egg*
jak, -a, -o *strong*
jakna *(f) jacket*
jasno *clear, understood*
javljati se, javiti se *to be in touch,*
  to contact
jedan, -dna, -dno *one*
jelo *(n) dish, meal*
jelovnik *(m) menu*
jer *for, since*
jesti *to eat*
jezik *(m) language, tongue*
još *else, more*
još uvijek *still*
jug *(m) south*
juha *(f) soup*
jutarnji, -a, -e *morning*
jutro *(n) morning*

k *towards (with dat. case)*
kabina *(f) booth*
kada *when*
kakav -kva, -kvo *what kind of*
kako *how*
  kako da ne *of course*
  kako to? *how come?*
kamion *(m) lorry*
kamo *where to*
kao *as, like*
kaput *(m) coat*
karta *(f) ticket, map*
  karta u jednom smjeru *one-way*
    ticket
  povratna karta *return ticket*
  karta prvog razreda *first-class*
    ticket
  karta drugog razreda *second-*
    class ticket

kartica *(f) credit card*
kasnije *later*
kašalj *(m) cough*
kašljati *to cough*
kat *(m) floor, storey*
kauč *(m) couch*
kava *(f) coffee*
kavana *(f) café*
kazalište *(n) theatre*
kazati *to say, tell*
kćerka *(f) daughter*
kemijski čistiti *to dry-clean*
kino *(n) cinema*
kiosk *(m) kiosk*
kiša *(f) rain*
kišobran *(m) umbrella*
klima *(f) climate*
klinika *(f) clinic*
klizanje *(n) skating*
ključ *(m) key*
knjiga *(f) book*
kod *at the house of (with gen. case)*
koji, -a, -e *who, which*
kola *(n pl) car*
kola za hitnu pomoć *ambulance*
kolač *(m) cake*
kolebanje *(n) hesitation*
kolega *(m) colleague, person at work*
koliko *how much, how many*
kolodvor *(m) station*
koljeno *(n) knee*
komforan, -rna, -rno *comfortable*
kompjutor *(m) computer*
kompjutorski, -a, -o *computer*
konačno *at last*
konobar *(m) waiter*
konobarica *(f) waitress*
kopija *(f) copy*
koristan, -sna, -sno *useful*
koristiti *to use*
kosa *(f) hair*
košarka *(f) basketball*
koštati *to cost*
košulja *(f) shirt*

koverta *(f)* envelope
kraj *(m)* area, end
kraj next to *(with gen. case)*
krasti, ukrasti to steal
kratak, -tka, -tko short
kratkoročan, -čna, -čno short term
kratkotrajan, -jna, -jno short lived
kretati, krenuti to set off
krevet *(m)* bed
kriška *(f)* wedge, piece
kriv, -a, -o wrong, guilty, at fault
kroz through *(with acc. case)*
kruh *(m)* bread
kucati to knock
kuća *(f)* house
kuglana *(f)* bowling alley
kuhati to cook
kuhinja *(f)* kitchen
kulturan, -rna, -rno cultural
kuna *(f)* kuna
kupaći kostim *(m)* swimming
  costume
kupaonica *(f)* bathroom
kupati se to bathe
kupiti to buy
kurs *(m)* exchange rate

lagan, -a, -o light
lak, -a, -o easy, light
laku noć goodnight
led *(m)* ice
leđa *(n pl)* back
lice *(n)* face
lift *(m)* lift
lignje *(f pl)* squid
lignje na ribarski način squid
  'fisherman style'
liječnica *(f)* doctor (woman)
liječnik *(m)* doctor (man)
lijep, -a, -o beautiful, nice
lijevo left
limun *(m)* lemon
lipanj *(m)* June
listopad *(m)* October

loš, -a, -e bad
lozovača *(f)* grape brandy
luka *(f)* harbour
ljeti in summer
ljeto *(n)* summer
ljubazan, -zna, -zno kind
ljudi *(m pl)* people, men
ljut, -a, -o angry
ljutiti se to be angry

magla *(f)* fog
majica *(f)* T-shirt
majka *(f)* mother
Makedonija *(f)* Macedonia
  makedonski, -a, -o Macedonian
  Makedonac *(m)* Macedonian
  man
  Makedonka *(f)* Macedonian
  woman
mali, -a, -o small
malo a little
mama *(f)* mum
marka *(f)* stamp
marketing *(m)* marketing
maslac *(m)* butter
medicina *(f)* medicine
mediteranski, -a, -o Mediterranean
međutim however
mehaničar *(m)* mechanic
meso *(n)* meat
mi we
mijenjati, promijeniti to change
miješan, -a, -o mixed
milijun *(m)* million
miran, -rna, -rno peaceful
misliti to think
mišljenje *(n)* opinion
mjenjačnica *(f)* exchange office,
  bureau de change
mjesec *(m)* month
mjesto *(n)* place
mlad, -a, -o young
mlijeko *(n)* milk
mlijeko za sunčanje suntan lotion

mnogo *many, much, a lot of (with gen. case)*
moći *to be able, can*
mogući, -a, -e *possible*
mogućnost *(f) possibility*
moj, -a, -e *my*
molim *please*
moliti, zamoliti *to ask for, to beg*
morati *to have to, must*
more *(n) sea*
morski, -a, -o *sea*
možda *perhaps*
mraz *(m) frost*
mrvice *(f pl) breadcrumbs*
muž *(m) husband*

na *on (with dat. case)*
na *to (with acc. case)*
na žalost *unfortunately*
nacionalni specijalitet *(m) national dish*
nadati se *to hope*
nalaziti, naći *to find*
nalaziti se *to be situated*
namjera *(f) intention*
namještaj *(m) furniture*
naplata *(f) fee*
napuštati, napustiti *to leave*
naravno *of course*
naručivati, naručiti *to order*
naselje *(n) housing estate*
naslonjač *(m) armchair*
nastavljati, nastaviti *to continue*
nastavnica *(f) teacher*
nastavnik *(m) teacher*
naš, -a, -e *our*
natrag *backwards, back*
navečer *in the evening*
ne *no, not*
nebo *(n) sky*
nedjelja *(f) Sunday*
negdje *somewhere*
nego *than*

neki, -a, -o *some, a few*
nema na čemu *don't mention it*
nestajati, nestati *to disappear*
nešto *something*
netko *someone*
ništa *nothing*
nitko *no one*
noć *(f) night*
noćenje *(n) overnight stay*
noćni klub *(m) night club*
noga *(f) leg, foot*
nogomet *(m) football*
nos *(m) nose*
nov, -a, -o *new*
novac *(m) money*
novčanik *(m) wallet, purse*
novine *(f pl) newspaper*
nož *(m) knife*
nuditi, ponuditi *to offer*
nula *(f) zero*
njegov, -a, -o *his*
Njemačka *Germany*
  njemački, -a, -o *German*
  Nijemac *(m) German (man)*
  Njemica *(f) German (woman)*
njen (njezin), -a, -o *her*
njihov, -a, -o *their*

o *about (with dat. case)*
obala *(f) coast*
obalan, -lna, -lno *coastal*
obično *usually*
obitelj *(f) family*
objekat *(m) facility, object*
oblačan, -čna, -čno *cloudy*
oblak *(m) cloud*
obrok *(m) meal*
očito *evidently, obviously*
od *from (with gen. case)*
odakle *where from*
odgovarati *to suit, to correspond*
odijelo *(n) suit*
odjel *(m) department*

odlazati, otići *to go away*
odličan, -čna, -čno *excellent*
odlučivati, odlučiti *to decide*
odmah *immediately*
odmarati se, odmoriti se *to rest,*
  to take a holiday
odmor *(m) rest, holiday*
oglas *(m) advertisement*
ohrabrivati, ohrabriti *to encourage,*
  to cheer up
oko *(n) eye*
oko *around (with gen. case)*
okolina *(f) neighbourhood, vicinity*
okrenuti broj *to dial the number*
on *he*
ona *she*
onaj, ona, ono *that*
onda *then, next*
oni, one *they*
opasan, -sna, -sno *dangerous*
opet *again*
oprema *(f) equipment*
oprostite *excuse me*
ordinacija *(f) doctor's surgery*
ormar *(m) cupboard*
osim *except (with gen. case)*
osjećaj *(m) feeling, emotion*
osjećati se, osjetiti se *to feel*
osoba *(f) person*
ostajati, ostati *to stay, to remain*
ostavka *(f) resignation*
ostavljati, ostaviti *to leave*
otac *(m) father*
otkad *from when, since*
otok *(m) island*
otvarati, otvoriti *to open*
otvoren, -a, -o *open*
ovaj, ova, ovo *this*
ovdje *here*
ozdravljati, ozdraviti *to recover,*
  to get better
oženiti se *to get married (of a man)*
oženjen *married (of a man)*

padati *to fall*
pakovati, spakovati *to pack*
palačinka *(f) pancake*
papar *(m) pepper*
park *(m) park*
parkiralište *(n) car park*
parkirati *to park*
pauza *(f) pause, break*
pažljiv, -a, -o *careful*
pero *(n) pen*
pesimist *(m) pessimist*
piće *(n) drink*
pire od krumpira *(n) mashed potato*
pisati, napisati *to write*
pismo *(n) letter*
pitati *to ask*
piti, popiti *to drink*
pivo *(n) beer*
pješice *on foot*
pjevati *to sing*
plaćanje *(n) payment*
plaćati, platiti *to pay*
plan *(m) plan*
planina *(f) mountain*
plav, -a, -o *blue, blonde*
plaža *(f) beach*
ples *(m) dance, dancing*
plivanje *(n) swimming*
plivati *to swim*
ploška *(f) slice*
po *around, through (with dat. case)*
početak *(m) beginning*
počinjati, početi *to begin*
podatak *(m) information*
podne *(n) noon*
podnositi *to tolerate*
područje *(n) region*
pogled *(m) view*
pogrešan, -šna, -šno *wrong*
pokazivati, pokazati *to show*
poklon *(m) present*
polaziti, poći *to set off*
polica *(f) shelf*

policajac *(m) policeman*
policijska postaja *(f) police station*
polovica *(f) half*
polupansion *(m) half board*
polje *(n) field*
Poljska *Poland*
ponašanje *(n) behaviour*
ponedjeljak *(m) Monday*
ponekad *sometimes*
ponovo *again*
ponuda *(f) offer*
pored *next to (with gen. case)*
poruka *(f) message*
posao *(m) work*
poseban, -bna, -bno *special,
  separate*
posjećivati, posjetiti *to visit*
poslije *after (with gen. case)*
poslovni sastanak *(m) business
  meeting*
postajati, postati *to become*
postojati *to exist*
pošta *(f) post office*
potpisivati, potpisati *to sign*
povratak *(m) return*
poziv *(m) invitation*
pozivati, pozvati *to invite*
pozivni broj *(m) code number
  (telephone)*
praktičan, -čna, -čno *practical*
prati, oprati *to wash*
pravac *(m) direction*
praviti, napraviti *to make*
pravo *(n) right*
predavati, predati *to hand over*
predgrađe *(n) suburb*
predjelo *(n) first course*
predlagati, predložiti *to suggest*
predstavnik *(m) representative*
pregovor *(m) negotiation*
prehlađen, -a, -o *cold (to have a
  cold)*
preko *across (with gen. case)*

prelaziti, prijeći *to cross*
prema *towards (with dat. case)*
preporučivati, preporučiti
  to recommend
prestati *to stop*
pretpostavljati *to suppose*
previše *too much*
pričati *to talk, to tell*
prihvaćati *to accept*
prijatelj *(m) friend*
prijateljica *(f) friend*
prijateljski, -a, -o *friendly*
prijavljivati, prijaviti *to
  announce*
prije *before (with gen. case)*
prijedlog *(m) suggestion*
prijevoz *(m) transport*
prilaziti, prići *to approach,
  to go up to*
primati, primiti *to receive, to accept*
primorje *(n) coastal region, seashore*
priroda *(f) nature, countryside*
pristanište *(n) quay*
pritisnuti *to pinch together*
privatan, -tna, -tno *private*
privredni, -dna, -dno *economic*
prizemlje *(n) ground floor*
priznati *to confess, to admit*
probati *to try*
problem *(m) problem*
prodavač *(m) salesman*
prodavačica *(f) saleswoman*
prodavaonica *(f) shop*
prodavati, prodati *to sell*
proizvod *(m) product*
proizvođenje *(n) production*
proizvođenje pod licencijom
  production under licence
prostorija *(f) space*
prošlost *(f) past*
protiv *against (with gen. case)*
provoditi, provesti *to spend (time)*
prozor *(m) window*

prst *(m) finger*
prtljaga *(f) luggage*
prvi, -a, -o *first*
pržiti *to fry*
puni pansion *(m) full board*
put *(m) way, road, journey*
putnički, -a, -o *traveller's, travel*
putnik *(m) traveller*
putovati *to travel*
putovnica *(f) passport*

račun *(m) bill*
računalo *(n) computer*
računovođa *(m) accountant*
raditi *to do, to work*
radni, -a, -o *working*
rado *gladly*
radovati se *to look forward to*
rakija *(f) brandy*
rame *(n) shoulder*
rano *early*
raspolaganje *(n) disposal*
raspoložen, -a, -o *disposed*
ravno *straight on*
razboljeti se *to fall ill*
razglednica *(f) postcard*
razgovarati *to chat*
razgovor *conversation*
razmatrati, razmotriti *to examine,*
  to discuss
razmišljati *to consider*
razumjeti *to understand*
razvijen, -a, -o *developed*
recepcija *(f) reception*
reci/recite *say, tell (imperative of reći)*
reći *to say, to tell*
reklamni odjel *(m) advertising*
  department
restoran *(m) restaurant*
rezervirati *to reserve*
riba *(f) fish*
ribarski, -a, -o *fishing*
riječ *(f) word*

rijeka *(f) river*
riva *(f) promenade (by the sea)*
roba *(f) goods*
roditelj *(m) parent*
rođen, -a, -o *born*
roštilj *(m) grill, barbecue*
rublje *(n) laundry*
ručak *(m) lunch*
ručati *to have lunch*
ručnik *(m) towel*
rujan *(m) September*
ruka *(f) arm, hand*
rukav *(m) sleeve*
rukomet *(m) handball*
rukometno igralište *(n) handball*
  pitch
Rusija *Russia*
  ruski, -a, -o *Russian*
  Rus *(m) Russian (man)*
  Ruskinja *(f) Russian (woman)*

s *with (with ins. case)*
s *from, off (with gen. case)*
sada *now*
sadržaj *(m) facility, content*
sala *(f) hall*
sala za konferenciju *conference hall*
salata *(f) salad*
salon *(m) salon*
salon za masažu *massage salon*
sam, -a, -o *alone*
samac *(m) bachelor*
samo *only*
samoposluga *(f) self-service shop*
samostan *(m) monastery*
sandale *(f pl) sandals*
sanjati *to dream*
sapun *(m) soap*
sastanak *(m) meeting*
sat *(m) clock, hour, class*
sav, sva, sve *all*
savjetovati *to advise*
saznati *to get to know, to find out*

sebe *oneself*
sekretarica *(f) secretary*
selo *(n) village*
sendvič *(m) sandwich*
sestra *(f) sister*
siguran, -rna, -rno *sure, certain*
sijati *to shine*
silaziti, sići *to get down, to get off*
sin *(m) son*
sir *(m) cheese*
sistem *(m) system*
siv, -a, -o *grey*
sjajan, -jna, -jno *wonderful, smashing*
sjećati se, sjetiti se *to remember*
sjediti *to be sitting*
sjesti *to sit down*
sjever *(m) north*
skijanje *(n) skiing*
skoro *almost*
skrenuti *to turn*
skup, -a, -o *expensive*
skupljati se *to gather together, to meet together*
slab, -a, -o *weak*
sladoled *(m) ice cream*
slagati se *to agree*
slati, poslati *to send*
slatko *(n) dessert*
Slavonija *(f) Slavonia*
slobodan, -dna, -dno *free*
Slovenija *(f) Slovenia*
  slovenski, -a, -o *Slovenian*
  Slovenac *(m) Slovenian man*
  Slovenka *(f) Slovenian woman*
slučaj *(m) event, case*
slušati *to listen to*
službenik *(m) clerk, counter clerk*
služiti se, poslužiti se *to be served*
sljedeći, -a, -e *next, following*
smatrati *to consider*
smještaj *(m) accommodation*
smješten, -a, -o *situated, sited*

snijeg *(m) snow*
soba *(f) room*
sok *(m) juice*
sol *(f) salt*
spajati *to link, to join*
spavaća soba *(f) bedroom*
spavati *to sleep*
spomenik *(m) monument*
sport *(m) sport*
sportsko-rekreacijski centar *sports centre*
spreman, -mna, -mno *ready, prepared*
spremati *to prepare*
Srbija *(f) Serbia*
  srpski, -a, -o *Serbian*
  Srbin *(m) Serbian (man)*
  Srpkinja *(f) Serbian (woman)*
srdačan, -čna, -čno *cordial*
sredina *(f) middle*
središnji, -a, -e *middle, central*
sretan, -tna, -tno *happy*
srijeda *(f) Wednesday*
stadion *(m) stadium*
stajati *to be standing*
stalno *continuously*
stan *(m) flat*
stanica *(f) stop*
stanovati *to live, to reside*
stanovnik *(m) inhabitant*
star, -a, -o *old*
stavljati, staviti *to put*
stizati, stići *to arrive*
stol *(m) table*
stolica *(f) chair*
stolić *(m) little table*
stolni tenis *(m) table tennis*
stomak *(m) stomach*
stran, -a, -o *foreign*
strana *(f) side*
stric *(m) uncle*
strina *(f) aunt*
studirati *to study*

stvar (f) thing
stvarno really
subota (f) Saturday
suh, -a, -o dry
suknja (f) skirt
sumaglica (f) mist
sumrak (m) dusk
sunce (n) sun
sunčan, -a, -o sunny
sunčati se to sunbathe
suprug (m) husband
supruga (f) wife
suradnja (f) cooperation
surađivati to cooperate
sušiti se, osušiti se to dry
sutra tomorrow
suviše too much
svadba (f) wedding
svaki, -a, -o each, every
svakodnevni, -a, -o everyday
sveučilište (n) university
sviđati se to like, to be pleasing
svijetlosmeđi, -a, -e light brown
svjež, -a, -e fresh
svoj, -a, -e one's own
svugdje everywhere
šalica (f) cup
šalter (m) counter
šampon (m) shampoo
šef (m) boss
šešir (m) hat
šifra (f) box number
škola (f) school
Škotska Scotland
šorc (m) shorts
što what, that
Stovani, -a Respected, Dear
   (in a formal letter)
šuma (f) forest
šunka (f) ham

tada then, at that time
taj, ta, to that

tako so
također also
taksi (m) taxi
tanak, -nka, -nko thin
tamo there
tanjur (m) plate
taška (f) bag, handbag
tata (m) Dad
tava (f) saucepan
tečaj (m) course
teleći, -a, -e veal
telefon (m) telephone
telefonirati to telephone
telefonski broj (m) telephone
   number
telefonsko buđenje (n) alarm call
temperatura (f) temperature
tenis (m) tennis
tepih (m) carpet
terasa (f) terrace
teren (m) pitch, court
tetak (m) uncle
tetka (f) aunt
težak, -ška, -ško difficult, heavy
ti you (singular)
tih, -a, -o quiet
tipičan, -čna, -čno typical
tisuća (f) thousand
tjedan (m) week
tko who
točan, -čna, -čno exact, precise
tokom during (with gen. case)
topao, -pla, -plo warm
trajati to last
tramvaj (m) tram
transfer (m) transfer
transportni odjel (m) transport
   department
trava (f) grass
travanj (m) April
tražiti to look for
trebati to need, to require
treći, -a, -e third

trend *(m) trend*
trenutak *(m) moment*
trg *(m) square*
tri *three*
trim kabinet *(m) exercise room*
tržište *(n) market*
turist *(m) tourist*
turistički, -a, -o *tourist*
turistkinja *(f) tourist*
tuš *(m) shower*
tuširati se, istuširati se *to shower,
  to have a shower*
tužan, -žna, -žno *sad*
tvoj, -a, -e *your (singular)*

u *in (with dat. case)*
u *to (with acc. case)*
u redu *OK, all right*
učenik *(m) pupil*
učitelj *(m) teacher*
učiteljica *(f) teacher*
učiti, naučiti *to learn*
udata *married (of a woman)*
udati se *to get married (of female)*
udoban, -bna, -bno *comfortable*
ugao *(m) corner*
ugovor *(m) contract*
uho *(n) ear*
ujak *(m) uncle*
ujna *(f) aunt*
ujutro *in the morning*
ukratko *in short, briefly*
ukus *(m) taste*
ulaz *(m) entry*
ulaziti, ući *to go in, to enter*
ulica *(f) street*
ulje *(n) oil*
ulje za sunčanje *suntan oil*
umoran, -rna, -rno *tired*
uopće ne *not at all*
upoznati *to introduce*
upravo *just now*
ured *(m) office*

uskoro *soon*
usluživati *to serve*
usna *(f) lip*
uspjeh *(m) success*
usta *(n pl) mouth*
ustajati, ustati *to get up*
uvečer *in the evening*
uvijek *always*
uvjet *(m) condition*
uvjetovati *to cause, to bring about*
uvoz *(m) import*
uzbuđen, -a, -o *excited*
uzimati, uzeti *to take*

valuta *(f) currency*
vaš, -a, -e *your (plural)*
važan, -žna, -žno *important*
WC *(m) (pronounced ve-tse) toilet*
večer *(f) evening*
večera *(f) dinner*
večerati *to have dinner*
već *already*
vedar, -dra, -dro *clear, bright*
velik, -a, -o *large, big*
veoma *very*
veseo, -la, -lo *jolly, merry*
vi *you (plural)*
vidjeti *to see*
vilica *(f) fork*
vino *(n) wine*
visok, -a, -o *tall, high*
više *more*
vjenčati se *to get married*
vjerojatno *probably, likely*
vjetar *(m) wind*
vjetar puše *the wind is blowing*
vlak *(m) train*
vlastit, -a, -o *own*
voda *(f) water*
voditi *to lead*
voditi razgovor *to have a
  conversation*
vojnik *(m) soldier*

voljeti *to like, to love*
voziti *to drive*
vozni, -a, -o *train*
vraćati se, vratiti se *to return*
vrat *(m) neck*
vrata *(n pl) door*
vrijeme *(n) time, weather*
vrlo *very*
vrsta *(f) sort, kind*
vrt *(m) garden*
vruć, -a, -e *hot*

za *for (with acc. case)*
za *behind (with ins. case)*
zaboravljati, zaboraviti *to forget*
zadovoljan, -ljna, -ljno *pleased, satisfied*
zadržavanje *(n) keeping*
zagrebački odrezak *(m) Zagreb schnitzel*
zagrijati *to heat, to warm*
zaista *really*
zaključak *(m) conclusion*
zaključavati, zaključati *to lock*
zalaziti, zaći *to go behind*
zaljev *(m) bay*
zamišljati, zamisliti *to imagine*
zamrzivač *(m) freezer*
zapad *(m) west*
zapisivati, zapisati *to note down*
zaprositi *to ask for girl's hand in marriage*
zašto *why*
zatim *then, next*

zato što *because*
zatvoren, -a, -o *closed*
zaustavljati se, zaustaviti se *to stop*
zauzet, -a, -o *busy, engaged*
zavisi od *depends on (with gen. case)*
zavjesa *(f) curtain*
završavati, završiti *to finish*
zdravo *hello, goodbye (colloquial)*
zelen, -a, -o *green*
zgrada *(f) building*
zima *(f) winter*
zimi *in winter*
značiti *to mean*
znanje *(n) knowledge*
znati *to know*
zoološki vrt *(m) zoo*
zračna luka *(f) airport*
zrakoplov *(m) aeroplane*
zrakoplovan, -vna, -vno *aeroplane*
zubar *(m) dentist*
zubna pasta *(f) toothpaste*
zvati, nazvati *to call*
zvati se *to be called*
žao mi je *I am sorry*
želja *(f) desire, wish*
žedan, -dna, -dno *thirsty*
željeti *to want, to desire*
žena *(f) woman, wife*
živjeti *to live*
život *(m) life*
žlica *(f) spoon*
žut, -a, -o *yellow*

English–Croatian vocabulary

able, to be **moći**
about **o** *(with dat. case)*
accept, to **prihvaćati; primati, primiti**
accommodation **smještaj** *(m)*
accountant **računovođa** *(m)*
ache, to **boljeti**
across **preko** *(with gen. case)*
address **adresa** *(f)*
admit, to **priznati**
advertisement **oglas** *(m)*
advertising department **reklamni odjel** *(m)*
advise, to **savjetovati**
aeroplane **avion** *(m);* **zrakoplov** *(m);* **avionski, -a, -o**
after **poslije** *(with gen. case)*
again **opet; ponovo**
against **protiv** *(with gen. case)*
agency **agencija** *(f)*
agree, to **slagati se**
agreed **dogovoren, -a, -o**
agreement **dogovor** *(m)*
airport **aerodrom** *(m);* **zračna luka** *(f)*
alarm call **telefonsko buđenje** *(n)*
all **sav, sva, sve**
all right **u redu**
almost **skoro**
alone **sam, -a, -o**
already **već**
also **također**
always **uvijek**
ambulance **kola za hitnu pomoć** *(pl)*
America **Amerika** *(f)*
and **i; a**
angry **ljut, -a, -o**

angry, to be **ljutiti se**
announce, to **prijavljivati, prijaviti**
another **drugi, -a, -o**
antibiotic **antibiotik** *(m)*
aperitif **aperitiv** *(m)*
apologize, to **ispričavati se, ispričati se**
approach, to **prilaziti, prići**
April **travanj** *(m)*
area **kraj** *(m)*
arm **ruka** *(f)*
armchair **naslonjač** *(m)*
around **oko** *(with gen. case);* **po** *(with dat. case)*
arrive, to **stizati, stići**
as **kao**
as far as **do** *(with gen. case)*
as soon as **čim**
ask, to **pitati**
ask for, to **moliti, zamoliti**
ask for girl's hand in marriage, to **zaprositi**
aspirin **aspirin** *(m)*
at (time) **u** *(with acc. case)*
at the house of **kod** *(with gen. case)*
athletic **atletski, -a, -o**
aunt **strina** *(f);* **tetka** *(f);* **ujna** *(f)*

bachelor **samac** *(m)*
back **leđa** *(n pl)*
backwards **natrag**
bad **loš, -a, -e**
bag **taška** *(f)*
balcony **balkon** *(m)*
bank **banka** *(f)*
bar **bar** *(m)*
barbecue **roštilj** *(m)*

basketball **košarka** *(f)*
bathe, to **kupati se**
bathroom **kupaonica** *(f)*
bay **zaljev** *(m)*
be, to **biti**
beach **plaž** *(m)*
beautiful **lijep, -a, -o**
because **zato što**
become, to **postajati, postati**
bed **krevet** *(m)*
bedroom **spavaća soba** *(f)*
beer **pivo** *(n)*
before **prije** *(with gen. case)*
beg, to **moliti, zamoliti**
begin, to **počinjati, početi**
beginning **početak** *(m)*
behaviour **ponašanje** *(n)*
behind **za** *(with ins. case)*
better **bolji, -a, -e**
better, to get **ozdravljati, ozdraviti**
big **velik, -a, -o**
bill **račun** *(m)*
black **crn, -a, -o**
block of flats **blok** *(m)*
blonde **plav, -a, -o**
blue **plav, -a, -o**
boat **brod** *(m)*; **čamac** *(m)*
book **knjiga** *(f)*
booth **kabina** *(f)*
born **rođen, -a, -o**
boss **šef** *(m)*
bowling alley **kuglana** *(f)*
box number **šifra** *(f)*
brandy **rakija** *(f)*
bread **kruh** *(m)*
breadcrumbs **mrvice** *(f pl)*
break **pauza** *(f)*
breakfast **doručak** *(m)*
briefly **ukratko**
bright **vedar, -dra, -dro**
bring about, to **uvjetovati**
brother **brat** *(m)*
building **zgrada** *(f)*

bureau de change **mjenjačnica** *(f)*
bus **autobus** *(m)*; **autobusni, -a, -o**
business meeting **poslovni sastanak** *(m)*
busy **zauzet, -a, -o**
but **ali, a**
butter **maslac** *(m)*
buy, to **kupiti**

café **kavana** *(f)*
cake **kolač** *(m)*
call, to **zvati, nazvati**
called, to be **zvati se**
can **moći**
car **auto** *(m)*; **kola** *(n pl)*
car park **parkiralište** *(n)*
careful **pažljiv, -a, -o**
carpet **tepih** *(m)*
case **slučaj** *(m)*
cash **gotov novac** *(m)*
cause, to **uvjetovati**
central **središnji, -a, -e**
centre **centar** *(m)*
certain **siguran, -rna, -rno**
chair **stolica** *(f)*
change, to **mijenjati, promijeniti**
chat, to **razgovarati**
checkout **blagajna** *(f)*
checkout operator **blagajnica** *(f)*
cheer up, to **ohrabrivati, ohrabriti**
cheese **sir** *(m)*
cheque **ček** *(m)*
child **dijete** *(n)*
children's **dječji, -a, -e**
chin **brada** *(f)*
Christmas **Božić** *(m)*
church **crkva** *(f)*
cigarette **cigareta** *(f)*
cinema **kino** *(n)*
class **sat** *(m)*
clear **vedar, -dra, -dro**
clerk **službenik** *(m)*
climate **klima** *(f)*

clinic **ambulanta** *(f)*; **klinika** *(f)*
clock **sat** *(m)*
closed **zatvoren, -a, -o**
cloud **oblak** *(m)*
cloudy **oblačan, -čna, -čno**
coast **obala** *(f)*
coastal **obalan, -lna, -lno**
coastal region **primorje** *(n)*
coat **kaput** *(m)*
code number (telephone) **pozivni
  broj** *(m)*
coffee **kava** *(f)*
cold **hladan, -dna, -dno**
cold (have a cold) **prehlađen, -a, -o**
colleague (man) **kolega** *(m)*
colleague (woman) **kolegica** *(f)*
colour **boja** *(f)*
come, to **dolaziti, doći**
comfortable **komforan, -rna, -rno;
  udoban, -bna, -bno**
company **društvo** *(n)*; **firma** *(f)*
computer **kompjutor** *(m)*;
  računalo *(n)*
computer **kompjutorski, -a, -o**
conclusion **zaključak** *(m)*
condition **uvjet** *(m)*
conference hall **sala za
  konferenciju** *(f)*
confess, to **priznati**
congratulate, to **čestitati**
consider, to **razmišljati; smatrati**
contact, to **javljati se, javiti se**
content **sadržaj** *(m)*
continue, to **nastavljati, nastaviti**
continuously **stalno**
contract **ugovor** *(m)*
conversation **razgovor** *(m)*
cook, to **kuhati**
cooperate, to **surađivati**
cooperation **suradnja** *(f)*
copy **kopija** *(f)*
cordial **srdačan, -čna, -čno**
corner **ugao** *(m)*

cost, to **koštati**
couch **kauč** *(m)*
cough **kašalj** *(m)*
cough, to **kašljati**
counter **šalter** *(m)*
counter clerk **službenik** *(m)*
countryside **priroda** *(f)*
course **tečaj** *(m)*
court (for games) **igralište** *(n)*;
  teren *(m)*
credit card **kartica** *(f)*
Croatia **Hrvatska**
    Croatian **hrvatski, -a, -o**
    Croat (man) **Hrvat** *(m)*
    Croat (woman) **Hrvatica** *(f)*
cross, to **prelaziti, prijeći**
cultural **kulturan, -rna, -rno**
cup **šalica** *(f)*
cupboard **ormar** *(m)*
currency **valuta** *(f)*
curtain **zavjesa** *(f)*

dad **tata** *(m)*
daily **dnevni, -a, -o**
Dalmatia **Dalmacija** *(f)*
dance **ples** *(m)*
dangerous **opasan, -sna, -sno**
daughter **kćerka** *(f)*
day **dan** *(m)*
decide, to **odlučivati, odlučiti**
Denmark **Danska**
dentist **zubar** *(m)*
department **odjel** *(m)*
depends on **zavisi od** *(with gen.
  case)*
desire **želja** *(f)*
desire, to **željeti**
dessert **slatko** *(n)*
detailed **detaljan, -ljna, -ljno**
developed **razvijen, -a, -o**
dial the number, to **okrenuti broj**
difficult **težak, -ška, -ško**
dining room **blagovaonica** *(f)*

dinner **večera** *(f)*
dinner, to have **večerati**
direction **pravac** *(m)*
directly **direktno**
disappear, to **nestajati, nestati**
discuss, to **razmatrati, razmotriti**
dish **jelo** *(n)*
disposal **raspolaganje** *(n)*
disposed **raspoložen, -a, -o**
distant **dalek, -a, -o**
do, to **raditi**
doctor **doktor** *(m)*
doctor (man) **liječnik** *(m)*
doctor (woman) **liječnica** *(f)*
doctor's surgery **ordinacija** *(f)*
don't mention it **nema na čemu**
door **vrata** *(n pl)*
dream, to **sanjati**
dress **haljina** *(f)*
drink **piće** *(n)*
drink, to **piti, popiti**
drive, to **voziti**
dry **suh, -a, -o**
dry, to **sušiti se, osušiti se**
dry-clean, to **kemijski čistiti**
during **tokom** *(with gen. case)*
dusk **sumrak** *(m)*

each **svaki, -a, -o**
ear **uho** *(n)*
early **rano**
east **istok** *(m)*; **istočni, -a, -o**
easy **lak, -a, -o**
eat, to **jesti**
economic **privredni, -dna, -dno**
egg **jaje** *(n)*
else **još**
emotion **osjećaj** *(m)*
empty **prazan, -zna, -zno**
encourage, to **ohrabrivati, ohrabriti**
end **kraj** *(m)*
engaged **zauzet, -a, -o**
engaged in, to be **baviti se**

England **Engleska**
English **engleski, -a, -o**
Englishman **Englez** *(m)*
Englishwoman **Engleskinja** *(f)*
enough **dosta** *(with gen. case)*
enter, to **ulaziti, ući**
entry **ulaz** *(m)*
envelope **koverta** *(f)*
equipment **oprema** *(f)*
evening **večer** *(f)*
event **slučaj** *(m)*
every **svaki, -a, -o**
everyday **svakodnevni, -a, -o**
everywhere **svugdje**
evidently **očito**
exact **točan, -čna, -čno**
examine, to **razmatrati, razmotriti**
excellent **odličan, -čna, -čno**
except **osim** *(with gen. case)*
exchange office **mjenjačnica** *(f)*
exchange rate **kurs** *(m)*
excited **uzbuđen, -a, -o**
exclusive **isključiv, -a, -o**
excuse me **oprostite**
exercise room **trim kabinet** *(m)*
exist, to **postojati**
exit **izlaz** *(m)*
expensive **skup, -a, -o**
export **izvoz** *(m)*
extension (telephone) **interni broj** *(m)*
eye **oko** *(n)*

facade **fasada** *(f)*
face **lice** *(n)*
facility **objekat** *(m)*; **sadržaj** *(m)*
fall, to **padati**
fall ill, to **razboljeti se**
family **obitelj** *(f)*
far **dalek, -a, -o**
far from **daleko od** *(with gen. case)*
fast **brz, -a, -o**
father **otac** *(m)*

fax **faks** (m)
fee **naplata** (f)
feel **osjećati se, osjetiti se**
feeling **osjećaj** (m)
few, a few **neki, -a, -o**
field **polje** (n)
finally **konačno**
find, to **nalaziti, naći**
find out, to **saznati**
finger **prst** (m)
finish, to **završavati, završiti**
firm **firma** (f)
first **prvi, -a, -o**
first course **predjelo** (n)
fish **riba** (f)
fishing **ribarski, -a, -o**
flat **stan** (m)
floor **kat** (m)
flour **brašno** (n)
fog **magla** (f)
following **sljedeći, -a, -e**
foot **noga** (f)
football **nogomet** (m)
for **jer; za** (with acc. case)
foreign **stran, -a, -o**
forest **šuma** (f)
forget, to **zaboravljati,
  zaboraviti**
fork **vilica** (f)
France **Francuska**
  French **francuski, -a, -o**
  Frenchman **Francuz** (m)
  Frenchwoman **Francuskinja** (f)
free **slobodan, -dna, -dno**
freezer **zamrzivač** (m)
fresh **svjež, -a, -e**
fridge **frižider** (m)
friend (man) **prijatelj** (m)
friend (woman) **prijateljica** (f)
friendly **prijateljski, -a, -o**
from **iz** (with gen. case); **od** (with
  gen. case); **s** (with gen. case)
from when **otkad**
frost **mraz** (m)

fry, to **pržiti**
full **pun, -a, -o**
full board **puni pansion** (m)
furniture **namještaj** (m)
future **budućnost** (f); **budući, -a, -e**

game **igranje** (n)
garage **garaža** (f)
garden **vrt** (m)
gather together, to **skupljati se**
general manager **generalni
  direktor** (m)
gentle **blag, -a, -o**
gentleman **gospodin** (m)
Germany **Njemačka**
  German **njemački, -a, -o**
  German (man) **Nijemac** (m)
  German (woman) **Njemica** (f)
get, to **dobiti**
get off, to **silaziti, sići**
get up, to **ustajati, ustati**
girl **djevojka** (f)
give, to **davati, dati**
gladly **rado**
glass **čaša** (f)
go, to **ići**
go away, to **odlaziti, otići**
go behind, to **zalaziti, zaći**
go in, to **ulaziti, ući**
go out, to **izlaziti, izaći**
go up to, to **prilaziti, prići**
God **Bog** (m)
good **dobar, -bra, -bro**
goodnight **laku noć** (f)
goodbye **do viđenja; zdravo
  (colloquial)**
goods **roba** (f)
grass **trava** (f)
green **zelen, -a, -o**
grey **siv, -a, -o**
grill **roštilj** (m)
ground floor **prizemlje** (n)
guest **gost** (m)
guilty **kriv, -a, -o**

hair **kosa** *(f)*
hairdressing salon **frizerski salon** *(m)*
half **polovica** *(f)*
half board **polupansion** *(m)*
hall **sala** *(f)*
ham **šunka** *(f)*
hand **ruka** *(f)*
hand over, to **predavati, predati**
handbag **taška** *(f)*
handball **rukomet** *(m)*
happy **sretan, -tna, -tno**
happen, to **dešavati se, desiti se**
harbour **luka** *(f)*
hat **šešir** *(m)*
have, to **imati**
have to, to **morati**
he **on**
hear, to **čuti**
heat, to **zagrijati**
heating **grijanje** *(n)*
heavy **težak, -ška, -ško**
hello **dobar dan; halo** *(on telephone)*; **zdravo** *(colloquial)*
her **njen (njezin), -a, -o**
here **ovdje**
here is **evo** *(with gen. case)*
here you are **izvolite**
hesitation **kolebanje** *(n)*
high **visok, -a, -o**
his **njegov, -a, -o**
hockey **hokej** *(m)*
holiday **odmor** *(m)*
holiday apartment **apartman** *(m)*
hope, to **nadati se**
hospital **bolnica** *(f)*
hot **vruć, -a, -e**
hotel **hotel** *(m)*
hour **sat** *(m)*
house **kuća** *(f)*
housing estate **naselje** *(n)*
how **kako**
how come? **kako to?**
how many **koliko** *(with gen. case)*
how much **koliko**

however **međutim**
hungry **gladan, -dna, -dno**
hurt, to **boljeti**
husband **muž** *(m)*; **suprug** *(m)*

I **ja**
ice **led** *(m)*
ice cream **sladoled** *(m)*
if **ako**
ill **bolestan, -sna, -sno**
imagine, to **zamišljati, zamisliti**
immediately **odmah**
import **uvoz** *(m)*
important **važan, -žna, -žno**
in **u** *(with dat. case)*
in front of **ispred** *(with gen. case)*
industrial **industrijski, -a, -o**
infection **infekcija** *(f)*
information **informacije** *(f pl)*; **podatak** *(m)*
infrastructure **infrastruktura** *(f)*
inhabitant **stanovnik** *(m)*
intention **namjera** *(f)*
introduce, to **upoznati**
invitation **poziv** *(m)*
invite, to **pozivati, pozvati**
Ireland **Irska**
iron, to **glačati**
island **otok** *(m)*
Istria **Istra** *(f)*
Italy **Italija** *(f)*

jacket **jakna** *(f)*
jam **džem** *(m)*
join, to **spajati**
jolly **veseo, -la, -lo**
journey **put** *(m)*
juice **sok** *(m)*
June **lipanj** *(m)*
just now **upravo**

key **ključ** *(m)*
kind **vrsta** *(f)*
kind **ljubazan, -zna, -zno**

kiosk **kiosk** *(m)*
kitchen **kuhinja** *(f)*
knee **koljeno** *(n)*
knife **nož** *(m)*
knock, to **kucati**
know, to **znati**
knowledge **znanje** *(n)*
kuna **kuna** *(f)*

landlady **gazdarica** *(f)*
language **jezik** *(m)*
large **velik, -a, -o**
last, to **trajati**
later **kasnije**
laundry **rublje** *(n)*
lead, to **voditi**
learn, to **učiti, naučiti**
leave, to **napuštati, napustiti;**
  ostavljati, ostaviti
left **lijevo**
leg **noga** *(f)*
lemon **limun** *(m)*
let out, to **izdavati**
letter **pismo** *(n)*
life **život** *(m)*
lift **lift** *(m)*
light **lagan, -a, -o; lak, -a, -o**
like **kao**
like, to **sviđati se; voljeti**
likely **vjerojatno**
link, to **spajati**
lip **usna** *(f)*
listen to, to **slušati**
little **mali, -a, -o**
little, a little **malo**
live, to **stanovati; živjeti**
living room **dnevna soba** *(f)*
lock, to **zaključavati, zaključati**
look (at), to **gledati; pogledati**
look (well), to **izgledati**
  (dobro)
look for, to **tražiti**
look forward to, to **radovati se**
lorry **kamion** *(m)*

lose, to **gubiti, izgubiti**
lots of, a lot of **mnogo** *(with gen.*
  case)
love, to **voljeti**
luggage **prtljaga** *(f)*
lunch **ručak** *(m)*
lunch, to have **ručati**

Macedonia **Makedonija** *(f)*
  Macedonian **makedonski, -a, -o**
  Macedonian (man)
    Makedonac *(m)*
  Macedonian (woman)
    Makedonka *(f)*
madam **gospođa** *(f)*
main **glavan, -vna, -vno**
make, to **praviti, napraviti**
man **čovjek** *(m)*
many **mnogo** *(with gen. case)*
map **karta** *(f)*
market **tržište** *(n)*
marketing **marketing** *(m)*
marriage **brak** *(m)*
married (of a man) **oženjen**
married (of a woman) **udata**
married, to get **vjenčati se**
married, to get (of a man)
  oženiti se
married, to get (of a woman)
  udati se
meal **jelo** *(n)*; **obrok** *(m)*
mean, to **značiti**
meat **meso** *(n)*
mechanic **mehaničar** *(m)*
medicine **medicina** *(f)*
Mediterranean **mediteranski, -a, -o**
meet together, to **skupljati se**
meeting **sastanak** *(m)*
menu **jelovnik** *(m)*
merry **veseo, -la, -lo**
message **poruka** *(f)*
middle **sredina** *(f)*; **središnji, -a, -e**
milk **mlijeko** *(n)*
million **milijun** *(m)*

Miss **gospođica** *(f)*
mist **sumaglica** *(f)*
mixed **miješan, -na, -no**
moment **trenutak** *(m)*
monastery **samostan** *(m)*
Monday **ponedjeljak** *(m)*
money **novac** *(m)*
month **mjesec** *(m)*
monument **spomenik** *(m)*
more **još; više**
morning **jutro** *(n)*; **jutarnji, -a, -e**
mother **majka** *(f)*
motorway **autocesta** *(f)*
mountain **planina** *(f)*
mouth **usta** *(n pl)*
Mr **gospodin** *(m)*
Mrs **gospođa** *(f)*
much **dosta** *(with gen. case)*; **mnogo**
  (with gen. case)
mum **mama**
must **morati**
my **moj, -a, -e**

name **ime** *(n)*
nature **priroda** *(f)*
near **blizu** *(with gen. case)*
neck **vrat** *(m)*
need, to **trebati**
negotiations **pregovori** *(m pl)*
neighbourhood **okolina** *(f)*
new **nov, -a, -o**
newspaper **novine** *(f pl)*
next **onda; zatim; sljedeći, -a, -e**
next to **kraj** *(with gen. case)*; **pored**
  (with gen. case)
nice **lijep, -a, -o**
night **noć** *(f)*
no, not **ne**
no one **nitko**
noon **podne** *(n)*
north **sjever** *(m)*; **sjeverni, -a, -o**
nose **nos** *(m)*
note down, to **zapisivati, zapisati**

nothing **ništa**
now **sada**
number **broj** *(m)*

object **objekat** *(m)*
obviously **očito**
occupied with, to be **baviti se**
October **listopad** *(m)*
of course **kako da ne; naravno**
off **s** *(with gen. case)*
offer **ponuda** *(f)*
offer, to **nuditi, ponuditi**
office **ured** *(m)*
oil **ulje** *(n)*
OK **u redu**
old **star, -a, -o**
on **na** *(with dat. case)*
on foot **pješice**
one **jedan, -dna, -dno**
oneself **sebe**
one's own **svoj, -a, -e**
only **samo**
open **otvarati, otvoriti**
open **otvoren, -a, -o**
opinion **mišljenje** *(n)*
or **ili**
order, to **naručivati, naručiti**
other **drugi, -a, -o**
otherwise **inače**
our **naš, -a, -e**
outside **izvan** *(with gen. case)*
overnight stay **noćenje** *(n)*
own **vlastit, -a, -o**

pack, to **pakovati, spakovati**
pancake **palačinka** *(f)*
parent **roditelj** *(m)*
park **park** *(m)*
park, to **parkirati**
passport **putovnica** *(f)*
past **prošlost** *(f)*
pause **pauza** *(f)*
pay, to **plaćati, platiti**

payment **plaćanje** *(n)*

peaceful **miran, -rna, -rno**

pen **pero** *(n)*

pepper **papar** *(m)*

perhaps **možda**

person **čovjek** *(m)*; **osoba** *(f)*

pessimist **pesimist** *(m)*

petrol **benzin** *(m)*

petrol station **benzinska
  stanica** *(f)*

pinch together, to **pritisnuti**

pitch **igralište** *(n)*; **teren** *(m)*

place **mjesto** *(n)*

plan **plan** *(m)*

plate **tanjur** *(m)*

play, to **igrati**

playing **igranje** *(n)*

playing area **igralište** *(n)*

please **molim**

pleased **zadovoljan, -ljna, -ljno**

pocket **džep** *(m)*

Poland **Poljska**

police **policija** *(f)*

policeman **policajac** *(m)*

police station **policijska postaja** *(f)*

possibility **mogućnost** *(f)*

possible **mogući, -a, -e**

post office **pošta** *(f)*

postcard **razglednica** *(f)*

pound **funta** *(f)*

practical **praktičan, -čna, -čno**

precise **točan, -čna, -čno**

prepare, to **spremati**

prepared **spreman, -mna, -mno**

present **poklon** *(m)*

price **cijena** *(f)*

price list **cjenik** *(m)*

private **privatan, -tna, -tno**

probably **vjerojatno**

problem **problem** *(m)*

product **proizvod** *(m)*

production **proizvođenje** *(n)*

promenade (by the sea) **riva** *(f)*

pupil **učenik** *(m)*

purse **novčanik** *(m)*

put, to **stavljati, staviti**

quay **pristanište** *(n)*

question, to **ispitivati, ispitati**

quick **brz, -a, -o**

quiet **tih, -a, -o**

quite **baš**

rain **kiša** *(f)*

read, to **čitati, pročitati**

ready **spreman, -mna, -mno**

really **stvarno; zaista**

receive, to **dobiti; primati, primiti**

reception **recepcija** *(f)*

recommend, to **preporučivati,
  preporučiti**

recover, to **ozdravljati, ozdraviti**

red **crven, -a, -o**

region **područje** *(n)*

remain **ostajati, ostati**

remember, to **sjećati se, sjetiti se**

rent, to **izdavati; iznajmljivati,
  iznajmiti**

reply, to **odgovarati, odgovoriti**

representative **predstavnik** *(m)*

require, to **trebati**

reserve, to **rezervirati**

reside, to **stanovati**

resignation **ostavka** *(f)*

respect **poštovanje** *(n)*

Respected (in a letter) **Štovani,
  Štovana**

rest **odmor** *(m)*

rest, to **odmarati se, odmoriti se**

restaurant **restoran** *(m)*

return **povratak** *(m)*

return, to **vraćati se, vratiti se**

right **desno; pravo** *(n)*

river **rijeka** *(f)*

road **cesta** *(f)*; **put** *(m)*

room **soba** *(f)*

Russia **Rusija**
    Russian **ruski, -a, -o**
    Russian (man) **Rus** *(m)*
    Russian (woman) **Ruskinja** *(f)*

sad **tužan, -žna, -žno**
salad **salata** *(f)*
salesman **prodavač** *(m)*
saleswoman **prodavačica** *(f)*
salon **salon** *(m)*
salt **sol** *(f)*
same **isti, -a, -o**
sandals **sandale** *(f pl)*
sandwich **sendvič** *(m)*
satisfied **zadovoljan, -ljna, -ljno**
Saturday **subota** *(f)*
saucepan **tava** *(f)*
say, to **kazati; reći**
school **škola** *(f)*
Scotland **Škotska**
screen **ekran** *(m)*
sea **more** *(n)*; **morski, -a, -o**
seashore **primorje** *(n)*
second **drugi, -a, -o**
secretary **sekretarica** *(f)*
see, to **vidjeti**
seem, to **činiti se**
self-service shop **samoposluga** *(f)*
sell, to **prodavati, prodati**
send, to **slati, poslati**
separate **poseban, -bna, -bno**
September **rujan** *(m)*
Serbia **Srbija**
    Serbian **srpski, -a, -o**
    Serbian (man) **Srbin** *(m)*
    Serbian (woman) **Srpkinja** *(f)*
serve, to **služiti, poslužiti; usluživati**
served, to be **služiti se, poslužiti se**
set off, to **kretati, krenuti; polaziti, poći**
shampoo **šampon** *(m)*
she **ona**
shelf **polica** *(f)*

shine, to **sijati**
ship **brod** *(m)*
shirt **košulja** *(f)*
shoes **cipele** *(f pl)*
shop **prodavaonica** *(f)*
short **kratak, -tka, -tko**
short lived **kratkotrajan, -jna, -jno**
short term **kratkoročan, -čna, -čno**
shorts **šorc** *(m)*
shoulder **rame** *(n)*
show, to **pokazivati, pokazati**
shower **tuš** *(m)*
shower, to **tuširati se, istuširati se**
side **strana** *(f)*
sign, to **potpisivati, potpisati**
since **jer; otkad**
sincerely **iskreno**
sing, to **pjevati**
sister **sestra** *(f)*
sit down, to **sjesti**
sitting, to be **sjediti**
situated **smješten, -a, -o**
situated, to be **nalaziti se**
skating **klizanje** *(n)*
skiing **skijanje** *(n)*
skirt **suknja** *(f)*
sky **nebo** *(n)*
Slavonia **Slavonija** *(f)*
sleep, to **spavati**
sleeve **rukav** *(m)*
slice **ploška** *(f)*
Slovenia **Slovenija** *(f)*
    Slovenian **slovenski, -a, -o**
    Slovenian (man) **Slovenac** *(m)*
    Slovenian (woman) **Slovenka** *(f)*
small **mali, -a, -o**
smashing **sjajan, -jna, -jno**
snow **snijeg** *(m)*
so **tako**
soap **sapun** *(m)*
society **društvo** *(n)*
sock **čarapa** *(f)*
soldier **vojnik** *(m)*

some **neki, -a, -o**
someone **netko**
something **nešto**
sometimes **ponekad**
somewhere **negdje**
son **sin** (m)
soon **uskoro**
sorry **žao**
sort **vrsta** (f)
soup **juha**
south **jug** (m); **južni, -a, -o**
space **prostorija** (f)
speak, to **govoriti**
special **poseban, -bna, -bno**
spend (time), to **provoditi, provesti**
spoon **žlica** (f)
sport **sport** (m); **sportski, -a, -o**
square **trg** (m)
squid **lignje** (f pl)
stadium **stadion** (m)
stamp **marka** (f)
standing, to be **stajati**
station **kolodvor** (m)
stay, to **boraviti; ostajati, ostati**
steal **krasti, ukrasti**
still **još uvijek**
stomach **stomak** (m)
stop (bus) **stanica** (f)
stop, to **prestati; zaustavljati se, zaustaviti se**
storey **kat** (m)
stormy **buran, -rna, -rno**
straight on **ravno**
street **ulica** (f)
strong **jak, -a, -o**
study **radna soba** (f)
study, to **studirati**
suburb **predgrađe** (n)
success **uspjeh** (m)
suggest, to **predlagati, predložiti**
suggestion **prijedlog** (m)
suit **odijelo** (n)
suit, to **odgovarati**

summer **ljeto** (n)
sun **sunce** (n)
sunbathe, to **sunčati se**
Sunday **nedjelja** (f)
sunny **sunčan, -a, -o**
suntan lotion **mlijeko za sunčanje** (n)
suntan oil **ulje za sunčanje** (n)
suppose, to **pretpostavljati**
sure **siguran, -rna, -rno**
swim, to **plivati**
swimming **plivanje** (n)
swimming costume **kupaći kostim** (m)
swimming pool **bazen** (m)
system **sistem** (m)

table **stol** (m)
table tennis **stolni tenis** (m)
take, to **uzimati, uzeti**
take a holiday, to **odmarati se, odmoriti se**
take part in, to **baviti se**
talk, to **pričati**
tall **visok, -a, -o**
taste **ukus** (m)
taxi **taksi** (m)
tea **čaj** (m)
teacher (man) **nastavnik** (m); **učitelj** (m)
teacher (woman) **nastavnica** (f); **učiteljica** (f)
telephone **telefon** (m)
telephone number **telefonski broj** (m)
telephone, to **telefonirati**
tell, to **kazati; pričati; reći**
temperature **temperatura** (f)
tennis **tenis** (m)
terrace **terasa** (f)
than **nego**
thank you **hvala**
that **da; što**

that **onaj, ona, ono; taj, ta, to**
theatre **kazalište** (n)
their **njihov, -a, -o**
then **onda; tada; zatim**
there **tamo**
they **oni, one**
thin **tanak, -nka, -nko**
thing **stvar** (f)
think, to **misliti**
third **treći, -a, -e**
thirsty **žedan, -dna, -dno**
this **ovaj, ova, ovo**
thousand **tisuća** (f)
three **tri**
throat **grlo** (n)
through **kroz** (with acc. case); **po**
  (with dat. case)
Thursday **četvrtak** (m)
ticket **karta** (f)
    first-class ticket **karta prvog**
      razreda
    second-class ticket **karta drugog**
      razreda
    one-way ticket **karta u jednom**
      smjeru
    return ticket **povratna karta**
time **vrijeme** (n)
tired **umoran, -rna, -rno**
to **na** (with acc. case); **u** (with acc.
  case)
toilet **WC** (m) (pronounced ve-tse)
tolerate, to **podnositi**
tomorrow **sutra**
tongue **jezik** (m)
too much **previše; suviše**
tooth **zub** (m)
toothpaste **zubna pasta** (f)
tourism **turizam** (m); **turistički, -a, -o**
tourist (man) **turist** (m)
tourist (woman) **turistkinja** (f)
towards **k** (with dat. case); **prema**
  (with dat. case)
towel **ručnik** (m)

town **grad** (m)
train **vlak** (m); **vozni, -a, -o**
tram **tramvaj** (m)
transfer **transfer** (m)
transport **prijevoz** (m)
transport department **transportni**
  odjel (m)
travel, to **putovati**
traveller **putnik** (m)
traveller's **putnički, -a, -o**
tree **drvo** (n)
trend **trend** (m)
trousers **hlače** (f pl)
truth **istina** (f)
try, to **probati**
T-shirt **majica** (f)
turn, to **skrenuti**
two **dva, dvije**
typical **tipičan, -čna, -čno**

umbrella **kišobran** (m)
uncle **stric** (m); **tetak** (m); **ujak** (m)
under **ispod** (with gen. case)
understand, to **razumjeti**
underwear **donje rublje** (n)
unfortunately **na žalost**
university **sveučilište** (n)
up to **do** (with gen. case)
urban **gradski, -a, -o**
use, to **koristiti**
useful **koristan, -sna, -sno**
usually **obično**

veal **teleći, -a, -e**
very **veoma; vrlo**
vicinity **blizina** (f); **okolina** (f)
view **pogled** (m)
village **selo** (n)
visit, to **posjećivati, posjetiti**

wait, to **čekati**
waiter **konobar** (m)
waitress **konobarica** (f)

wake up, to **buditi se,
probuditi se**
wallet **novčanik** (m)
want, to **htjeti; željeti**
warm **topao, -pla, -plo**
warm, to **zagrijati**
wash, to **prati, oprati**
water **voda** (f)
way **put** (m)
we **mi**
weak **slab, -a, -o**
weather **vrijeme** (n)
wedding **svadba** (f)
wedge **kriška** (f)
Wednesday **srijeda** (f)
week **tjedan** (m)
west **zapad** (m); **zapadni, -a, -o**
what **što**
what kind of **kakav, -kva, -kvo**
when **kada**
where **gdje**
where from **odakle**
where to **kamo**
which **koji, -a, -e**
while **dok**
white **bijel, -a, -o**
who **koji, -a, -e; tko**
whole **cijeli, -a, -o**
whose **čiji, -a, -e**
why **zašto**
wife **supruga** (f); **žena** (f)
wind **vjetar** (m)
window **prozor** (m)

wine **vino** (n)
winter **zima** (f)
wish **želja** (f)
with **s** (with ins. case)
without **bez** (with gen. case)
woman **žena** (f)
wonderful **divan, -vna, -vno; sjajan,
-jna, -jno**
word **riječ** (f)
work **posao** (m)
work, to **raditi**
working **radni, -a, -o**
worry, to **brinuti se**
worse **gori, -a, -e**
write, to **pisati, napisati**
wrong **kriv, -a, -o; pogrešan,
-šna, -šno**

year **godina** (f)
yellow **žut, -a, -o**
yes **da**
you (singular) **ti**
you (plural) **vi**
young **mlad, -a, -o**
young lady **djevojka** (f);
gospođica (f)
your (singular) **tvoj, -a, -e**
your (plural) **vaš, -a, -e**

Zagreb schnitzel **zagrebački
odrezak** (m)
zero **nula** (f)
zoo **zoološki vrt** (m)

Grammar index

The numbers following each entry refer to the relevant unit(s) in the book.